A
798
THE U,S EQUESTRIAN TEAM BOOK OFRIDING
STEINKRAUS, WILLIAM

DATE DUE		
APR 3 0 1981	AUG - 5 1992	
JUN 3 1 1981	APR 1 4 1993	
OCT 4 1982	NOV 7 1994	
OCT 2 1 1982	DEC 994	
APR 2 2 1983	DEC 994	
JUN 1 4 1989	OCT 1 9 2000	
MAY 6 1991		
JUN 6 199	SEP 0 5 2002	
JUN 2 2 199	AUG 1 2 2003	
AUG - 6 1991	JUL 3 1 2007	
FEB 1 1992		

DISCARD

THE U.S.
EQUESTRIAN TEAM

BOOK OF RIDING

The First Quarter-Century of the USET

EDITED BY WILLIAM STEINKRAUS
FOREWORD BY WHITNEY STONE

SIMON AND SCHUSTER · NEW YORK

DESIGNED BY EVE METZ
MANUFACTURED IN THE UNITED STATES OF AMERICA

1   2   3   4   5   6   7   8   9   10

LIBRARY OF CONGRESS CATALOGING IN PUBLICATION DATA
THE U.S. EQUESTRIAN TEAM BOOK OF RIDING.

1. UNITED STATES EQUESTRIAN TEAM.   2. SHOW JUMPING—
ADDRESSES, ESSAYS, LECTURES.   3. THREE-DAY EVENT (HORSE-
MANSHIP)—ADDRESSES, ESSAYS, LECTURES.   4. DRESSAGE
TESTS—ADDRESSES, ESSAYS, LECTURES.   I. STEINKRAUS,
WILLIAM.   II. UNITED STATES EQUESTRIAN TEAM.
SF310.U63G5887   798'.23'0973   76–13495
ISBN 0-671-22371-2

DEDICATION

To all the loyal supporters, contributors and staff members whose labors and generosity in behalf of the United States Equestrian Team enabled it not only to survive for twenty-five years, but to grow and flourish . . . and particularly, to certain remarkable people no longer with us who did so much more than their fair share to help:

> *Brigadier General John T. Cole*
> *Walter B. Devereux*
> *Amory L. Haskell*
> *Major General Guy V. Henry*
> *Jacques Jenny, D.V.M.*
> *Ernst Mahler*
> *Andrew M. Montgomery*
> *Alvin Untermyer*
> *J. Spencer Weed*

NOTE TO THE READER

The three organizations most deeply involved in American international equestrian sport all have rather unwieldy names, and are commonly referred to by their initials. Instead of spelling out each name every time it occurs, we have followed this same practice in this book. The actual titles of the organizations involved are as follows:

USET = United States Equestrian Team, Inc.—the nonprofit, voluntary organization that exists for the express purpose of training, selecting and financing the amateur equestrian teams that represent the United States in world competition, including the Olympic Games.

FEI = Fédération Équestre Internationale—the Brussels-based governing body of international equestrian sport, which formulates the rules under which all international equestrian competition is conducted.

AHSA = American Horse Shows Association—the governing body of horse-show sport in America, which formulates rules for all domestic equestrian competition and is our official member of both the FEI and the United States Olympic Committee.

CONTENTS

THE U.S. EQUESTRIAN TEAM BOOK OF RIDING

DRESSAGE & GENERAL CONSIDERATIONS

APPENDIX

Foreword

WHITNEY STONE

Whitney Stone, chairman of the board of directors of the United States Equestrian Team, Inc., was one of its founding directors and its president for two decades from 1952 through 1972. A distinguished breeder of Thoroughbreds—his Morven Stud produced the brilliant Shuvee, the only mare ever to win the Jockey Club Gold Cup, which she did twice—Stone has long been a member of the Jockey Club and a key figure in both the National Horse Show and the American Horse Shows Association. For many years he also headed one of the nation's most prominent international engineering and construction firms.

WHEN WE FIRST STARTED what is now the United States Equestrian Team, some twenty-five years ago, we certainly didn't have much idea of what we were getting into. Surely we had no thought of year-round training centers, or chartering planes to fly horses to Tokyo or Moscow. In fact, we even had trouble figuring out what to call ourselves, and our first effort—the International Equestrian Competitions Corporation—soon proved such a mouthful that we changed it the following year to the present form. We've been able to live with that.

Those of us who still remember the birth pains of the infant IECC/USET can take considerable satisfaction from its accomplishments since then, for it's come a long way from those days when we had only a handful of borrowed horses, a group of riders who were almost totally unfamiliar with the rules under which they were competing, and hardly any money in

9

the kitty. The challenges of the next twenty-five years can hardly prove any tougher.

Before I get ahead of myself, however, let me outline the circumstances in which the USET was created, so that the reader will have a general background for the various personal accounts that follow. The whole thing really started after the 1948 Olympic Games, for it was only then that the U.S. Army finally and irrevocably mechanized the last vestiges of its horse cavalry. Our country had been represented by an Army team at the 1948 Olympics, as it had all the way back to 1912, and the Army Horse Show Team had also always provided the teams that represented the United States in all other official international competitions, such as our own National Horse Show, Toronto's Royal Winter Fair and the big foreign shows. The only civilian to ride for our country during all those years was a Millbrook, New York, fox hunter named Frederic Bontecou who rode with the Army team in Europe in 1924–1925. (He represented us civilians admirably, even winning the George V Cup, but since he rode in his reserve officer's uniform, nobody could tell the difference.)

In any case, all of a sudden there was no Army team to compete at the National Horse Show, and in 1949 there was only one lonely reserve officer (Lieutenant Gordon Wright) at Madison Square Garden to ride against the teams from Canada, Mexico, Ireland and Chile, and it was obvious to everyone that something had to be done. Before the show was over, lawyer Robert Lee Henry had drafted the papers for incorporating in the State of New York a nonprofit, membership corporation that would "select and obtain for the United States the most competent amateur representation possible in international equestrian competitions . . ." and undertake to finance it.

By June of 1950 the application for incorporation had been approved, and seventeen men met at the Down Town Association near Wall Street in New York to put the new organization into operation. Not all of the true parents were present at its birth, but even so, a great many of the people who were to figure prominently in the team's affairs did in fact attend that very first meeting—Generals Albert Stackpole and Alfred G. Tuckerman, Drew Montgomery, Amory Haskell, Alvin Untermyer and J. Spencer Weed, to name but a few. By the time the smoke had cleared we'd unanimously voted Colonel John "Gyp" Wofford, a veteran of the 1932 Olympics, our president, and Spencer Weed our chairman of the board. I thought I got off easy as chairman of the executive committee, but two years later they got even by naming me president to succeed the ailing Wofford, and it took me quite a while to get out of that one.

The minutes of that first meeting noted that "discussion was had concerning finances and methods to be employed in the raising of funds for the Corporation" and that Messrs. Weed, Stone and Haskell had been asked to report back on "the entire financial situation and to make recommenda-

The USET executive staff, circa 1953: (from left) Andrew M. Montgomery, secretary-treasurer; Whitney Stone, president; Brig. Gen. Frederic W. Boye, executive vice-president.

tions." Eventually we engaged a well-known fund-raising firm to help run our 1952 Olympic drive, and soon discovered that it could only provide direction, while we still had to do all the work. Anyhow, we managed to scrape together enough money to select and train teams for the fall circuits of 1950 and 1951, and to send a full complement of horses and riders to Helsinki for the 1952 Olympics. We were very proud when our initial teams won their share of classes on the fall circuit, and especially proud of the two bronze medals they won at Helsinki. And that was only the beginning, as you will find related in some detail elsewhere in this book.

As I think back on those "hardy pioneers" who helped the team get started, few of whom are still with us today to enjoy the team's performances now, I am struck by how lucky we were to be able to draw together so many outstanding sportsmen for one common cause. As a group they shared a profound belief in the value of amateur sport in general and the horse in particular, and they were unstinting in backing this conviction with time, energy and money. Without them, and those who have picked up the burden of team support from them, the USET would not exist at all today. Equally important to the team have been those whose contributions took the form of horses, services, facilities or simply blood, sweat and tears. Bless them all.

Yet while the USET has been fortunate in drawing support from many more people than I could acknowledge individually here, in another sense—in terms of the present size of our U.S. equestrian community—the group that is keeping the team alive remains perilously small. And whatever else happens to the team during the next quarter-century, this has got to change.

Key men in the 1960s: (from left) Brig. Gen. F. F. Wing, Jr., executive vice-president; Whitney Stone, president; Stefan von Visy, three-day coach; Bertalan de Nemethy, coach of the jumping team.

That squalling baby we wet-nursed in the 1950s is now an adult, with an adult appetite for funds, while the kind of patron who could support what he cared about and damn the tax considerations has pretty much been legislated out of existence. Or to put it another way, these days we're fielding strong, truly national competitive teams, and they both demand and deserve equally strong, truly national support.

I rather doubt that I'll be around to see how the USET's second quarter-century turns out, and if the year 2000 is anything like the movie versions, I wouldn't understand it anyway. I can only hope that those who guide the USET's destinies from now to then get half the fun and satisfaction out of it that I've had up to now.

Editor's Introduction

Since this is a rather unusual book about a rather unusual organization, it may be helpful to start off with a few explanations and clarifications. Perhaps even the concept of *The USET Book of Riding* will perplex those readers who insist on categorizing things, for what is it? Written both by and about the U.S. Equestrian Team, it is neither an objective history, a collection of personal reminiscences nor a book of instruction, yet it includes elements of all three. Technically, it probably comes closest to what the Germans term a *Festschrift*—a commemorative volume of varied contents, assembled to mark some special anniversary or date. Our excuse in the present case is that the USET was twenty-five years old at the end of 1975, and a quarter-century represents an important milestone in the life of something as ephemeral as an equestrian team.*

In terms of man's relationship with the horse, a quarter-century is hardly a hoofbeat, of course. Even the horse's use in sport traces far back into the mists of oral history, centuries before the first Olympic Games in 776 B.C. The modern forms of international equestrian sport, however, date only from the early years of the present century, and the emergence of show jumping and eventing as important spectator sports in some of the world has been pretty much a television-induced, post–World War II development.

*Editor's note: There was a temptation to exceed this mark in order to include the results of the 1976 Olympic Games at Montreal. However, these few addenda would have caused the entire project to be deferred into the following year, while the Montreal results are sure to have been amply covered by other sources in the interim. Thus it finally seemed most sensible to conform to the avowed twenty-five-year period.

The sand ring at the USET's Gladstone, New Jersey, training center, permanent head-quarters of the team since 1961. (The rider is Bill Steinkraus on Snowbound.) The beautiful stables are leased to the team by the estate of the late James Cox Brady.

This rapid rise in the public's interest in equestrian sport since 1950 has co-incided with the decline of military support for it, for even the most diehard cavalrymen could no longer refute, after World War II, the practical advantages of armor plate and internal combustion. Accordingly, the challenge to the postwar equestrian teams of the world has been to develop a new, "civilian" base of support, or perish. Sadly, a number of formerly important teams have done the latter, and thus the fact that the United States among others has successfully done the former constitutes an accomplishment of some significance.

What, then, is this U.S. Equestrian Team? In practice the acronym USET refers both to the civilian, nonprofit corporation created in 1950 to finance our international amateur equestrian teams and to the competitive teams themselves. These are three in number, one for each of the principal international equestrian disciplines: show jumping, combined training and dressage. What these consist of will be amply explained on the pages that follow, which are organized into the same three sections.

How many riders are there on the competitive teams? A complete entry for the Olympic Games totals fourteen, including three reserves: five each for show jumping and combined training, and four for dressage. Many

14

people are surprised to learn that there is never a permanent team, as such, in any discipline; each team is selected anew for a particular competition or series of competitions. Since there are always also riders standing in the wings, as it were, and few team members can afford to devote the entire year to amateur equestrianism, in the course of the average year as many as two dozen riders may participate on one or another of the USET's competitive teams. Of course, it is also true that certain riders remain interested in and eligible for team participation for long periods of time, and even more important, manage to keep themselves adequately mounted; thus they can be selected for team after team until they seem like fixtures on it. Nonetheless, nobody is ever named to a squad for as long as a year at a time, and team captains too are named only after the particular squad has been selected.

The word "amateur" has been mentioned several times, and since this has become a rather complicated factor in the equestrian world, let me next touch on that. The Olympic Games, which are the USET's primary competitive objective, have always been restricted exclusively to amateur participants and remain so today. When the team was founded in 1950, this was also true of almost all other official international competitions; hence the USET's charter of incorporation restricts its activities to amateurs, and its preferred tax status, too, depends on that basis. But then in 1972 the interna-

Headquarters for the three-day team since 1974: front view of the office and stables at South Hamilton, Massachusetts, given to the team by Forrester A. Clark. The center is located in the heart of the beautiful Myopia Hunt country, not far from the Ledyard Horse Trials course.

tional equestrian federation, recognizing that a rather hypocritical "shamateurism" had become quite prevalent in the sport, voted to largely eliminate the restrictions against professionals in most non-Games competitions. In response to this change, a number of nations started including both professionals and amateurs on their official teams, and it hardly seemed reasonable to deny the same opportunity to our own top professionals. However, this created a rather curious situation: our country was free to name a professional rider to its international team (and did, in the person of Rodney Jenkins, who has contributed significantly to the team's success on a number of recent occasions). But technically speaking, since the USET cannot subsidize any professional participation, it should take no credit for his accomplishments on its behalf.

Fortunately, this situation has been less confusing in practice than on paper, though of course it would be simpler still if no such complications existed at all. Let me add, however, that I am personally very skeptical about the wisdom of abandoning the amateur-professional distinction entirely, as some have suggested. My reasoning is (and I can no more than touch on it here) that there is a fundamental difference between professional and amateur sport: the ultimate goal of the former is revenue from paid admissions, while the ultimate goal of the latter is the benefit to the participant. Thus it seems to me that Baron de Coubertin, founder of the modern Olympic movement, knew exactly what he was doing when he placed his major emphasis on the value of "taking part" and included within the structure of the Games many so-called minor sports—yes, like riding—that are marvelous for the participant even though they are not especially attractive to the sports promoter. Forced to compete in the open marketplace of professional sporting entertainments, some of these would not long survive, much less flourish, and that would be sad indeed.

Finally, a few apologies are necessary. First, to the generous souls whose loans or gifts of horses to the team have kept something between its riders and the ground—well, most of the time—and often very high-class transportation at that. Without them there would be no team, and the fact that their names do not invariably appear when their horses are mentioned should by no means suggest that we fail to appreciate that simple fact. Next, to those who will search in vain for any reference to a favorite horse or rider, or an episode in which they themselves participated. This is a big book as it stands, but I agree that as far as telling the *whole* story of those twenty-five years is concerned, it hardly scratches the surface. Many of my own favorite horses, people, pictures and anecdotes are missing too, and I would be much happier if the present volume were twice as big and three times as good. Nonetheless, it gives some idea of some of the USET's major high points, and if it were as complete as I would like it to be, few could afford the money to buy it or the time to wade through it. In any case, I am quite sure that the present contributors, all of whom are more at home in the saddle than at the desk, will happily defer to another generation of riders in producing the next volume.

Last of all, the editor must apologize for whatever errors of fact have found their way into these pages. He has caught some, but no doubt others have escaped him, and he can only hope they are as benign as they are unintentional. In extenuation, he might point out that few of the contributors have had written records to refer to, and memories can be fallible. We hope the fact that most of us have also hit the ground with some regularity during our riding careers is only incidental.

W.C.S.

SHOW JUMPING

Innocents Abroad:
The USET's Early Years

ARTHUR J. McCASHIN

A highly successful show rider before World War II, Arthur McCashin be-
came the first riding captain of the USET's jumping squad, and played a
major role with it right from the start. A member of the first USET fall-
circuit, Olympic and Pan American Games teams, McCashin became a
sought-after course designer after his retirement from competitive riding,
doing the international courses at New York's National Horse Show for
many years. One of his sons, Frederic McCashin, V.M.D., now shares the
USET veterinary responsibility.

BACK IN WHAT SEEMS like the Stone Age before World War II, the activities
of our Army riders in the European horse shows were pretty much a mystery
to most American horse-show exhibitors, and I was no exception. However,
thanks to the international classes at the National and a few trips to Dublin,
I had at least an idea of what Irish-American international jumping was like,
and had even done a little of it myself. This came about because of an unusual class they had in the old National, the De Valera Challenge Cup,
which called only for teams of three jumpers under one ownership. It was
designed primarily for the military teams, of course, but anyone who qualified could enter, and it just happened that I rode jumpers in those days for a
man named Julius Bliss who had three crackerjacks—Greyflight, Will Gallop
and Modernistic. No better jumper ever looked through a bridle than the

first one, and the other two were no slouches, either. In 1938 their score for six trips around the old Garden with rubs to count was exactly one fault.

Anyhow, I was lucky enough to win the De Valera Cup back to back in 1937 and 1938, riding against the Irish, U.S., Argentine and Canadian military teams, and because of this, I got an inquiry about my possible interest in riding in the 1940 Olympic Games. John Tupper Cole—then, as I recall, a major—told me I might be invited to the trials, but wondered aloud if I could go on competing against professionals in the regular shows without endangering my amateur status. Before that ever really got cleared up the war had come along, the Games were cancelled and I had no occasion to even think about the Olympics again until almost ten years later.

Horse shows were suspended during the war because of gas rationing, and I switched from horses to airplanes for the duration. When I started fooling with horses again after the hostilities, it was mostly with racehorses and hunters. (I had a training track on my place in Connecticut, and one summer I got a local kid named Steinkraus to do some galloping for me.) However, I still showed jumpers every now and then, and followed them closely. I well remember thinking what a shame it was when we had no U.S. team on the fall circuit in 1949, but I didn't know exactly what I could do about it. I was to find out shortly!

By the following spring it became clear that the Army would give its horses no reprieve, and soon I heard that some of the staunch supporters of the National were forming an organization to take over the job of preparing our international teams. Colonel John Wofford (better known as "Gyp" when he instructed at West Point) was named president of the new International Equestrian Competition Corporation, as the USET was called the first year.

To get things started, a number of riders from the New York area were invited to come to Gordon Wright's Secor Farms in White Plains, New York, to be evaluated as candidates for the new team. A last-minute problem prevented me from attending, but because of my past experience I was told on the telephone that I was rated as a "B" rider. (I've always enjoyed needling Steinkraus about the fact that he rode in the evaluation and made only a "C.")

It took a while for the new IECC to figure out what it was trying to do; at the beginning, some of its organizers were thinking in terms of zone teams and an interzone final trial. Eventually, however, it was decided to have formal individual trials for the selection of a fall-circuit jumping team. Thanks to the influence of General Albert Stackpole, then president of the Pennsylvania National show, the Pennsylvania National Guard barracks at Indiantown Gap were made available for the purpose.

Facilities there were a bit spartan, and I'm just as glad that my exposure to them was only a couple of weeks. However, all the candidates joined in the spirit of the thing, and we had a lot of laughs before it was all over. In addition, I made many new friends, among them a Kansas girl named Carol Durand who was to become not only a teammate, but practically a member of my family before her untimely death in a riding accident in September, 1970.

The trials consisted of three separate courses, and I rode an honest old roan horse named Paleface, then lent to us by H. J. O'Connell, and later by Sam Campbell. After the smoke had cleared, the selection committee named three riders to make up the team for the fall circuit (then consisting of Harrisburg, New York and Toronto) and three young riders as a reserve squad to show in the regular open classes and gain experience. Carol Durand, Norma Matthews and I were named to the official team, and Hugh Wiley, Norman Brinker and Bobby Fraser were the reserves. As it turned out, our reserves came in handy for the Irish team, for when Bill Mullin broke a wrist out fox hunting, Hugh Wiley filled in for him—and very creditably, too.

Not much was expected of us that first fall circuit, since Mexico's 1948 Olympic champions with the then Colonel Humberto Mariles had proved almost invincible the year before, and there were also teams from England, Chile, Canada and Ireland. However, we had three pretty useful horses; Carol's Reno Kirk was good enough to make anyone's team, even today, and Norma's big spotted horse, Country Boy, was fine as long as the fences didn't look too spooky.

We didn't seriously challenge Mexico's domination, but we did win five competitions, among them New York's Low Score finals and Toronto's International Team Challenge Cup (predecessor of the Nations Cup), and nobody thought we'd disgraced ourselves. After the shows we disbanded to "wait for next year," when the trials would select not only a fall-circuit team, but also our squad for the 1952 Olympics to be held in Helsinki, Finland.

The 1950 squad was terribly thin in backup horses—hardly anyone remembers our second string, and it's just as well—but the next year we got a big lift when Gyp Wofford was able to latch on to the last of the Army string for the princely consideration of $1 apiece. The group included six jumpers from the 1948 Olympic squad, and though they all had a lot of age and some physical problems, too, they also had invaluable experience under European conditions.

Star of the group was Democrat, whom Colonel F. F. Wing had ridden to fourth place in the 1948 Olympics in London. Democrat was eighteen and not too sound, but still a marvelous jumper. Other proven horses were the German-bred Totilla, with whom Wing had won the Grand Prix of Aachen; Rascal and Rattler, from Colonel A. A. Frierson's Olympic string, and Swizzlestick, a favorite of Garden crowds when Captain Charles Symroski had ridden him for the Army. In addition to the horses from the 1948 Army squad we had a rider, Captain John Russell, who though still on

The first civilian U.S. Equestrian Team, winners of the Low-Score Competition at the National Horse Show in 1950: (from left) Norma Matthews (now Mrs. R. S. Shely) on Country Boy, Arthur McCashin on Eager Beaver and the late Carol H. Durand on Reno Kirk.

active service was given permission to try out for the team. Johnny brought along a useful young horse named Blue Devil, and because of his seniority, as it were, he was also given the ride on Democrat for the trials.

Another lucky break for the team was the acquisition of the brilliant mare Circus Rose by Gussy Busch at the 1950 National Horse Show. Busch had always liked Carol Durand's riding, and with Carol now on the team, he bought the mare with her in mind and renamed her Miss Budweiser. (The FEI now frowns on this kind of thing and prohibits it in the Olympics, but when Miss Bud was the only one, nobody paid much attention to it.)

The 1951 USET trials were held at the old Army Cavalry School in Fort Riley, Kansas. Not long before the trials were to commence, the Republican River went into flood and nearly washed away the Hippodrome, the beautiful showgrounds where the trials were to be held. Fortunately, the footing dried out sufficiently for the trials to start on time, though things did look a bit bedraggled.

Twenty-odd entries competed in the trials, including Carol Durand and Norma Matthews from the 1950 team and Norman Brinker from the 1950 reserve squad. Hugh Wiley found himself without a horse and was not present, but Bill Steinkraus, who had not competed at Indiantown Gap, appeared on the scene with Don Ferraro's Black Watch, a horse who could jump a big fence despite rather clumsy conformation.

Though the trials were open to women, there was a big question as to whether the FEI would permit them to ride in the jumping events in the Olympic Games. Petitions had been submitted to the FEI, and we and the

British were pressing hard for them, but as of the summer of 1951, no final decision had been reached.

Team selection in the trials was based entirely on aggregate scores, and after the final course the standings were headed by Johnny Russell with Democrat, followed by me with Totilla, Carol Durand with Miss Budweiser and Steinkraus with Black Watch. The first three were named to start the fall circuit, with Steinkraus riding in the civilian classes in reserve. Norman Brinker, the next-highest male rider in the trials, was named an additional reserve to cover the possibility that women might be prohibited from jumping in the Olympics.

Thanks to the stronger string of horses, our fall circuit went even better in 1951 than in 1950, and we picked up seven victories against teams from Mexico, Ireland, Canada and Brazil. Steinkraus, who had been lent the old Army horse Gray Fox to back up Black Watch, won the open jumper championship at Harrisburg with him, and on the strength of this was given a spot on the team in Toronto—his first appearance as a USET rider. In addition, he was invited to join Russell and me on the team that was named to compete in Mexico after the fall circuit at a big show that Mariles, then at the height of his power and influence, had organized at Monterrey.

The trip to Mexico is one I could never forget if I lived to be a thousand.

Arthur McCashin schooling Paleface outside Fort Riley's West Riding Hall, just prior to the 1951 Olympic Trials.

All the teams for the fall circuit were there except for Canada, and the invitation also included the French Cadre Noir, which had done the show numbers in New York and Toronto, as well as a bunch of Mariles' friends and acquaintances from the North American shows. Right after we arrived, everyone was whisked off to Acapulco to sight-see—everyone, that is, except for the Mexican riders, who stayed in Monterrey and schooled. As riding-team captain I stayed behind and kept our horses going, because I couldn't see conceding that kind of advantage to the Mexicans, even if they were only killing us with kindness. Mariles was pretty cagey that way.

When we arrived at Monterrey Stadium for the first class, the riders thought Mariles was playing a joke, because the fences were all near the top of the standards. The funny thing was that he *wasn't* joking! After the visiting-team captains all protested, he lowered the fences for the first class, which was just a preliminary, after all. With the fences lowered there were still only two or three clear rounds, but as it turned out, they were to be the only clear rounds in the whole show! I suppose it was sport, but it seemed more like riding for your life. No team finished the course for the second day of the low-score competition, in which you jumped the course one way on your first horse and then in reverse on your second. The course was terribly complicated, and with only about three minutes to learn it, I almost took a wrong turn on my second horse. I felt a little better when Mariles—who had designed all the courses himself—did go off course on Arete. (Even the jury couldn't figure out the course, and after Mariles went wrong they let him jump half a dozen fences and finally fall before they got around to blowing him out.)

Though Monterrey couldn't run an official Nations Cup—it wasn't an official international show under FEI rules—it ran a class under the same conditions and called it something else. To everyone's surprise, the winner was the USET, with the resounding total of 77 faults (and believe me, this was pretty good). Bill Steinkraus and Reno Kirk had the low individual score with 8 faults in each round, but the jury decided to award the individual trophy for the lowest *single* round, which just happened to have been scored by d'Harcourt of Mexico with 4 faults. Anyway, our Mexican hosts generally could not have been more generous, and all in all it was an experience I'll never forget.

The Olympic year of 1952 was to prove even more unforgettable, in a variety of ways. During the winter the FEI voted against permitting women to jump in the Games, so our 1952 Olympic squad consisted of Russell, Steinkraus and me with Brinker as reserve. (Only three riders started in the Nations Cup in those days.) Carol was, of course, terribly disappointed, but generously let me add Miss Budweiser to my string, leaving Reno Kirk, whom she'd ridden so successfully on the fall circuit, to Steinkraus.

The team assembled at Camden, South Carolina, to train for Europe with Gyp Wofford as overall *chef d'équipe* and Bob Borg helping with the three-day and dressage training. I liked Camden, having spent some time there during my active steeplechasing days, but our training there was fraught with difficulties. Stable-personnel problems were a real headache, and our eventual stable manager, Harry Moss, took over only a few days before we departed for Europe. The only way at that time to transport horses to Europe was by ship, which meant that after you'd got them fit, you had to let them down again to stand the inactivity of the trip, and then pick them up slowly on the other side. We didn't get the last groom we needed until we were right at the dock, where an old racetracker had been instructed to meet us. ("Doc" Alpers kind of liked his beer, but he sure knew how to ship horses, having been coast-to-coast with racehorses dozens of times; before the experience was over, he proved a great help.)

We had shipped Totilla from Camden two days early so that he could stop off en route at Belmont Park and have his heel nerves done (again) by Dr. William Wright, who also generously supplied the team with all the medicine it needed as his contribution to our Olympic effort. So there I was, leaving for my first European tour and the Olympic Games with one green six-year-old mare and one patched-up old stager we were hoping might get by just one more time if we needed him.

The horses arrived in Germany safe, but thin, and went right to Munich-Riem, where our Army team had trained, which became our training base too. (I'm told that it was hardly recognizable as the same place in 1972, when it was the site of the equestrian events at the Munich Olympics.) Munich was then still pretty much in a shambles, having been hard hit by the war, and there was rubble everywhere.

After several weeks in which the horses regained some condition, we started off by rail on a brief tour of German pre-Olympic shows, consisting of Wiesbaden, Düsseldorf and Hamburg. All three cities were still digging out and rebuilding, for the German postwar recovery was only starting. However, the shows were impressively well organized, and as someone who had been around horse shows all his life, I was a bit surprised to find myself like a fish out of water.

Until I got to Germany, I'd been pretty confident about knowing what I was doing with the team (except for the experience in Mexico, which was so abnormal that it didn't count). After all, I'd been showing jumpers all my life, and the fall circuit was no different from what I'd been seeing at other good U.S. shows. German show jumping, however, was a revelation. Seeing the big outdoor courses at Düsseldorf and Hamburg, and watching how the best foreign riders handled them, made me realize how much we had to learn, and how little we challenged the ability of our best horses at home. Our touch classes put so much stress on riding accurate approaches and jumping fences absolutely cleanly that we never got around to exploiting our horses' ability to jump big fences freely and fluently. Suddenly I felt like a novice again, and even Gyp's experience with this kind of competitive situation was too scanty to be of much help.

Competitively, however, we weren't doing all that badly. In fact, we won the big pre-Olympic team class in Düsseldorf over Germany, and I won a class with Miss Bud there. (The trophy was a gold ring in the form of a Saint George that I wear to this day.) Russell won the famous Hamburg Derby with Rattler, the first non-German rider ever to do so, and we won a lot of ribbons everywhere we went. Nonetheless, deep down inside we knew that we were basically beginners in doing some of the things at which the Europeans were already experts. I couldn't wait to get home and start schooling my horses all over again, starting with some different basic ideas and a lot of new natural obstacles—banks, ditches, waters—that I'd have to build. Yes, the whole thing was a real revelation.

In the meantime, however, we had the Helsinki Olympic Games to contend with. I wish I could say that it was the high point of my USET career, but in some ways it was almost the opposite. In fact, I got so frustrated by our haphazard stable organization and the internal friction that had developed that at times I was ready to chuck the whole thing. Sure, we were new hands at an old game, and away from home, and you could make excuses for some of our difficulties. Still, I don't believe in glossing over problems, or walking into mistakes that you can see coming, and I'm afraid I didn't grin and bear it very well. The best thing I can say is that it didn't last forever, and the team operates very differently today.

Despite our pre-Games problems, the Games themselves went surprisingly well. The Finns built what we thought was an enormous course for the Prize of Nations, but our horses jumped their hearts out, and with a little luck we might have won it all. I rode Miss Budweiser; Russell, Democrat, and Steinkraus, Hollandia. (In those days, there was no fourth rider, and all

The USET's 1952 Olympic jumping team, surprise winners of the pre-Olympic team competition at Düsseldorf: (from left) Arthur McCashin on Totilla, Captain John Russell on Rattler and Bill Steinkraus on Hollandia. Several weeks later Russell became the first foreign rider ever to win the famous Hamburg Derby.

Arthur McCashin and Miss Budweiser, starting the morning round of the Prize of Nations at the Helsinki Olympics in 1952. They finished thirteenth in a field of fifty-nine, helping the USET win a bronze team medal on its first attempt.

three scores counted.) At the end of the first round, our total of 23 faults was a couple of knockdowns better than those of the British and the Chileans; but at Helsinki the Prize of Nations was, for the first time, a two-round competition. In the second round, the British and Chileans went considerably better, we not quite as well, and so we ended up with the team bronze instead of a shinier medal. Nonetheless, it was something, and since the three-day team had also won a bronze, the USET's Games debut was regarded as a great success.

A few images from Helsinki will never leave me—some still rather rankling, others simply funny. I'll never forget Fritz Thiedemann coming to the schooling area one day and building an oxer that was almost six feet square. He trotted around once or twice and then jumped it, forward and backward—and this on his *reserve* horse! Once the Games were under way, the performances of the great Czech distance runner Emil Zatopek could never be forgotten. He won three gold medals, and the first time I saw him run I had to single him out as having the worst running style in the race!

Finally, I'll never forget bicycling up the long hill from the warm-up area to the stables, in boots that were suddenly much too tight on that warm day, to find that the horses hadn't even left the barn, though I had only fifteen minutes to warm up and get to the stadium a couple of miles away! All I can say about that is that we never made quite the same mistake again.

After the Olympics our team competed at Dublin. There wasn't time to ship our own horses from Helsinki, so we rode second- (third-?) string Irish horses, which proved to be quite an experience. Reunited with our own

29

horses we then finished our tour at London, where we had a reasonably good show but made no waves.

For the North American fall circuit after the Games, the Olympic individual gold-medal winner, Pierre d'Oriola, and the rest of the French team competed, along with the perennial (in those years) Irish and the Canadians. Looking at our courses again in the context of what I'd seen abroad, I could clearly see for the first time how backward and primitive our form of international jumping was, in many ways.

There were a lot of falls at Harrisburg that year, basically because the courses contained a lot of traps. Many were there by accident, but some were intentional, too, for many show managers still thought, Build something flimsy and awkward, and see if anyone can make it. I longed to see us show the American public the kind of jumping we'd seen in Europe, but we sure didn't do it that year.

In a certain way, of course, our old-fashioned courses helped us competitively, for we knew that game, and we had an excellent fall circuit. Carol Durand replaced Russell, who stayed in Europe with his unit, and we dominated the shows for the first time. Steinkraus took over from Russell on Democrat and hit it off immediately with him, winning eight individual classes. We also won the Low Score Aggregate, which was a bigger deal than the Nations Cup in those days, at two of the three shows.

After Toronto we returned our borrowed horses to their owners, retired old Democrat to pasture—he'd certainly done more than his share—and disbanded the team until the following year. Having paid its Olympic-year expenses, the infant USET didn't have the finances or the organization to do anything else. However, thinking about the whole thing that winter, I began to realize that we'd probably never get anywhere in the show-jumping big time until we started building more European-type courses at home, and preparing for them right from the ground up.

In 1953 the team ran trials at the end of the summer in Quentin, Pennsylvania, where I rode a big saddle-bred chestnut horse named Rusty. I was happy to have him, too, but it does kind of indicate that we hadn't really solved the horse problem that summer. Carol Durand, Ronnie Mutch and I were named to represent our country against teams from England, Ireland and Canada, the Mexicans being involved in some kind of political squabble. Returning for the second time, Harry Llewellyn and Pat Smythe of England were a bit more outspoken, and Pat described our courses to some journalist as "prehistoric." The remark made many people angry, but I wanted to cheer, for basically she was right—there was a tremendous gap between us and Europe in the course department, and it was time we faced it. Actually, we were never permitted to walk a course in those days, and it wasn't until Pat started complaining that our officials reluctantly agreed to it.

Though we trained for the fall circuit for only a few weeks and had four

Arthur McCashin riding his own Mohawk at the London International Show at White City in 1955. Note the sheepskin pad under Mohawk's girth, a protection he required to keep him from cutting himself with his caulks.

completely new horses to go along with the veteran Reno Kirk and Paleface, we managed to get by pretty well, winning ten classes out of thirty-two, and being the leading team at Toronto. Deep inside, however, we knew that the handwriting on the wall was still there: establish some real continuity of training and get some decent horses, or perish competitively.

The summer of 1954 found the USET holding Pan American Games trials at Oak Brook, Illinois, and this time a big effort was made to provide courses that would more nearly resemble what we could expect to find abroad. To this end the team engaged as course designer a former Hungarian cavalry officer named Bertalan de Nemethy, whom I had met the previous year through a former pupil of his, Gabor Foltenyi, one of the better jumper riders at the shows. Bert's courses at Oak Brook stressed scope so much that we had to really start riding forward instead of looking for a short stride, and I was extremely impressed by them and by him. There was some preliminary discussion about other ways in which he might help the USET, but unfortunately, nothing came of it at the time.

Four riders were to start in the Nations Cup at the Pan American Games in Mexico City, so five riders were picked at the trials, including three newcomers. Joining Steinkraus and me were Charley Dennehy from Chicago with the brilliant but rather erratic Pill Box; Lieutenant John Wheeler, an active artillery officer with the Army-trained Little Mac—a real marvel for his age, small size and limited experience—and Gyp's eldest son, Jeb. (Jeb later dropped out, but went to Mexico as a member of the three-day squad, for which he had also qualified.)

Steinkraus, Dennehy and I were named to ride on the 1954 fall circuit against strong teams from Germany and Spain plus the two regulars, Mexico and Canada. As we might have known, there was no way our improvised string of mostly green horses could cope with this kind of field after only a few weeks' training in my backyard at Pluckemin, New Jersey. The Germans, Spanish and Mexicans won thirty classes among them, and we were lucky to be shut out only once on the circuit (at Harrisburg). But it was sure a long circuit that year.

The 1955 Pan American Games were scheduled early, so we trained all three squads at Camden again, under the watchful eye of Tupper Cole, who served as *chef d'équipe*. I liked this, since I had a useful hurdle horse to play with in my spare time, and the training session went well. Nemethy and Foltenyi helped us out by building some nice courses to school over at Southern Pines, North Carolina, and Tupper Cole, a fine horseman as well as a fine person, was a great asset in schooling.

However, it took more than that to solve our horse problem. Of our four best horses—Pill Box, Little Mac, my Mohawk and Norman Coates's Volco's Duke, lent to Steinkraus—not one was a real Games horse, and only Pill Box was even very close. Perhaps it didn't make much difference anyway, for as it turned out, the course in Mexico gave off strong echoes of Monterrey; the Mexicans won the competition with more than 70 faults, and we were lucky to get out of town with our skins still intact. Fortunately, Wally Staley and Bob Borg salvaged some USET prestige by winning individual gold and silver medals in three-day and dressage, respectively, as described elsewhere in this book.

By this time it was obvious to many people that making a few European shows before the 1956 Olympics in Stockholm wasn't going to be nearly enough to turn things around this time, even though we'd gotten away with it in 1952. It was also pretty obvious that the person who could probably help us most in our training would be Bert de Nemethy, if we could get him. Doing so took considerable negotiation, both with Bert and with his then employer, the famous Boston sportswoman Eleonora Sears, but get him we did, just in time to go with us to Europe for a tour of five European shows that summer. It was the best move the USET ever made.

Bert at last gave the USET Prix squad a shortcut to the collective experience of the European trainers, and a sound and systematic method of developing horses and riders and teaching them to cope with European

The 1955 USET squad at London: Arthur McCashin on Mohawk, Bill Steinkraus on Night Owl, Hugh Wiley on Nautical and John Russell on Florett. The riders look pensive, and well they might; they are about to tackle a big Nations Cup course with four green horses. Three years later, Nautical and Night Owl helped collaborate on the first of three consecutive USET wins in this famous class.

conditions. In addition, he continued to exert a big influence on my thinking and others' in regard to course design. (Thus he became partly responsible for the fact that once I'd finished riding on the team, I let myself get stuck with the job of building international courses for the Washington and New York shows for a number of years.)

Of course, there wasn't time for Bert to accomplish much before we shipped to Europe in 1955, and when he saw the green-as-grass stock we were taking, he must have wondered what he had gotten into. (We *had* to make some changes after Mexico, but we didn't have much to choose from. Only two of the horses we were sending to join two of Russell's that were already over there had any real experience—my Mohawk, and Wiley's recently purchased Nautical. Steinkraus' Wonabet was only a year off the

33

racetrack, Wiley's Blue Ridge was really a working hunter and my backup, Sortie Sunday, had shown only in local shows and was none too sound.)

The 1955 European tour was no bed of roses. The major European teams were already well along in their rebuilding programs, and we no longer had any of the experienced Army horses to help us out. By the end of the tour, at Rotterdam, we didn't even have three sound horses to enter in the Nations Cup, and overall results from the tour were anything but impressive. The main thing was, however, that we were starting to get an idea of what we were doing and what had to be done, and in that sense, 1955 was a real turning point.

After returning from Europe I knew that I didn't have an Olympic horse, and that both my family and my farm had been neglected for a long time. I stayed home that fall, and as it eventually turned out, that was the end of my riding participation in USET, though I've been involved since then in lots of other ways.

Others can tell the story of what happened thereafter better than I. The 1956 Olympic squad had to struggle to place fifth, but things were already improving. With Bert as permanent coach, the team did not disband after the fall circuit, but took a nucleus of horses to Tryon, North Carolina, to continue training. Bert spent the summer of 1957 looking at new horses and riders at the new training center the team set up on the Greenwich, Connecticut, estate of the late Alvin Untermyer. By the time the team returned to Europe in 1958, they were a whole lot less "innocent" than that first team I was on only six years earlier, and proved it by winning almost a score of classes, including such major wins as London's Nations Cup, the Grand Prix of Rotterdam and the George V Cup.

Today when the USET goes to Europe it's a far cry from that first trip in 1952. The flight on a 727 jet takes only a few hours, as compared with eight or ten days on a ship. Even the freshman riders and horses are usually competitive right from the beginning, having jumped comparable courses at home many times at our own shows. The jumping team has won an individual Olympic gold medal and a couple of team silvers, the last one (at Munich) only one-quarter of a fault away from the gold, which can't elude us forever.

It's a very big change, and I'd love to have had a crack at it the way it is now. On the other hand, I'm glad I played a role the way it was then, and had something to do with changing it.

From Horse Cavalry to USET

JOHN W. RUSSELL

Johnny Russell was a member of both the last Army Olympic Equestrian Team in 1948 and the first "civilian" USET squad in 1952. Though he ended his own competitive career in 1955, Colonel Russell has remained a part of the international competitive scene as coach of the U.S. Modern Pentathlon Team at four Olympics, and has also kept his hand in at judging and course designing. Russell lives in San Antonio, Texas, and still coaches the pentathletes at Fort Sam Houston.

IMMEDIATELY AFTER WORLD WAR II, the U.S. Equestrian Sports Committee began looking for horses and riders for the 1948 Olympics. This committee, which was all military, had been appointed by the U.S. Olympic Committee. By 1947, the Army had already assembled quite a formidable squad. Some horses were shipped in from Germany, while the best-known U.S. Army horses were called in from the various posts and remount stations. Being stationed in Italy at the time, I requested orders for Fort Riley, Kansas, to try for the team. On the strength of my European horse-show record, permission was granted and my orders were cut.

I had shown pretty much all over Italy, Austria and Germany and was fortunate enough to win a lot of big classes on two horses I had liberated from the enemy toward the end of the war: Don Pedro, a medium-sized dark brown warmblood, who won the Prize of Nations in Vienna and Milan and was the high-point open horse of Italy; and Blue Devil, a smaller chestnut Italian Thoroughbred named for my division, the 88th Blue Devil Division, one of the best event and speed-class horses of his time. Naturally, I wanted these two horses to come to the States with me, but the Army refused to ship them; the division commander, General Moore, agreed to hold the horses until I could get back to Europe.

The Army Olympic squad was commanded by Colonel Earl F. Thomson, a silver medalist in 1932 and 1936 for the three-day event, who went on to win a gold team medal for the three-day event and a bronze in Grand Prix dressage in the 1948 Games. I believe he is the only American to have won medals in both the three-day event and the Grand Prix dressage in the same Olympic Games. The squad consisted of fifteen riders, many of whom had been pretty sure shots for the 1940 Games, which had to be cancelled because of World War II.

By catch-riding, I soon had up to seven or eight horses behind my name on the rider–horse list. On this squad, all riders except those doing Grand Prix dressage trained for both the three-day event and the Prize of Nations jumping team. For me it made training more interesting. The team met every morning, and each horse had a schedule. This could be changed only by discussion with the team leader and the veterinarian, Dr. Harvey Ellis, who seldom missed a formation. A typical day might consist of dressage work for all horses; then one would be galloped on the flat, another scheduled for cross-country or steeplechase and a third for road work. Some days were just stadium jumping. In my case I usually had at least three horses in both the three-day and stadium-jumping categories. My rider/groom helped me with the conditioning work by riding one and leading one for the long walk-and-trot cross-country sessions while I schooled my jumpers. In the afternoons I would work the problem horses, or one that required extra training for one reason or the other, again.

Because of my recent European show experience, I was also responsible for all course construction for both three-day and Prize of Nations. Fort Riley was a course designer's dream. The Hippodrome, as the outdoor training ground was called, had four distinct areas: Aachen, Lucerne, Dublin and a general area. Each of the great shows for which they were named has its particular course idiosyncrasies; since these were duplicated at Fort Riley, horses that trained there could go anywhere in the world and be at home. (The only jump I ever found in Europe that we had not trained over was the one the Germans call Pulvermans Grab [grave] and that in Hungary is called the Budapester.) Being the junior officer, I was also detailed to teach the officers' wives and all visiting ladies, of whom there seemed to be an endless stream. This took valuable time away from my training, but occasionally had its attractions.

On October 1, 1947, we had a full trials with the three-day horses. My horse (by assignment, and not by choice) was one I shall never forget. Dites-Moi was one of the few horses I ever rode that could not jump. On the steeplechase course we brushed through all the way up to my knees. He

The 1948 Army Horse Show Team, winners of the Aga Khan Cup (the Nations Cup) at Dublin just following the London Olympics. The riders are Wing, Symroski, Frierson and Russell on Air Mail, who clinched the win with the best individual performance of the day.

went to his nose on the first cross-country fence, and shook my teeth on every one that followed. Somehow we managed to finish. The next day, to my surprise, he was sound, and after another minor miracle we placed fifth overall. Lieutenant Charles Anderson won the trials with Reno Palisade and later a gold medal in the 1948 Games.

For the Prize of Nations trials held on the Paul Butler estate, at Oak Brook, Illinois, near Chicago, I was assigned a German horse called Brown Gander, a horse with a lot of jump but a real puller, and Rattler, a Texas-bred Quarter Horse by Rattlesnake Tom. (This little horse in 1952 made me the first foreigner ever to win the Hamburg Spring Derby.)

Somehow I qualified to make the trip to Europe, where the final selections would be made. Eleven officers, eleven grooms and thirty-one horses shipped out in late October, 1947, setting up training in Munich-Riem, site of the 1972 Olympics. Seventeen horses were already in Europe, and my speed horse, Blue Devil, also joined our group. (Unfortunately, my other horse, Don Pedro, had had too many weekend warriors ride him during my absence and finally went completely lame.)

The string assigned me by Colonel Thomson were all jumpers—Blue Devil, Rattler, Air Mail and Roll On. Because of lack of motivation toward my dressage work, I was not going to have a chance at the three-day event, but I had a whale of a jumper string. In Lucerne, Air Mail won the individual Prize of Nations, and with my four horses I was easily the leading rider of the show. (Here is one sure instance where the training at Riley paid off, for the Lucerne banks stopped a lot of foreign riders.)

The method of travel in those days was by train for both horses and riders. This was done in pretty good style, for we were usually assigned a special train with a U.S. Army transportation officer in charge who literally ran the railroad. As the junior officer, I usually went with the horses. There were four to six horses to a car, which meant that each horse had a really good box and could lie down, and surprisingly enough, most did. One groom stayed in each car at all times. My only complaint about this duty was Blue Devil's snoring. He hit the sack as soon as the train started rolling.

The team had a car for sleeping and a well-stocked dining car and bar. As this was 1947 and 1948, when food and liquor were strictly rationed in Europe, every time the train slowed or stopped the population of the train would double. The train officer would discover the newcomers after we were well out in the country, so there was nothing to do but have a great party until the next city. There he would dutifully unload all the stowaways off one end while we welcomed a new batch at the other. We had been strictly instructed on the importance of good public relations with Europeans, and we were doing our best to comply! Our team captain was also very much concerned with press relations, protocol, etc.; anyone incorrectly turned out or ignoring local customs and courtesies was in grave trouble. In this regard, one of our colonels taxed him to the limit. At the racecourse we used for galloping, the Germans had the horses ridden left and right on alternate days: Monday the horses galloped right, Tuesday left, and so on. This colonel could never remember which day was which and consistently galloped in the wrong direction, causing great havoc. Finally, the German jockeys decided to give him something to remember. As our absentminded teammate cantered contentedly down the track in the wrong direction, as usual, we heard the sound of hoofbeats coming. Galloping toward him full out, head to head, completely across the track, was every jockey at the racetrack. Even Custer couldn't have had a worse moment. True to his training, the horse held his course while his thunderstruck rider stared at the oncoming wave. We witnesses were sure he was dead when his horse, at the last second, wheeled and with speed borne of desperation, outran the field. Needless to say, our teammate became unconfused from then on about those days.

Although running the team for the team captain was a big responsibility, being a member of the team was wonderful fun and tremendous training. There were good horses, the best of equipment and good riders for teammates—such good riders that the final selection of those who would start in the Games was not easy. (On one occasion Washington politics appeared to enter the decision, as one rider had really not won enough to be chosen.)

The Army Olympic Team of 1948 won the bronze medal in dressage, with Lieutenant Bob Borg placing fourth individually. The three-day team

Captain Russell and Air Mail, his Olympic mount in 1948, competing in the Nations Cup at Lucerne, won by the United States.

won the gold medal, with Lieutenant Colonel Frank Henry second individually and Lieutenant Anderson fourth. Colonel Franklin Wing was fourth individually in the Prize of Nations, but because of the elimination of Colonel Frierson and Rascal, the Prize of Nations team did not place. (There was no discard score in those days.) Since we had won almost every big competition in Europe that spring, including the Grand Prix of Aachen, the Prize of Nations at London and the Prize of Nations in Dublin, it was a bitter pill.

Despite the good showing of the group, the Army proceeded to disband the equestrian team. Immediately after the London Games, all riders were assigned to Europe. I was very fortunate to go back to Munich headquarters commandant of the 2nd Constabulary Brigade. All the good foreign horses were also shipped to Munich and came under my command, so it turned out to be a delightful three years. Also under my command were all enlisted men of the Headquarters and the Aviation section. One of them spoke perfect German and had been a groom with the equestrian team, so I put him in charge of the stables in Munich-Riem, and then started showing all over Germany. With two bronze-medal dressage horses, several three-day-event horses and a half-dozen German jumpers, I was fairly well mounted.

Colonel Wing commanded a brigade in Augsburg, Lieutenant Colonel Henry was with a senior headquarters, Colonel William F. Greear was chief of staff of Berlin (thus opening up the great Berlin Show) and an old friend, Colonel Throckmorton, was secretary to the General Staff. I kept them

39

mounted and they kept me out of trouble. We showed all over Germany, France and Ireland that summer. Washington had disbanded the official team, but we had organized our own in the hope that if we did well, word would get back and somehow the team might be brought to life again. We won the Prize of Nations in Ireland, Paris and Vichy. The word did get back, all right, but the reaction was not what we wanted—we were told in no uncertain terms to get back to our tanks and start riding iron horses.

With my tour up, I took a Stateside assignment. On my way to report for duty I stopped off at the Pennsylvania National Horse Show in Harrisburg and saw Colonel Wofford. He told me that he was heading up the newly formed civilian equestrian team and that if I wanted to be on the team, all I had to do was find several Olympic-caliber horses and get the Department of the Army to let me go on temporary duty to train with the team. By this time I had ten years' service, but except for the war years, the real Army had seen very little of me. My chances of getting permission seemed very slim. At any rate, I took up my duties as adviser and instructor for the Army Reserve at Altoona, Pennsylvania. The schedule there called for mostly night training sessions, which left the days free for horse hunting and time to ride the few I had already found.

A year later, as luck would have it, I ran into an old friend, George Wilson, in the sports office of the Department of the Army, and he helped me get permission to go to Riley for the equestrian-team trials. To destroy any myths surrounding the old saying "The Army takes care of its own," I was told that I was not to expect to get any horses from the Army even if I had formerly ridden and trained them. At Riley, Arthur McCashin was already in training with Totilla and Swizzlestick. Carol Durand, the first woman on the team, had Reno Kirk and one of my former horses, Rattler. My old horse, Blue Devil, was in quarantine with a suspected communicable disease and was to be put down. Fortunately, he was retested and spared. Democrat, Colonel Wing's Olympic horse, was sore. I had a horse with me called By Day, an attractive but hot and careless chestnut lent to me by W. Haggin Perry.

As I began training for the trials, it suddenly hit me that this was not the Army team anymore. I had been accustomed to an organized training squad that met promptly every morning at a given time to find a program laid out for each of its members. If you had a problem horse, you and your coach discussed the problems and went to work on solving them, which might include a change of rider. Things were a lot more casual with the civilian group, and the stay at Riley was relaxed and pleasant, ending with, I believe, three trials. Democrat had a small operation, but was back in action at least enough to win the trials and put me on the team. For horse-show purposes I took Swizzlestick and Blue Devil, who never regained his 1947–1950 form. Swizzlestick was about half the horse he had been in 1948.

40

Major Russell, in "civvies," and Blue Devil, competing at New York's National Horse Show in 1951, where they won the Drake Challenge Trophy.

Democrat was off and on in his soundness, so Colonel Wofford and I decided against using him for Stateside shows, even though I knew he was my best horse.

We showed that fall (1951) in Harrisburg, New York, Toronto and then Mexico. My participation was somewhat less than brilliant. I won several classes here and there, but it is certainly true that "the better the horse, the better the rider." My best friend on the circuit, General Humberto Mariles, was also having problems, and without each other's help, we both might have ended up with broken necks.

One of the problems was never being able to train. When you have only old jumpers, mostly lame, the primary concern is having something sound enough to go in the ring. We had not heard of the drugs that now exist—all we had were Antiphlogistine, mothballs to melt in the feet and white gas to stand them in. Hormone shots were supposed to give the old geldings more energy.

We went into winter training at Camden, South Carolina, which was very pleasant, but I had nothing to train. I spent the winter hacking through the pines and did a little stick-and-ball at the polo field, always hoping a nice fresh new jumper would appear. None did.

In the spring we shipped to Europe, and back to Munich-Riem, my second home by now. The team now consisted of Billy Steinkraus with Hollandia and Reno Kirk, Arthur McCashin with Miss Budweiser and Totilla, Norman Brinker with Paleface and me with Democrat and Rattler.

Again, training was light; except for Reno Kirk falling in a double ditch and breaking Billy's arm, things were pretty dull. We showed at Wiesbaden, Düsseldorf, Hamburg and several small shows before shipping to Helsinki. We won the Prize of Nations at Düsseldorf and won a class here and there at the other shows. Rattler and I won the Hamburg Derby, a famous class over a course that has not changed since 1920. Rattler was the first foreign horse and I was the first non-German rider ever to win this class. The course really suited Rattler, with large banks, ditches and the famous "Pulverman's Grave." Rattler, being from west Texas, plus his year at Riley, thought it a breeze.

When we arrived in Helsinki for the 1952 Olympic Games, Democrat was really hurting. He was so sore that very much flat work was impossible, and jumping out of the question. Even so, it was obvious that if we were to do well in the Games, the horses to use were Miss Budweiser, Hollandia and Democrat. This was a mighty shaky outfit, and the wrong course could kill us. Miss Budweiser had bank and ditch problems; Hollandia, a good jumper, had his squirrely side and Democrat was a sore horse with no conditioning.

At any rate, we won the bronze medal as a team. Gustav Rau, the man who put the German team together after the war and had a great deal to do with the German team's being what it is today, wrote: "The Americans are three completely different type individuals, all with different type horses, but they are the most cold-blooded riders in the Games. Each knows exactly what they must do and they will do it." This is the way I always felt, riding with Billy Steinkraus and Arthur McCashin. No matter what horses we started, one of us usually came through, and we managed to pick up lots of ribbons.

After the Games, I already had orders to Frankfurt as headquarters commandant for V Corps. The Army was wasting no time putting me back to work, but with the Russell luck, in weeks I was showing all over Germany with Josef Neckermann, the now-famous dressage rider. In the 1950s he was a first-class jump rider. His son-in-law Hans Pracht and another friend, Henri François-Poncet, lent me their jumpers to show. Another source of horses for me was one of the big German dealers who would let me show his sale horses that were entered in the big shows. This could be one or a dozen. I was able to buy and sell my way to a good German mare called Lonie. She first jumped for Germany, then was sold to the French, with whom she developed a real stopping problem. Because of this I was able to buy her. With some reschooling we began to win classes. In 1953 we were fourth in the German National standings. One of her biggest wins was the Ladies' Hamburg Derby with my wife. (This was another first, to have both Derbys won by the same family.)

My military assignment was also interesting; being commandant of the I. G. Farben building and V Corps Special Troop, I handled everything from

42

Major Russell at the 1952 Olympics in Helsinki. By the last fence the second time around, the nineteen-year-old Democrat was struggling against fatigue, but his courage never gave out.

maneuvers to the general's hunting trips. A corps alert could come at three o'clock in the morning; my job was to awaken the troops and move the entire corps headquarters to the field, including telephone and lights. I also had to have breakfast ready to serve by the time the commander arrived. If this was not done fast enough and with a minimum of damage to government equipment, I had to do it all again.

Meanwhile, I had been told by Colonel Wofford that he was sending Bill Steinkraus, Arthur McCashin and Hugh Wiley over and that he would like for me to join them if I could get loose from the Army. This was 1955, and I again asked for extended temporary duty to ride full-time with the team. I was told rather pointedly how many actual days I had spent working for the Army and how little I knew about the operation of a tank, but was finally granted permission to ride with the team.

I had now a good string of horses—Lonie had done well at all the major shows; Bally Bay, a nice five-year-old, picked up ribbons wherever he went, including Aachen, and I also had a six-year-old mare, Isolde, green but very talented. But just a few weeks before I joined the team, Lonie broke a bone in her foot, and Isolde developed lung trouble and never jumped again. Almost overnight, I was practically walking. I bought another horse from Hans Winkler that I really hated. He was one of those horses that knocked down every wall or gate if you left from a nice spot. The only way to get him to jump clean was to make him feel that his life was in danger. Every first round, if the jumps were not built like fortresses, I had to put him in trouble at all the verticals. The best way to get his attention was a short ride around the back of the barn.

Anyhow, with him, Bally Bay and a lame Lonie, I joined the 1955 squad. This was my first meeting with Bert de Nemethy. It was soon obvious that Bert wanted to have some training sessions and to get things a little more organized. He and Bob Freels got the stables in order and Bert started running supervised warm-ups and training sessions. He didn't have

43

Major Russell and his Bally Bay at Ostend, Belgium, in 1955. This was Russell's last tour as a rider.

much in the way of horseflesh to work with, and we didn't have much success at the shows, but as I look back over the years, that was the beginning of the first-class civilian team we have today. And making the transition from an army to a civilian team is by no means a simple matter. After Mariles, no one in Mexico has ever been able to pull the Mexicans together, even though they buy terrific horses. France has never successfully made the change from a military to a civilian team, and in my opinion, the Irish stuck too long with the old-timers and waited too long to change their methods and organize a modern team. Even Italy will be a long time finding replacements for the d'Inzeo brothers. However, with their fine coaching and permanent training centers at Gladstone and Hamilton, the USET should have a good foundation to work from for years to come.

At any rate, my riding career was about to end. I had made a promise to myself that thirty-five was the magic age at which to stop competitive riding. I had seen too many good riders continue until they were hurt, or had lost the desire to ride over big courses. I was determined to stop early, but Uncle Sam also let me know that I was a thirty-five-year-old major with all the earmarks of becoming a much older one. We finished the tour with Hugh Wiley and Nautical becoming a pair to watch. It was not a very exciting finale for me, except for falling in the water jump at White City, but I'd already had my share of thrills.

I was back in the Army again, heading for a brilliant military career without horses, when less than a year later I was called to the Pentagon. My new assignment, they told me, was to teach some soldiers how to ride. I packed my bags again and headed for Fort Sam Houston, Texas, as officer in charge of the United States Modern Pentathlon Team. But that is a whole other story.

44

POSTSCRIPT

Through the years many people have asked me to comment on the differences between military teams and those supported by independent civilian agencies, and perhaps a few words on this subject would not be out of place here.

I will start by describing the military team. Actually, this should probably be called the state-supported team, for when a team is supported by the army it really means the country; not only are the facilities of the armed forces at your disposal, but those of most government agencies as well.

As a military athlete you are first fed, equipped, housed, transported and trained, which is quite different from depending on your own private funds. In the case of the Army Equestrian Team you could add horses and veterinary service to the "furnished" list. Our training facilities at Fort Riley were second to none. They included two riding halls; a jumping stadium with all the various European-type obstacles, such as banks, ditches, water; a full-length cross-country containing every kind of obstacle you might run into and a flat track and steeplechase course, with dressage rings all over the infield. (Fort Sill, Oklahoma, probably still has the most up-to-date and beautiful jumper course in this country, built for training the 1940 Olympic Team.)

With the military team you had the full-time Army grooms, seven days a week. ("Fuddy" Wing sometimes found his in Democrat's stall on Sunday morning, but at least he was there.) There were also a full-time supply sergeant, a full-time blacksmith and enough extra bodies so that building a course or painting the jumps was no big item. When it came to moving the horses, the transportation office was called; your trucks or train were arranged; the stable officer and groom moved the outfit and set it up upon arrival. As riders we were usually furnished orders giving us the option of flying, driving or taking the train. When a military team arrived in any foreign country, you immediately paid a courtesy call on your embassy. This usually assured you of transportation, PX and medical support, plus a good start on the social side of things.

Even on tour the military athlete is free from the pressure of expense, and you seldom hear money matters discussed. The Army makes sure that you don't make any money traveling, but you should not need to dip into your own funds. Training riders, like any other team, depends on the coaching staff. In my case I was always furnished the best. My first international coach was a Count Keckler, one of Mussolini's Black Shirt riders before World War II. In my opinion, he was the best speed coach in the world. Machese Fabio Mangilli, another Italian, taught me a great deal about three-day. Captain Barnekow, who rode on the German 1936 Olympic Team, was also most helpful. The military never hesitated to hire or seek information from others if it helped their effort. Colonel Thomson hired Richard Wätjen as a full-time coach when we were hardly speaking to the Germans. Under Army discipline the matching up of horses and riders could be pretty impersonal; if the team leader felt another rider could do a better job on a particular horse a switch was made, whether you liked it or not. Our training discipline was simple and fair: be on time and do your job. However, I have heard stories about teams before my time that were pretty unpleasant, and I can understand how this could be, considering the power a military commander has at his disposal.

During my time on the Army team, training was varied and interesting. We all did all the disciplines—three-day, jumper and dressage. The program was worked out months in advance, and you could tell by looking at the schedule when you would be required to ride a dressage test, go cross-country, jump a course, etc., and on what horse. Afterward you could expect to be told what you did right, and surely you would be told your weak areas and given suggested ideas for improvement.

Another plus for most military teams is the feeling of comradeship. The fact that all your teammates belong to the same club may not make you ride better, but you win better and lose better. Often we got as much pride and satisfaction out of a teammate's victory as we did out of our own.

Despite the good points of having an Army team, in my opinion a number of weak points partially overshadow the advantages. The methods of team selection and getting assigned to the team could be very unsatisfactory. It was also very difficult to pursue a riding career and maintain your promotion status at the same time, while having your immediate commander refuse to release you for training could stop you dead in your tracks. I know of a number of officers who sought unsuccessfully to obtain a tryout. The Army had many good enlisted riders. To my knowledge none made the teams, though of the thousands who served with horses, surely some must have had some talent. Top-quality riders are hard to come by, no matter how good the training program, but entering a competitive sport such as riding after graduation from one of the military academies is a rather late start when your competitors have been competing since infancy. The military depended on an elaborate network of regiments, schools and remount stations to develop the young horses. In the modern Army this does not exist; had the Army continued to provide our equestrian teams, either horses would have become a major weakness or one of the world's largest breeding programs would have had to be put into operation.

Now to evaluate the civilian team as I see it, starting with the good points. The civilian coach has his pick of the best in the nation, which includes the military. In spite of what many think, tryouts are much easier to get into in the civilian setup. Moreover, every time you show in major competitions you are trying out for the team, and you require permission from no one. More top-quality horse–rider combinations are available to the civilian coach, mostly fully trained and ready to put on the plane. At the very least, you know they can jump a big course. Every professional has the opportunity to develop Olympic-type horses and sell them to prospective Olympic riders or even to the team.

This means, in effect, that USET has hundreds of trainers all over the nation producing horses and riders. The civilian rider may devote all or part of his time to his riding. He may drop out at will and pick up again when he feels he has the right horse. All the civilian rider need do is be the best in the nation in his event and he, in spite of what you sometimes hear, will be on the team. No coach goes to the games with second-class performers if better ones are available, regardless of his personal feelings.

On the minus side. Unless a horse is owned by the team, the civilian coach has little control of the horse and rider except on tour, where in most cases it is too late or too risky to make many changes. In addition, it is obviously rather difficult to take a rider off a horse he bought with his own money to ride. However, today I believe this problem is minimal. Most of the good winning combinations today need very little juggling. Money to train, transport and compete is probably the one advantage of the military athlete. Owning and showing as an individual can be very expensive.

Some sports today have enough money to financially support outstanding athletes prior to their selection at national and Olympic trials. Perhaps, sometime in the future, this may be possible for horses and riders. We also need a selection method that is so clear that everyone directly or indirectly concerned can tell who has made the squad. In practice, the best riders generally *are* selected; however, any system that cannot be explained in simple terms will always create dissatisfaction, which hurts the sport. Some teams designate certain competitions and give a point value for places. The competitors with the most points join the team; then the coach and committee select the Olympic starters. This has many drawbacks, too, but at least it is a system that people understand, and it has a certain amount of P.R. value.

In conclusion, as a competitor under both systems, I found it much more comfortable and economical to compete under the military, but believe that with the civilian concept we have more winners and have more horses and riders participating.

The Horse
with the Flying Tail

HUGH WILEY

Hugh Wiley was on special leave from the U.S. Navy, training for the Olympics, when he decided that Nautical would be a more appropriate name for his favorite mount than Injun Joe, but Walt Disney came up with a better one still; millions of Americans thrilled to the story of the "Horse with the Flying Tail" from New Mexico who got to meet the Queen. One of the star performers of the USET's first decade, Hugh Wiley retired from active competition after the Rome Olympics. He is now a well-known instructor in Virginia.

IT WAS A BEAUTIFUL MORNING, that Wednesday in July, 1959—unusually bright and warm for London. The doorman was humming "Yankee Doodle Dandy" (tongue in cheek, I am sure) as he opened the door for me at the Hyde Park Hotel. I suppose by his observations I was a Yankee and I was in London riding on a pony. *Some pony,* I thought, as I descended the steps to the street, for Nautical was sweeping the boards at the White City that year. We couldn't do a thing wrong, class after class.

As I walked toward Piccadilly I thought, Tonight's the big one, the one I want the most—The King George V Gold Cup. Strangely enough, I felt that it was a foregone conclusion—that we couldn't lose; or at least, that Nautical couldn't lose, for he was at his peak. In fact, I had to caution myself not to be overconfident.

Actually, I always felt I could win every class I entered, even though, conversely, I knew I could lose it, too. There's sort of a balance which keeps tugging away: take only calculated risks, or go for broke? The latter was Nautical's philosophy. At least, it seemed to be his thinking, for many a wild ride I had on that Palomino. You would think he was the one who had walked the course, for if he thought I was too slow in pointing him at the next fence, he would break for whatever was in front of him. He was always incredibly brave, and now, after four years of Bert de Nemethy and Wiley, he was slightly more trusting. He was beginning to listen and to wait a little on his turns.

In my crazy daydreams that morning I had already won the Gold Cup and was now winging to victory in the 1960 Olympics in Rome. At least, that was what Walt Disney Productions had said we must do for the movie it was making of Nautical's life. (The Disney people had been filming us all that summer in Europe. Just before big competitions they would remind me that they had six cameramen at all angles covering my every move—which was a bit off-putting, to say the least. I sometimes found myself trying too hard to win for Disney.) At any rate, it was a tall order to win a gold medal, but why not? I'd been lucky enough to get this far, so why not all the way?

London is a wonderful city, I thought as I passed Hyde Park Corner. The Queen's Horse Guard was moving sedately toward Buckingham Palace, the cabbies were hysterical as usual and I could see Bert de Nemethy at a distance coming my way. Bert stopped to chat and pass on the stable news; he said that all was well.

This was unusual, believe me, for things were seldom all well with our little group of twelve horses, four riders, four grooms, a stable manager and a coach. "Surely, Bert, that's impossible," I said. "Well, *almost* everything is all right," he said reluctantly. "The grooms are complaining about their hotel, the blacksmith didn't show up and I can't find anyone to ship us to Ireland."

"Well, that's fair enough," I sighed. "At least things are normal." Bert had already longed Nautical that morning, and reported him in top form. I could tell by the twinkle in his eye that Bert was confident Nautical would do well this evening.

As we parted, I thought again that without Bert, there would be no high hopes for Nautical that night. He had taken me and that rogue of a horse and after four years of drill and discipline had come up with a winning combination. I would be the one in the spotlight if we won, but I knew, better than anyone else, who deserved the credit.

Today, fifteen years later, I am still often asked about Nautical. Where is he? Was the movie about his life true? Who were the bad guys? Bill Steinkraus suggested that this USET book might provide a good opportunity to tell the straight story about a wonderful horse named Joe.

I entered Injun Joe's life only in his eleventh year, so I am not much of an authority on his early life. The part in the Disney film about his starting with the Nortons in New Mexico is true, and his original name was Peter de Oro, after his sire, Muchacho de Oro. He passed through several different hands before he came East, and I do know that the late Joe Green and Cappy Smith both had him for a while in Virginia. To the best of my knowledge, however, the "heavies" in the film who knocked him around were mostly figments of the Disney poetic license; Disney liked to have something *happen* every few minutes in his films, even if nothing much happened in real life, and he felt no compunction about adding a dramatic incident or two.

In any case, my connection with Injun Joe dates from the spring of 1955, and in particular from a telephone call I received one day from General F. W. Boye, then the USET's executive vice-president. "Hugh," the General said, "would you be able to go to Europe with the team in four weeks?" Almost without thinking, I agreed. Anything to get out of that Maryland hayfield was my rationale. General Boye told me that I must have two good horses equipped and ready to report at Arthur McCashin's in New Jersey in three weeks.

On hanging up, I knew that I only had one horse that could possibly go to Europe, and he wasn't really top-caliber. (He was my working hunter, Coq de Guerre.) I wasn't going to tell this to General Boye, so the only thing to do was find another good horse, quick.

I called my good friend Sally Randolph Mills for advice, and without hesitation she recommended a Palomino owned by Millarden Farms called Injun Joe. I had seen this horse, but remembered him as being awfully difficult. Pat Dixon had been riding him, and though he had won a great deal, you could hardly call him consistent. Thus it was with great reservations that I went to see him again at a show in Hanover, Pennsylvania.

I watched him in one class and suddenly knew that he was the horse for me. He didn't win, but some of his jumps were unbelievable. He could leave out strides and be 2′ over the biggest oxer. He's a real crowd pleaser, but a scary one to ride, I was thinking.

Within several days, Injun Joe had a new home in my stable, and a new name, Nautical, in honor of my maritime career. Much to my dismay, riding him proved even more difficult than I had expected. Pat Dixon told me that he thrived on work, but he seemed to me to be a complete nut. If he even saw a fence, he exploded. The only thing that gave me any hope at all was that he was very gentle in the stable—he didn't kick or bite, and was a good doer. Since I had to report shortly to New Jersey, I didn't know what to do except cross my fingers and hope that somehow or other, it would all work out.

I arrived at Arthur McCashin's with Nautical and Coq de Guerre and was welcomed by Arthur, Bert de Nemethy and Bill Steinkraus. So far so

Nautical and Hugh Wiley during the first trip abroad for both of them, at Rotterdam in 1955. After overcoming his initial apprehensiveness, Nautical became a consistently spectacular water jumper.

good, I thought as we unloaded the horses. Bert was anxious to see my horses perform, so he scheduled me to work them both the following morning.

Arthur and Billy had both had international experience. They had ridden in the 1952 Games in Helsinki and in numerous other international events on the fall circuit. Bert had been on the Hungarian team before the war and as a young officer had ridden in Rome. My only exposure was to have been an alternate on the U.S. team in 1950 for our international indoor shows. It was interesting that evening to hear them chat about the European big time; now I was about to become a part of it.

I retired late that night thinking how I would dominate Joe in the morning. He would do what I wanted, or else! (Or else I would do what *he* wanted, which is about how it went for the next two years.)

The following morning I worked with Bert for the first time. He had just taken over as coach of the U.S. jumping squad and was something of an unknown quantity to me. After my performance that morning, he had no place to go but up. We didn't exactly have a brilliant string that year, but my new star, Nautical, must have seemed the bottom of the barrel.

I remember it as if it were yesterday. Bert wanted to see my two horses jump water and a bank. At first, Nautical would have no part of either and stopped repeatedly. Then Arthur finally got behind him with a whip, and he jumped so big I thought we would never come down. That one jump was impressive, but everything else that morning was too horrible to be true. I was embarrassed and Bert was polite, but there was no turning back now. We would leave for England in several days.

We spent our first few weeks in England that summer going to small national shows, which gave us a chance to see what we had in the way of talent. It wasn't much, but to my relief, I found that we didn't have the only green horses; in fact, there were many horses less experienced than ours. As a team we were about in the middle that year. This gave us hope.

Bert could always see potential greatness in Nautical, and he never gave up. I suppose most of you who are reading this little tale have heard the expression "slow work." Well, that is what we did with Nautical, day after day for many, many months. Transitions, circles, straight lines, bending, flexing—but very little jumping. Bert rode him most of the time, and gradually Nautical learned to accept him. But though his flat work improved, he was still a nut over fences as far as I was concerned, and would consistently run away. In order to look less like a fool, I just sat quiet and went along for the ride. I didn't know it at the time, but that was the secret to riding Nautical.

The following year, 1956, was not a good year for Nautical. While we were training for the Olympics in Tryon, North Carolina, he developed a sand crack in his left front hoof. The veterinarian practically cut his hoof off. The crack was very high, so the only cure was to cut above the crack so he could grow a new foot. This would put him out of work for the remainder of the year. As luck would have it, I got two very good horses, Trail Guide and Master William, to ride instead. I did not miss my yellow charger in the least.

The long convalescence proved a blessing in disguise. Nautical came back strong, after what was probably his first vacation in twelve years. I had to stay at home that winter, so Bert put him back into training himself. His letters kept saying how well Joe was responding and that I would not recognize him in the spring. And so it was—the breakthrough came at last. The lines of communication were established; Joe was accepting the rider's legs, hands and seat. It had taken just two years. Who else but Nemethy would have taken the time?

The year after the Stockholm Games we did not go to Europe, so I competed with Nautical around the United States. He started winning more and more consistently, and by the fall indoor circuit he was a formidable contender. He had become a very good time horse and looked as if he might be a Prize of Nations horse as well. We were all looking forward to our 1958 tour of continental Europe and England.

A new addition to our group was Jack Kettering. Jack was much more than a groom, for when he became personally responsible for Nautical's care, he also took it upon himself to keep me on the straight and narrow path. Jack was the last person I would see on entering the field of battle and the first I would see upon returning. He would always congratulate me with a smile or chastise me with his silence. It was to Nautical's credit if we had a clear round and to my discredit if we had a fence down. I must say, it would have been harder to face the strain of competition without Jack.

That summer turned out a lot differently from our earlier European tours in 1955 and 1956. The 1958 squad was composed of Steinkraus, Frank Chapot, George Morris and me, and we proved a strong team. We were all well mounted this time, and somewhere in the string we had a horse who could cope with almost any kind of competition. We won a lot of classes that summer, including some important ones—London's Nations Cup, and no fewer than five Grands Prix.

Gradually, the Europeans were developing an awe of Nemethy. How could he have put together such a team of riders from the cowboy country? For ours was the first team to compete in Europe since the war that really looked like a team, rode like a team and behaved like a team. The other teams were like a collection of individuals.

Of course, despite an outward appearance of complete harmony, we had our tense moments. We all had our little idiosyncrasies that started to grate after months of being together; my habit of slurping hot tea finally got to Billy, and his fiddle playing finally got to me. Nor can I forget the

Hugh Wiley and Bert de Nemethy, talking over riding tactics at Cologne in 1956. The civilization of Nautical was a collaborative effort for both.

great and universal depression one morning in Aachen when Bert refused to raise our laundry allowance by $1.50 a week! But on the whole, it was a marvelous summer.

Nautical had continued his improvement that summer. He was now much more disciplined and consistent in his performance. We could count on him more and more for a clear round when the going was difficult. After we got back to America, he won a great deal at Harrisburg and the Garden that fall. He was now a pleasure to ride, and I felt he could jump anything. It seemed a long winter, because I couldn't wait to get back to competing again.

In 1959, we went to Europe early, because the Rome show was the first days of May. We needed all of April to prepare ourselves for one of the most difficult shows in Europe. The 1960 Games would be held here, so we needed the exposure. We prepared ourselves well, for we won the Nations Cup on the last day. Nautical was the last horse to go, and he clinched the victory with a clear round. That was a wonderful moment after so many disappointments and frustrations. I do believe Nautical had arrived, for the Romans loved him.

After Italy we moved on to several shows in Germany. All of our horses were going satisfactorily. Ksar d'Esprit won every puissance he competed in that year, all over 7' high. We won most of the Nations Cups and looked like the team to beat in 1960. The German team seemed to be our only contender.

After the Aachen show we crossed the channel to England and the Royal International in London, held outdoors in those days in the White City Stadium. I believe this was my favorite show and by far my favorite city. The courses rode tight, and a horse was kept busy. This was what Nautical liked. He was proving this to be true, for we were carrying the Sash of Honor.

Nautical had qualified for the George V Cup on Wednesday night. Somehow this competition has a glamour unlike all the others. There is a tension that night that horse, rider and spectator share. The royal box is full, as is the stadium. The class was to be televised, and Disney camermen, too, were everywhere.

We had all walked the course. It was predictably high; there was little room for error. I was nervous and edgy as I watched the first five horses jump the course. It looked difficult. I was to go toward the end, which is good tactically but bad for a nervous stomach. You wonder if you can do it. Suddenly you feel limp all over and fluttery in the stomach. You tighten your muscles to stop the twitching and try to pretend nonchalance.

I strolled out to the warm-up ring and it was bedlam. All the riders must have felt the same way—in a daze. Why wasn't Bert there? Where was Nautical? Darn Jack, he was late. Just then I was nudged from behind and

Nautical and Hugh Wiley at Wiesbaden, Germany, in 1959, showing the form that made them the top combination on the squad for that tour.

Jack said, "Where have you been? Are you ready?" "Yes, of course," I said.

As Nautical was unblanketed my confidence returned. He looked strong and sleek in the dim light. My nervousness fled as I mounted and moved into the crowd of riders. Bert was waiting for me at a warm-up fence. There was no last-minute strategy. We jumped a couple of small fences and stopped. I got off, and Jack led Nautical to the starting enclosure. Bert and I followed. My number was called. Two more to go before me. Bert reminded me to go steady at the treble, wished me luck and disappeared into the crowd.

Now I started to take deep breaths. I needed oxygen. The night air was cool, but I was hot. The horse in the ring had had a wreck, which gave me a few more seconds. The starter wanted me to stand at the ingate. I wouldn't, knowing that Nautical would get upset. I was trying to relax him as best I could. He was about to explode. I was longing to start. At last my number.

Jack was at the ingate to pat me twice on the left knee, as he always did; I made a quick sign of the cross and saluted the royal box as I entered the ring. At that point there were no nerves, no hesitation as I went into my circle and on to the first fence. We could see our distance many strides out, the pace was perfect and the impulsion was always in reserve.

We finished the course with no faults. I was exhausted, for Nautical pulled all the way. This had happened before; the more he jumped the stronger he became. He must have been excited by the lights and the applause, although I suspect he was slightly showing off, because as we left the stadium he became soft and gentle.

There were six clear rounds to go in the first jump-off, and I was last. Time would not be a factor until the second jump-off. Another clear round was needed.

As I entered the ring the second time, the tensions were mounting. The

Spaniard Paco Goyoaga had already gone clear. The silence was overwhelming. My senses became remarkably acute. The slightest noise was amplified many times. I could feel Nautical's heart beat, as he must have surely felt mine. The starting bell sounded and he surged forward into my hands and onto his hocks. I would not let him get away from me this time, I thought as we approached the first line of fences.

He was brilliant, soaring around the course without touching a pole. Two clear rounds, Paco and me. Another jump-off, this time against the clock.

Goyoaga had the misfortune of going first, trying to be both clear and fast. Things went badly for him. In his haste he had one rail down and then another for a total of 8 faults. This will be an easy one, I thought as I entered the arena to salute.

As I made my circle, I knew something was wrong. All Nautical needed was to have fire coming out of his nostrils, for he had gone mad. He was full out over the first fence, and I was standing and literally swinging on his mouth at the second. The course had been shortened, so the treble was next. *Go steady,* Bert had warned. I was spent. On the turn I tried with some success to bring Nautical back, but his stride got longer as we approached the treble. I wrenched him to the right to break the stride. He faced the treble just one stride out, but the stride was right and he was in balance for the leap in. We got through, somehow, but from then on it was a game of chance. All I could do was point him.

The last line was the water and two parallel oxers. I knew he would try to end with a flair. We made the turn toward the water and he started grabbing ground, as they say. The thrust was like a jet as we jumped the water, landing at least 5′ beyond the tape. I had no choice now but to ask for an even longer stride to adjust for the remaining distance. We made it and flew on to the last oxer, full out, for a brilliant finish. The crowd was ecstatic, the applause tumultuous, and Disney at last had a good win for his movie.

EPILOGUE

The team returned to the United States that summer and went on to win the gold medal at the Chicago Pan American Games. Nautical had the best individual score, though no individual medal was awarded that year. On the fall circuit he continued to go well, and we won the International Stake in New York for the second year in a row. He wintered well, and I was full of optimism as we took off for Europe the following spring to complete our Olympic preparation abroad.

The toast of London in 1959: Hugh Wiley and Nautical, winners of the George V Cup and three other competitions at the Royal International Horse Show to receive the Sash of Honor.

As luck would have it, Nautical's career was over. During our flight to Germany he developed pneumonia, and he never fully recovered. My big hopes for the Olympic Games had vanished.

We tried him in several classes at the Garden that fall, and he even won a class, but he was weak in the knees. His heart was as big as ever, but he fell on landing after a big fence, and we decided to retire him.

He had an official retirement ceremony at the Garden the following year, when he was seventeen years old. The next six long years he spent doing what he loved most—just being a horse. He stayed at the team's training center in Gladstone, New Jersey, and on Dr. Jacques Jenny's farm near Philadelphia for four years. He was still very much a celebrity and was visited constantly by his admirers.

Nautical finally came home to my farm in Maryland. He was a pleasure to have in the stable and was now, I might add, a very good hack. My wife and I would ride him all over the Maryland countryside and he was a perfect gentleman, but show him a fence and the spark would be rekindled.

The last morning was sad. He had not touched his feed. He had a rather distant look in his eye and appeared to be having trouble keeping his balance. He was not suffering at all. I led him from the stable to an outside paddock. He would not stop, but just staggered forward and fell to the grass. He was breathing heavily, and his eye had lost all expression. As I knelt beside him I could feel his heart beat, very much as I had that night in London so many years ago. The cadence was slower, but it was just as determined. It fell to a gentler and softer murmur and, finally, was silent.

Equipping Yourself for the USET

GEORGE H. MORRIS

One of the many USET riders who first attracted national attention as an equitation winner, George Morris left the jumping squad after a fine performance in the Rome Olympics to take a fling at an acting career. However, it was not long before he was back with horses and achieving spectacular success as a teacher, and since then he has had the pleasure of seeing a number of his pupils follow in his footsteps both as outstanding equitation riders and, later, as members of the team.

YOU NEVER CAN TELL; that is my motto. There was no one more surprised than I that first summer in 1957 when I was asked to work with Bert de Nemethy and the USET jumping squad at home and at the summer shows. After all, I (and most others) had thought myself the most least-likely-ever-to-succeed!

My earliest recollection of any horse is being picked up by the shirt by my sister's horse while he was grazing on the front lawn. This was a bit scary, as reports at the dinner table had it that this same horse had once reared over backward with my father, and later bolted through the streets of New Canaan, Connecticut, pulling a cart in which my mother was a passenger. He was disposed of shortly thereafter.

However, this dinner-table conversation got me off on a wary foot with horses, even though intuitively I loved them. My apprehensions were confirmed when my sister started putting me up on a neighbor's "sweet, gentle"

Shetland pony named Black Beauty, who always managed to dump me within a quick minute or two.

My first organized association with riding started at age nine at Margaret Cabell Self's New Canaan Mounted Troop. We always rode Wednesday, for this was a half-day at the New Canaan Country Day School and the bus would take us directly to troop with our brown-paper-bag lunches. Unfortunately, I could never eat lunch—partly because I was scared to death of horses (and this was a riding school), and partly because I didn't like the marching program either (and it was a marching school, too!). After six months of whining and sniveling, I didn't have to go to troop anymore.

The next school year came around, and I was still deathly afraid of horses but nonetheless in love with them. Needless to say, my ability as a horseman had not progressed one iota since the previous spring, for I had not ridden since. However, my family tried again and we joined the Ox Ridge Hunt Club in Darien, Connecticut. There I met someone with patience! Miss V. Felicia Townsend kept me on the lead line for the whole winter, the longest lead-liner in her long career as a riding instructress, riding two dead-but-still-alive horses named Mitzi and Mittens. They certainly were quiet; a standstill canter was their highest form of animation, and this could be achieved only after a good deal of encouragement.

However, several breakthroughs came within the next year or so to provide encouragement. I succeeded in staying on Gaylark during one of that horse's bucking sprees in a wide-open field, and Miss Townsend proclaimed that I would make it as a rider. I also followed my teacher's instructions to a T (out of fear) when she screamed, *"Reach!"* and successfully negotiated my first jump. Another great accomplishment at this time was surviving a trial ride with the late Otto Heuckeroth. This was not only a feat of nerve but also one of sheer strength. At any rate, things were looking up, and I was finally permitted to enter my first Ox Ridge member horse show. Actually, the only thing I clearly remember about the show, outside of the fact that I won a ribbon, was that I wore cowboy boots over my jodhpurs.

Alas, before long my nerve started to crumble again. This time the cause was Otto's enthusiasm for bigger fences. Finally it came down to a choice—either give up riding (which, curiously, I still loved), or try another teacher. And so off we packed to Gordon Wright.

Gordon was a very astute fellow. His prescription: a horse so sluggish it required a stick, and *only* cross-rail jumping for about six months. This sounds like Dullsville, but it was just what the doctor ordered. For although Gordon never taxed one's muscles or nerve, he surely made the brain work. And it took only a few lessons for me to realize that I was with a technician, learning a craft. This approach was right up my alley, and I started to become a very happy, confident human being as well as a passable rider.

Being a passable rider can take you quite a long way if you are also being taught weekly by Gordon Wright, have a fabulous junior horse, are blessed by luck at every turn and have a family that cares! By the age of fourteen, I had won both the AHSA and ASPCA finals at Madison Square Garden.

Not only was this a great boost psychologically for a wallflower type, but it drastically curtailed what was left for me as a junior show rider, encouraging me to look farther ahead toward possible riding goals. I vividly remember saying to Victor Hugo-Vidal, another of my helpful teachers, that I would someday ride in the Olympic Games. Though at the time this was a ridiculous statement, I knew it would happen. Shortly thereafter, riding a near-pony named Bubble Gum, I won a junior Olympic jumping class at the Fairfield show; I was hooked on riding jumpers!

It was just a summer later, during my sixteenth year, that my career with open horses really began. We traded in my wonderful junior hunter, Game Cock, for a green jumper named The Gigolo. He turned out to be a saint who forgave me over and over again for the mistakes I made, both in riding and in training. I also got to ride Gordon Wright's great horse, Royal Guard, who went on to the USET under the name of Saxon Woods. (My big problem with this horse was not jumping the course; it was getting him into the ring. He got my number and became an ingate rearer.) Finally, I had a lovely mare, War Bride, whom we purchased when her brilliant career as a green hunter was cut short because she began to make a noise. These

George Morris and The Gigolo schooling at Tryon, North Carolina, in 1955, before the Olympic trials. Morris didn't make the team that year, but it was already clear that he would.

Morris with Mrs. Harry Morris' War Bride at Wiesbaden, Germany, in 1959. The previous year he rode War Bride to his first international victory, at the big Aachen show.

were my teachers too, and if any one of these early jumpers had been a lemon, my confidence would probably have been severely damaged, and I never would have survived.

Another big day arrived in the early winter of 1955 when it was decided that I should go to the USET's Olympic Trials in Tryon, North Carolina. I guess it was really Mrs. William Joshua Barney who decided for me by offering to lend me Magnify (a team veteran) and Master William (a dead-green horse with a huge jump) to use in the trials. This gave me four horses to use, and an enviable string it proved to be. Though I wasn't selected in the trials to be a member of the 1956 Olympic squad (thank heavens!), I had a wonderful six weeks of learning and competing.

In retrospect, things couldn't have worked out better, even though I was disappointed not to be riding abroad that summer. For in place of a European trip, I took a Mexican trip and had six weeks of riding with General Mariles. Things were very different down there; and while I was sorry for not learning much technically, I was pleased with the opportunity to see and do with horses in another country. It helped me to appreciate, when I got home, how much our American horsemen had to offer.

One of my greatest breaks came the following fall while I was attending the University of Virginia in Charlottesville. Bert de Nemethy was spending the winter at Whitney Stone's farm and invited me to leave my horse War Bride with him and to come there and ride. I remember so well riding the mare the day after Bert had worked her; she was perfect, so supple and soft. I was afraid to touch her and ruin it. That winter I learned a lot—more with Bert than in school, I'm afraid.

During the following summer, Bert invited me to come with the squad to some of the shows. Then at the end of the summer, at the Piping Rock Show as a matter of fact, he introduced me to Richard Wätjen and arranged for me to go up to Sunnyfield Farm to work during the winter with Wätjen. As only Bert would put it, "You need the winter to learn how to sit." And you know, he was right; I wasn't such a bad rider, but still hadn't really learned where and how to sit!

After that winter, I had all the ingredients I needed, and during the three years of 1958, 1959 and 1960 I was given the chance to put it all together while riding on the team both at home and in Europe. War Bride made the first European trip with me, but I was also lucky enough to be given several other marvelous horses to ride, among them the Olympic veteran Night Owl, who in 1960 won the Grand Prix af Aachen, and the brilliant Sinjon, my Olympic mount in Rome that year. It was an unforgettable experience.

After the Rome Olympics I decided to develop a strong latent interest in the theater, but finally reverted to something I found even more satisfying—trying to pass on to others the riding knowledge that was imparted to me. Actually, my first riding protégé, Bill Robertson, started working with me at Ox Ridge while I was still in drama school, and rode on the jumping team for five years starting in 1961. Since then I have worked with many young riders who have regarded their junior participation in hunter-seat equitation as a possible stepping-stone to riding in the jumper division and hopefully, perhaps, making the team.

What I try to teach them and ask them to do is very much drawn from the experiences I have just related.

The sequence of events that shaped my riding career seemed so right, as I look back, and worked so well for me, that now I try to bring pupils along in a similar step-by-step fashion. In fact, I'm quite concerned if any of the steps with which chance provided me are bypassed by any of my up-and-coming young riders. For luckily, this country can afford a very comprehensive background for anyone who wishes to ride internationally in show jumping or combined training.

My first piece of advice to a parent or a youngster coming along is to begin with a teacher who is well grounded in the basics of hunter-seat equitation. Not only is this seat balanced and devoid of exaggerations, but it teaches one first and foremost to be a practical, workmanlike rider and to deal with a horse in a forward, rather than a collected, manner.

Many good qualities are developed through this kind of start, principally elasticity, firmness and tact. (I prefer it to starting off with dressage training, for in practice I feel that the latter often tends to produce a bit of

George Morris and Ellen Dineen's Sinjon, competing at Rome in 1959. A year later they were fourth individually in the Olympic Games, jumping in this same stadium. Sinjon was later purchased for the team by Walter B. Devereux.

stiffness.) Once the young rider is solid in the basics of a hunter-seat position, use of aids and employment of punishment and reward, both on the flat and over jumps, he is ready to enter the show ring, competing not only in the equitation but also in the hunter division. I've never pushed a junior rider into the jumper ranks whom I haven't first grounded in these other two divisions; I simply don't believe in it.

Showing a hunter is valuable for the jumper rider, not only as a preparation but because it develops skills he will use for the duration of his career: first, tact and smoothness remain a habit; and second, judgment of distance is kept more accurate and versatile from the very subtle demands made upon the hunter rider. (Jimmy Elder of the Canadian team told me, a year or so ago, that he wouldn't think of giving up his hunter riding because it helped him so much on his jumpers.) So really as a starting division at the horse shows, and as a refresher division all along, one can't overlook the value of showing our American hunter.

There is no doubt that before you graduate into showing jumpers, you should become versed in the rudiments and truths of basic dressage. I spend a great deal of time working my young riders on the flat, so that when they reach this stage and age, they are familiar with such concepts as impulsion, tempo, straightness, bending, half-halt, volte, shoulder-in, etc. They are very well set up to start pushing their horses together a bit more, to put them more accurately on the bit and to start controlling their haunches to a greater degree than was needed for equitation or hunter work. However, let me repeat that a premature emphasis on collection is usually like putting the proverbial knife in the monkey's hand. If the rider's conception and feel are not yet developed enough, he'll often become stiff and overbearing in his work. The dressage I appreciate most is soft, sympathetic and supple, built on a foundation of knowing and feeling a horse and his reaction to pressure.

My student is now in high school. He's had the wonderful, fluid background of galloping and jumping the straightforward horse and is now ready for the intricacies and variations of jumper riding. The basic dressage has given him the habit of collecting and gathering his horse. The best way of incorporating collection into jumping is through gymnastics, both on the straight line and on the turn. This is where the rider can learn the advanced controls and sophisticated moves of jumping high, wide and fast; and there is no doubt that this level is the epitome, the realm of the technician and the artist. The rider must be able to put all his knowledge and feel together and do it with split-second timing.

The last exercise I give a rider before encouraging him to try out for the USET and its great demands is to more or less let him go it alone. Self-sufficiency is a must for the top-class jumper rider; many good pupils have not made it because they have never learned to think and do for themselves. An invaluable experience for someone with a strong background and basic education is to spend the summer going to the shows with two or three jumpers by himself, having to win a few dollars to keep going.

This teaches the qualities of ingenuity and competitiveness like nothing else; and every good horseman at one time or another has known the feeling. When one is up to participating with an organization such as the USET and working with a great coach like Bert de Nemethy, one must be able to work and compete while striking a balance between taking direction and using self-intuition. When one or the other attitude takes over and the balance is lost, the team member can no longer be as valuable to himself or his fellows. Only the riders who find this balance can make it to the top.

Good luck and good riding!

George Morris and Mrs. John Galvin's Night Owl, winners of the Grand Prix of Aachen in 1960.

Tactics and Courses

FRANK D. CHAPOT

The year 1975 ended Frank Chapot's second decade as a USET rider, making this five-time Olympian the legitimate successor to Bill Steinkraus' "veteran" title as well as his role as team captain. A versatile rider of great courage and resourcefulness under pressure, Frank has excelled equally at speed and puissance competitions, and found time to win timber races as well. Married in 1965 to Mary Mairs, twice his Olympic teammate and a rider of almost equal celebrity, Frank remains active with horses on a New Jersey farm not far from Gladstone.

I N 1956, MY FIRST YEAR IN EUROPE with the USET, the difference between the jumping conditions there and what I was familiar with at home was very great. In fact, I can remember wondering, at the first show we competed in, how we'd ever win a class. It was Cologne, and three German horses tied for first in the puissance, all clearing 2 meters—6'7". They didn't bother to jump off the tie because it was an Olympic year. I was wrong in my doubts, for I even won a class myself before it was all over, but I'll never forget that demonstration of how different the standard was in our two countries.

Things have changed a lot since then—for me, for the USET and for American show jumping in general. Twenty years ago if you wrote about jumper courses and the tactics of preparing for them and riding them, you'd have had to make sharp distinctions between what happened in Europe and what we were doing on this side of the Atlantic. Today a great many things are the same, and there are really only two significant differences between what happens in American shows and what happens in Europe.

65

The main difference is that the European shows are basically financed by the public in the form of paid admissions at horse shows, while in the United States, it is the exhibitors themselves who make it possible for shows to operate by paying high entry fees.

The other principal difference is that in Europe, all classes are run under FEI rules with only knockdowns to count, while in this country, many shows still offer "rub classes" in which touches as well are scored. These are carry-overs from our old rules, when touches were scored in all classes except the knockdown-and-out and the high jump.

In most parts of the United States, rub classes conducted under AHSA Table I are used mainly for the green and inexperienced horses. Though some people feel that we should adopt FEI rules completely, I think Table I classes are still very useful for novices because this avoids making these horses jump very high or run very fast to win. In addition, a clear result is usually produced within a minimum amount of time, a point that is very important to management.

The main objection to rub classes is that they promote rapping or poling. This is perhaps true, but in my experience, poling done correctly and not overdone is not harmful. Moreover, green horses that are any good are usually more careful about hitting jumps in their early years than at any other time. I think more harm can be done to young horses by overfacing them with big jumps or by trying to go very fast with them, thus making them quick or perhaps incurring a wreck that shakes their confidence.

In preparing for a rub class, you have to consider what goal you are striving for. Are you just giving your horse experience over the obstacles on the course, or are you trying to win? If you are trying to win, you want your horse to be as sharp or careful as possible, yet without going to the extreme. You certainly don't want him to stop, or get so high over the spread jumps or in combinations that he gets into trouble. This is a judgment you must

Frank Chapot and Trail Guide, the best pair on the USET's silver-medal-winning squad at Rome in 1960.

Compilers of a remarkable record: Frank Chapot and Mrs. John Galvin's San Lucas, winners of almost three dozen international classes and competitors in a record forty-three Nations Cups. They were fourth individually, less than two seconds away from a medal, in the 1968 Olympics.

make from your own experience with each individual horse. With some horses, a light tap with a bamboo pole or a jump over a bamboo-pole offset (in front of a low jump) will be enough to produce a careful performance, while another horse wouldn't try if you hit him with the side of the barn. (The latter horse doesn't usually amount to much!)

In the old days when most classes in this country were judged on rubs, the fences were mostly vertical. Now the courses are far more sophisticated, with many spread fences and combinations. This makes it very important for you to use good judgment in not overdoing sharpening techniques or you will find your horse stopping or having a real confidence-shaking wreck.

With the gradual disappearance of the rub class for older horses, speed classes have become more popular. These are competitions in which the horse is asked not only not to knock down the jumps, but to complete the course faster than anyone else. These classes are very useful for many horses with limited jumping ability, as the jumps need not be high to produce a result. Therefore, a horse that doesn't have the scope to compete at the Grand Prix level may find a place where he can win in speed competitions. At present, in this country, most shows offer a limited number of jumper classes, and generally only one class, if any, is run as a speed competition. However, with the recent large increase in jumper entries at some of the major shows, more and more are finding it possible and practical to run two open jumper classes a day, a low-speed class and a jump-off class over a larger course.

Obviously, the single most important tactic in winning speed competitions is to find the fastest way around the course. Here again, your own judgment must be used. Should you let your horse run and jump, or try to save time by making sharp turns? In some cases, the shortest way is *not* the fastest. If the rider has to pull his horse up very short to go inside an obstacle to maintain the "shortest line," he may well take up more time than if he had galloped all the way around. There is no hard-and-fast rule that I know of to govern these situations, and one must decide for himself which route best suits the course and his horse. For the most part, on an experienced horse, the shortest way is best.

To be successful in speed competitions, you must go through the start as fast as you ever plan to go on the course, and in the direction of the second fence. Time wasted going through the start can never be made up later if you are in high-class competition. If the course is set up so that you can get through the start and jump the first fence at an angle that leaves you already headed for the second fence, precious time can be saved. Always notice which timer, if any, is closer to the first or last fence and favor that one in starting and finishing.

In walking speed courses, you will often find places where your horse

Speed merchants par excellence: Frank Chapot and Cheeca Farm's Good Twist— probably the fastest combination ever to represent the United States, as well as the fastest show jumpers in the world for most of their joint careers. The picture shows them in Madison Square Garden, site of many of their victories.

can leave out a stride between two fences. This will save time, but you must be careful that you do not ruin a turn by doing this. Many times putting in a short stride in front of a fence just before a short turn can enable you to start that turn on leaving the ground. Asking a horse to stand way back at a fence just before a turn usually lands you far out from the fence and makes the turn slower.

When you're riding against the clock it is most important to go from one fence to the next without pulling up. If it is necessary to make any adjustment or set your horse up for a fence, do it when you get to the jump, not just after jumping the previous fence. In other words, gallop from one fence to another without interfering with the stride. In doing this, you will often find no reason to check, thus saving a lot of time.

The start order in a speed class is also a factor. The competitors who go at the end of the competition have the advantage of seeing the other riders' mistakes and also their smart moves. It also helps "get your blood up" to see someone really burn up a course. One doesn't often have any say as to what order he competes in, but when you are lucky enough to go near the end, take advantage of it. It is unusual for the first horse in a speed competition to win it.

The distaff side of the Chapot family: Mary Mairs Chapot, the first woman ever to win a Games gold medal in jumping (at the São Paulo Pan American Games), and twice an Olympic teammate of Frank's, riding her own White Lightning at Hickstead in 1967. Five years later this home-bred mare was Frank's mount at Munich.

Perhaps the most important tactic in competing in speed classes over a period of time is how to use your horse. If you try to win every class you go in, you will probably blow your horse's mind or at least shorten his useful career in some way. Speed horses burn out fast if used improperly. Some horses are better over long galloping courses and others over twisty, trappy courses. Some horses you can try with in the first class and others take a class or two before they are ready to win. Try to know what suits your horse best. Try to win when you have an edge, or the competition itself is important.

Generally the schooling ring is not the place to teach your horse to go fast. All the basics should have been done at home, long before the show. When you're schooling for a class on an international level, the horse generally has a pretty good idea of what he's about. With horses such as Good Twist and White Lightning, it is enough that they are loosened up and fresh. A practice turn too many in the schooling area with horses such as these can often make them too sharp, and they will turn too soon in the ring rather than too late. This does not mean that certain horses do not benefit from a "roll-back" here and there. Again it must be the rider's judgment and knowledge of his horses that dictates schooling procedure.

Except for Nations Cup and puissance-type classes, most jumper competitions are won against the clock at some point. The more important classes usually stress the horse's jumping ability and the rider's skill in handling distance problems rather than speed. But because most classes end up against the clock, it is important to walk the jump-off course when you walk the original course. You will not get another chance to do so before the jump-off.

The good course designer will try to separate the good rider on a good horse from the poor rider on a good horse, rather than just test the strength of the horses. One has to try to figure out just what the course designer had in mind in preparing courses for Grand Prix or important competitions. For example, one might find a number of ramp or triple-bar jumps on a course which are easy to override without penalty, but watch out for the vertical or straight fence later on! Also, beware the jumps that ride so nicely on the long stride; horses tend to get flat over them. Most of the good riders will put in the extra stride in these circumstances, if the distance is more than four or five strides.

Distances in combinations make the difference in your approach. A normal oxer combination with a long distance in between the oxers will call for a faster or livelier approach than a vertical combination with a tight distance in between. If the course designer makes difficult related distances between fences and difficult distances in his combinations, the preparation of your horse becomes very important. It is not enough to have a very talented horse with scope if the courses prove your horse is not broke well enough to handle the distance problems.

Ideally, you have to teach your horse to go forward and come back readily with his head in the right place and not lose his mind at the same time. The mind is the most important. If we didn't have to worry so much about that, we could solve most problems with sharp spurs and severe bits. Here again, good judgment and the knowledge of just what you can do with each particular horse is important. We will all make thousands of mistakes in this area and know the answer the minute before we die.

Nations Cup courses are usually long courses with a tighter time limit than other classes. The most important tactic here is to find a good rhythm that you won't have to vary much. Since the course is so long, early big moves that break the rhythm can get you into trouble at the end. This is one way in which the course designer may test you. He may set problems that

Frank Chapot and Main Spring, donated to the USET by William D. Haggard, III, jumping the water at Hickstead en route to a third-place finish in the 1974 World Championships.

must be handled smoothly early in the course, thus perhaps causing trouble later on.

The Nations Cup course in the Olympic Games is even more difficult. The course is designed to test the best horses and riders in the world. It is set inside the 440-yard running track of the Olympic stadium. Horses walk into this strange situation for the first time on the day of the competition, the bell rings and they are expected to perform over this most difficult course with no further pause for looking around. At normal horse shows, the horses compete in the arena a few times before the Nations Cup takes place. Not so in the Games. The stadium itself is also a problem, in that no other horses are in sight or even nearby while a horse is performing. Many horses will turn and whinny for other horses when they get into the stadium. It takes a very seasoned horse to walk into this situation and do well.

The puissance class is designed to test the strength and jumping ability of the horse and is an example of still another type of course. The class usually ends over two fences, a big spread and a big vertical, usually a wall. The wall generally gets very high. The best tactic in trying to jump a very high wall is to try to get close to the base of it. Most horses don't jump very high fences well by standing off. Try to play an angle on the wall for two reasons. First, you can get to the fence at the proper takeoff point by opening or closing your angle of attack without disturbing the horse's impulsion. Also, the blocks on the wall stay on better if hit on an angle rather than straight on. Try not to jump the wall directly in a line toward the outgate, as many horses tend to get quicker in that direction.

Both your horse's ability and prior preparation are crucial in jumping the difficult courses presented today. When you're jumping courses on an international level there is not much margin for error. Shows just don't give out second chances. I have been very lucky to have horses of the caliber of Trail Guide, San Lucas, Main Spring, Good Twist, Manon and White Lightning to ride and someone with the ability of Bert de Nemethy to help prepare them. However, horses and riders don't last forever, and the new stars must come from the preliminary and junior ranks of shows held every day in this country. Nothing is more rewarding than to bring a young horse along from scratch to international caliber. Granted, few make it that far, but that hope is surely one of the things that make this sport so consistently interesting for so many people.

From Uncle Max to a Medal

NEAL SHAPIRO

The USET's second Olympic individual medal winner in jumping—he won the bronze at Munich—Neal Shapiro, has always had a talent for the big occasion, as his Grand Prix of Aachen and President's Cup wins also testify. Valued by his teammates for his irrepressible sense of humor and steadiness under pressure, Neal is also a skilled pilot and an enthusiastic trotting-horse owner/trainer/driver. He and his wife, Suzy, live in Long Island and spend their spare time looking for potential Olympic jumpers.

Ed Fisher's Riding Academy in Hempstead, Long Island, might seem an unlikely place to find candidates for the USET, but that's where it all started for me; as a child of five, I made my debut there aboard White Sox, one of the hourly rentals. When my family moved to Brookville we began to accumulate horses of our own and soon fell into the horse-show routine. In an attempt to develop my equestrian talents, my parents tried to enroll me in the local school of horsemanship. The owners apparently felt that there was little talent to develop, for I was rejected and forced to fend for myself. Nonetheless, for the next few years I rode my backyard horses in local shows and eventually began winning ribbons in the hunter and jumper divisions. I knew, however, that my horses wouldn't get anywhere at the bigger shows.

On the Fourth of July weekend in 1961 a horse trailer was pulled into our driveway. Much to our surprise, we found that the big gray horse inside was being delivered to us. Upon questioning the driver, my father learned that our man, Jack Amon, had made this unauthorized purchase. The Shapiros were now the somewhat reluctant owners of a former rodeo horse named Charlie Grey. By unanimous decision we renamed the horse Uncle Max after our favorite uncle.

We quickly learned that Max possessed several serious quirks which we would need to iron out. My number one problem was mounting. As soon as Max knew I was aiming for the saddle he would be off and running. We decided that the element of surprise would be our only hope. It was not uncommon to see me leaping onto the saddle from the hood of a car, a bale of hay or even a rooftop. At the shows a groom would lead Max past the tack room where I would be hiding, hopefully in a position to spring into the saddle. Many times I could be seen galloping through the stable area hanging around Max's neck. Once he got wise to all of our surprise attacks we resorted to the rodeo method of dropping onto the saddle from above the stalls. Fortunately, he eventually allowed me to mount in a more conventional manner with the aid of only one person. Max and I soon learned to understand each other and went on to be a rather successful team.

It was at this point that I began to take my riding career more seriously. In 1961, at the age of fifteen, I became the youngest rider to win the AHSA green-jumper title with Uncle Max. In 1962 Max was reserve Professional Horsemens Association champion to Ben O'Meara's Jacks or Better. In 1963 these same two horses reversed positions, with Max winning the championship title. At the end of the year we purchased Jacks from O'Meara to join forces with Uncle Max. The following year, 1964, Uncle Max and Jacks or Better repeated their previous year's success, the first time that the PHA champion and reserve both came from the same stable. The real highlight of the year came when I was selected to represent the U.S. Equestrian Team at Harrisburg and New York. I rode Jacks or Better and another uncle, Uncle Tom, at Harrisburg. Our international debut was marked by three international wins, and because of our success I also got to ride at New York.

The team did not go to Europe in 1965, but to my delight, I was selected for the European tour the following summer. It took Jacks and me most of the tour to adjust to the long and demanding courses in Europe. He had a short, shuffling gait which was not well suited to the long galloping courses we were confronted with. But bit by bit we made enough adjustments to enable us to get around. Aachen, Germany, was our last major European show, and it was here that our work paid off. I was determined to win something before we left for home, but had no idea that my determination would lead to winning the Grand Prix of Aachen after five rounds. If OTB had covered any bets on me that day, the payoff would have equaled the national debt!

Unfortunately, Jacks was not able to compete internationally after that summer because of an injury the following spring. He did, however, compete quite successfully on a much lighter schedule and ended his career by winning the Blitz Cup at Piping Rock in 1968. He is still living the life of

What a way to score your maiden victory! Neal Shapiro winning the Grand Prix of Aachen with his Jacks or Better in 1966 to register his very first win with the USET.

Riley at home on Long Island, and at the age of twenty-four still jumps out of the paddock to make an occasional visit to some of his pals down the block.

I had spent the winters of 1965 and 1966 training at Gladstone, where Bert de Nemethy struggled to revamp my self-taught riding style. As a kid I had watched many different riders in the show ring and had taken things from them which I felt I could incorporate into my own style. I greatly admired Benny O'Meara, whose style was characterized at first by long stirrups and high hands. Naturally, I too experimented with this technique, until I looked more like a gaited-horse rider than a jumper rider. Sonny Brooks and Dave Kelley were other successful jumper riders during my most impressionable years, and from them I adopted the "swing the leg back over the jump" technique. By modifying these techniques and a few others I managed to find a style that worked for me, but I was hardly the classic rider you'd find in Mary Chapot or Bill Steinkraus.

Bert undertook to rearrange my style without sacrificing what I had learned through natural feel and instinct. I had to relearn How as well as learn Why. But I realized that I would have to abandon most of my old techniques and learn new ones if I was to further my career.

Hour after hour was spent on the longe line, Bert hollering orders at one end and me wearing out the seat of my breeches at the other. It always seemed that he picked the roughest horse and the coldest morning for these sessions. At first I not only had trouble with the "new riding," but often couldn't even understand Bert. He was forever telling me to be gentle with the mouse, to put my spurn on the horse and get the hacks under him. (Translation: Be gentle with the horse's mouth, use your spurs and put his hocks under him.) But gradually, I started to get the idea.

The summer of 1967 brought another European tour. With Jacks out of action, the only horse I had left was Uncle Max. Despite his success in the

Mrs. Ernst Mahler's Night Spree and Neal Shapiro at Aachen in 1967. Later that year this combination won the coveted President's Cup at the Washington International.

United States, however, Maxie wasn't foolproof enough to take to Europe. He still had funny quirks, like jumping everything clear and then stopping at the last fence. Bert felt that I'd learn more by riding an experienced horse in Europe that summer, and assigned me to ride San Pedro, lent to the team by Mrs. John Galvin. Then for a second horse he put me on a promising younger horse, Night Spree, who had been lent to the team by Mrs. Ernst Mahler.

Bert was right, and the summer was a valuable one for me even though I didn't make any headlines. I started to feel really at home on those long, galloping courses, and realized that those painful sessions on the longe line were finally paying off. I had a new foundation of balance and control in place of my old style, and I will forever be grateful to Bert for having taken the time and trouble to change me over.

The fall shows of 1967 proved to be a good test for Night Spree. At the Washington International she won the coveted President's Cup, and the next week at New York she won the Democrat trophy. We ended the year on a good note by winning the Gamblers Stakes at Toronto. Again I found myself on the wrong end of the longe line for another winter in Gladstone, but this time I underwent the sessions willingly.

The following summer (1968) the team went to Europe again as part of its Olympic preparation, and this time, owing to a shortage of horses, I made the trip with my old friend Uncle Max. Things worked out quite well. We never did win a class, but Max hung in to be second several times in good competitions. In the Hickstead Derby, he ran true to form. The Derby course is formidable—there are lots of big fences, lots of ditches and waters, and one of the largest banks to face show jumpers anywhere. Max was jumping in exceptionally good form that day and actually never rubbed a fence the whole way around. However, though he jumped up the front side

76

of the big Hickstead Bank, which is 10'6" high, and neatly jumped the fence on the top, instead of sliding down as he was supposed to he took a flying leap from the top and landed in a heap at the bottom. It was like stepping into an elevator shaft—I was on the ground before I knew what was happening. We completed the course with no further faults, but the fall put us back to sixth place.

One of the British riders, Ted Edgar, kept trying to buy Max from me throughout the summer. I had my reservations about selling him, but Bert agreed that Max's team potential was limited. Moreover, I could tell that Ted really liked and understood Max—someone said that if Max were reincarnated in human form, it would be as Ted. Finally, we decided to leave Uncle Max in England, and I'm happy to say it worked out fine for everyone.

With neither Max nor Jacks left in my string, I then went through a coasting period. Fortunately, in a sport like ours a two-or-three-year slack period does not take its toll on a rider as it would on a football player or a boxer. Show jumping isn't like swimming or running, in which youth is all-important; in riding, experience and patience count for even more. It wasn't until the fall of 1969 that a horse came along which I felt might be the one every rider waits for. I was luckier than most, for with Sloopy, my dream would become history.

One morning during the Piping Rock Horse Show, Patrick Butler sat in our breakfast room with my parents and chatted over coffee. I remember Mr. Butler asking my father, "Doc, if you were going out to buy a jumper today, what would you buy?" My father didn't think long, removed his cigar from his mouth and said, "I'd have to buy Sloopy." To this day I don't know exactly how it came to be, but I'm forever grateful to Patrick Butler and Bert, for when spring came, Sloopy and I became a team.

I guess each horse has his own personality, but I've yet to meet one

Uncle Max, attempting the famous Hickstead bank "his own way" in 1968, with Neal Shapiro up (and about to be down). A great favorite with spectators, this ex-rodeo horse often managed to find "something different" to do on course.

who could match Sloopy's. He was sure no push-button horse. My first few rides at Gladstone, as soon as Sloopy had had enough, he would let me know by stopping in a corner and rearing up, or trying to spin me off. When he saw that I wasn't leaving the saddle he would lunge in the air again and again, getting madder and madder. This exhibition of flying leaps and fancy footwork continued for three or four sessions until finally Sloopy had to learn that he was not the boss.

About the fifth day, when he started his little act, I came right back at him. With every buck he got a good swift kick in the sides in return. This made him furious and he would give it right back to me. The harder I kicked the harder he would buck. He would leap higher and higher, trying to get away from me, but when he hit the ground again I was still with him. He got tired of the ordeal after a while and made a low sigh as if to say, "You've won this one, buddy, but I'll get back at you one day." Get back is just what he did, too—and he picked the day we were flying to Europe as the day for revenge.

Sixteen horses were at the airport, all ready to go—all except Sloopy, that is. He went into the shipping box without any trouble, but then he decided to come out. While we stood watching, his front legs came out over the top of the box and he started to get the rest out, no matter how. Because he could see over the top of the box he knew he could get out of it, and he continued to thrash. There had been a delay in loading due to an adjustment that had to be made to the aircraft, and by this time Sloopy's tranquilizer was wearing off. Planes were now landing over his head, and he became terrified by the noise. In this state it is not wise to administer more tranquilizer, because it can have a reverse effect. Also, if a horse throws such a fit on a plane, it endangers the lives of the others on board. As a result, the reluctant consensus was that Sloopy was to be left home, and with this decision the summer of 1970 looked long and lonesome for me.

Since the Olympic Games were in 1972 and Sloopy had never seen a European course, it was essential that he get some European experience in 1971. For this reason Bert decided to take no chances with an airplane flight and to send Sloopy to Europe by ship. Arrangements were made to obtain a special stall in which Sloopy would live until we reached our destination.

On May 5, 1971, we left the calm New York harbor. I remember the day well because I was sure that it would be my last. *The Poseidon Adventure* was a joyride compared with this one. The ship did not stop rolling from the moment we left New York until the time we docked in Le Havre, France. The trip took seven days—seven of the longest, most nauseating days of my entire life. Of the 168 hours on board I spent 100 flat on my back in my bed; I hung over the deck's railing for 32 hours, and the other 36 hours were passed staggering to the bathroom. Sloopy ate the whole time on board and got off the ship as fat as a pig. I was minus fifteen pounds and never so glad to see dry land in my life.

Upon losing my sea legs I made a miraculous recovery and met the rest of the team in Fontainebleau two weeks later. It was there that we had our first competition, two weeks after their arrival. Sloopy's style charmed the French crowd, and I still remember the "oohs" and "aahs" that came from the stands when he jumped his first course. The new environment made him jump everything with a foot to spare. Spectators soon began to call out, "Sloopy for President!" He would have had a lot of votes, mine included.

The next stops of the tour were in Hamburg and Cologne, Germany, where Sloopy showed me that neither the height nor the width of the big courses posed any problems to him. He had a wonderful attitude toward his work, and once he got onto the course it was all business.

Our next stop was Aachen, and it was here that Sloopy showed us what he was made of. The Aachen courses are always big, as big as you will find anywhere, and you can get a good idea of what your horse can or cannot do by his performance over these courses.

You've heard of "horses for courses," and Aachen was Sloopy's place. He jumped three clear rounds in the Nations Cup to help tie and then beat the British team. Then on the last day of the show he hit only one fence, a wall set at seven feet, in the fifth round of the Grand Prix. The jury decided to end the class there and tied two horses equal first, Sloopy and Sans Souci of France, ridden by Marcel Rozier.

It had been a great thrill to win this famous class in 1966, and it was just as good the second time around. When we rode in for our ribbons,

Patrick Butler's Sloopy under Neal Shapiro, making the kind of jump that made audiences gasp at Fontainebleau in 1971.

Sloopy and Sans Souci came in side by side, and when we lined up, Sloopy was second in line. He bounced from side to side until he worked his way over to the other side of Sans Souci, making him first in line. He stood there like a ham while his pictures were taken, obviously pleased with himself.

The old expression "One day you're up and the next you're down" certainly applies to all of us who have to rely on animals as fragile as show jumpers. The next year Sloopy shipped to Europe beautifully, on the same plane as everyone else, but on Grand Prix day at Aachen I found myself sitting in the stands watching the competition instead of riding in it. Sloopy was back at the barn with a fever, and it was feared he might not recover in time to jump in the Games eight weeks hence. His illness lingered for two more weeks, and we did not seem to be able to pinpoint just what it was. One vet would tell us one thing, and in another country another vet would tell us something else. Finally Bert and Mr. Butler arranged for Dr. Danny Marks to fly over and see if he could find the answer. Danny met us at La Baule, France, but his luggage never made it and all his drugs were lost. He spent the day of his arrival sewing up Snowbound, who had cut his head in a freak accident. It seemed that everything was against us, and the Games were far too close for comfort. However, Danny got new medicines, and soon Sloopy's temperature came down. Now he had to be strengthened up for the big job ahead of him.

Sometimes it seemed pretty futile. The other teams were putting the finishing touches on their horses, and here we were patching and hoping. Even if we made it, would we be prepared to go two or maybe three rounds against horses who were fit, healthy and prepared to be their best on September 3? We were there to do a job, and having waited ten years to do it, I didn't want to wait for another shot. Sloopy began improving to the point where he looked like his old self, and Peter Zeitler, his caretaker and the man who knew him best, said he would make it.

Finally, a month before the individual, I was able to ride Sloopy and we started to cram into four weeks what you would like to do in four months. The cliff-hanger wasn't over yet.

Arriving in Munich, we trained more intensively and planned a school for Sloopy on August 29. He was still not quite as fit as we would have liked, but he would be in condition to go one or two rounds. During the schooling session we jumped enough to get ourselves together again and we went to school over the water. It was a deep water and a little suspicious-looking, and the first time we galloped up to it, Sloopy left long and his hind legs went in. To our horror, we found that he also put a slice into his left hind leg that required about thirty of Danny Marks's neat little stitches to close. We could not believe that we were intended for all this bad luck.

Tough is tough, and Sloopy was tough with a capital T. He came out sound the next morning, and we still had five days before the individual. In

Neal Shapiro and Sloopy at the Munich Olympics in 1972, on the way to a bronze medal in the individual Grand Prix. In the Nations Cup eight days later, their faultless performance in the second round helped the USET win the silver team medal as well.

the middle of the night Danny and I would go out to check his bandage and treat the wound, and it was healing well. September 3 finally came, and we knew Sloopy felt fine when he lifted his groom, Peter Zeitler, off the ground by his thumb. As I walked the course and looked up at the "houses" built into it, I wished we had been a little luckier with our preparation. But Sloopy was a super athlete, and the designer had not built anything that he couldn't jump. The course consisted of fourteen obstacles with seventeen jumping efforts and no major traps except several turns which required great precision. Fifty-four riders from twenty-one nations were to start, the top twenty competitors returning for a second round and a jump-off, if necessary.

Sloopy jumped the first round with no difficulty, though it was not "play" for him as many competitions were. He had to try at the combinations and make real efforts at the big oxers. Still and all, it was not a major problem for him to get the distances or jump the fences. Our only problem arose at the water which was situated at the end of the stadium after a sharp left-hand turn from a vertical. As soon as you landed after the vertical you had to make your move at the water, which stretched out 16'. Sloopy met it well but upon landing put a hind foot on the tape for 4 faults. This was the only penalty he received in the first round.

In the second round the course was raised and shortened to ten obstacles with thirteen jumping efforts. In that round I had the second-to-the-last oxer down and emerged with 8 faults total from the two rounds. There were still three clear horses to go the second time and a flock of 4-faulters, so at first my total of 8 didn't look very good. Finally we got a bit of luck when one of the clear horses came back to gain 16 faults, and all three 4-fault Germans faulted out of contention. Anne Moore of England and Graziano Mancinelli of Italy had both been clear, but both had 8 faults for their second round. The three of us were now tied and would enter into a jump-off against the clock. This was the first time since 1952, in Helsinki, that the Olympic individual gold-medal competition had gone to a jump-off.

I was first in the jump-off, and my horse at this point was pretty tired. I had to try to be clean and fast to put the pressure on Anne and Graziano. If I could do it, they would have to take a cut to catch me. I started on my way and made some good sharp turns and got over the fences where I was cutting my corners. In the middle of the combination, however, fatigue took its toll and Sloopy rolled a rail off the middle element. Two more oxers lay before us and he rolled another rail off one of them. We had a total of 8 in the jump-off, and the rest of it was now out of my control.

With only Anne behind him, Graziano took his time and jumped a cautious but clear round. Anne pulled all the stops and went for the gold. She had crashed through the combination in the second round, and this time her horse said "no go" and ran past it. She whipped around to it again and finished without further fault. She and Psalm ended up with 3 faults—good enough to beat my score of 8; but Mancinelli won it all.

During the presentation I was quite satisfied to see Prince Philip coming toward me with the bronze medal; but Sloopy must have taken a shine to the gold, for he took a mouthful of the Prince's jacket and gave a healthy chomp. As we made our victory gallop around the stadium that day, I breathed a sigh of relief that we had made it and it was over. A lot of people had earned a piece of that medal hanging around my neck—Bert, Mr. Butler, Peter Zeitler and Danny Marks—and I would be forever grateful to them for their contributions. A portion of my life's ambition had been fulfilled that day, and without their help and their dedication it could never have been possible. We still had one more lap to go. The team event was in one week, and it was that day that we had to focus on now.

The Nations Cup took place in the main stadium and was the final closing event for the Olympic Games. It was also "curtains" for many of the top riders. The course can be described by three letters—B-I-G—and the scores showed it. All the fences produced knockdowns, and the double, 4a and 4b, and the triple, 12a, b, c, produced many refusals. The weather conditions were not the best; there was a light but constant drizzle, and it had turned quite cold besides. I was the eighth horse to go and the first of our team. As I jumped the first fence, Sloopy slipped a bit and it was obvious that the footing was slick. He jumped the second all right, and at the third, an oxer 5′3″ high by 6′6″ wide, he threw a shoe and had a rail down. We headed for the fourth fence, the "trouble double," and as he began to leave the ground he lost his footing and slid through the first part of the combination. He almost went down, but managed to scramble back onto all fours, and I got back into position as they reset the fence.

As I stood there waiting for the fence to be rebuilt, all I could think was, This isn't going to happen to me. I've got to finish, and finish in the time allowed. I'm not going to let this happen to me. I had three team members behind me depending on me and I could not let them down. The horn blew signaling me to continue, and the heat was on. I quickened Sloopy's pace in an attempt to stay within the time allowed and also to let him know I meant business. He completed the rest of the course with no further faults and within the time. However, under FEI rules, if a fence is dislodged by a refusal, six seconds are added to the score. With the penalty seconds we had 1¼ time faults, giving us a total of 8¼ faults. If I had been only two seconds faster, it would have been 7¾, and what a difference that could have made!

At the end of the first round we were running a very close race with the Germans. Steinkraus and Main Spring had made one of the only two clear rounds in the first round, and I managed to regain some ground by jumping the only clean round of the afternoon. As it turned out, it brought us close, but not close enough. We were still that quarter-fault behind the Germans and only good enough for the silver medal. We were all somewhat disappointed to be so near but yet so far, but we were happy to win the first team medal for the Prix squad since 1960. The Germans had been the heavy favorites, and it was a thrill to have given them such a close race. The summer had been filled with troubles, but our efforts paid off in the end.

The Untouchable Dream

KATHY KUSNER

From the beginning, the USET has been noted for its outstanding amazones, but of all these fine distaff competitors, Kus has had the best record. A three-time Olympian, she was the Ladies' European Champion in 1967 and second in the world title in 1965, but often beat the boys as well, having twice led all international riders at New York, and garnered such prestigious trophies as the President's Cup and the Irish Trophy at Dublin. Aside from her team activities, Kus has ridden races, scuba-dived, piloted jet airplanes and traveled almost everywhere.

LOOKING BACK OVER THE YEARS in which I've been connected with the team, I can still pinpoint the exact week in which it all started for me: the Pennsylvania National Horse Show at Harrisburg in 1956. A friend of mine was showing there that year, and I'd agreed to be the groom as a means of seeing the show. The team was there too, of course, and the obvious occurred: I watched them.

It was the first time I'd seen the team in action, and I was frankly dazzled. Actually, the whole show dazzled me, but especially the international classes. And the team seemed to do everything so well—not only were they going well in the ring, but they were turned out beautifully, and even back in the stable area everything was done just to perfection. I thought the USET was great, and knew I wanted to be connected with it.

From that time on, I had a sort of dream which I refused to compromise in any way: somehow, I was going to be a part of the team. But though I never doubted that this was what I wanted to do, or that it was the best

84

thing you could possibly do with jumpers, for a long time I was pretty weak on ideas of how to get there; it seemed terribly far out of reach.

As far back as I can remember I'd always been fascinated by horses. My earliest memories are of pony rings, where I'd lead in order to get more rides. I was always nagging my parents for a pony of my own, repeating the request at approximate twenty-minute intervals during all waking hours, and when I got to be twelve, I finally wore them down. The result was a $150 Western pony named Champ, who was self-supporting because I sold pony rides on him when I wasn't zooming around, bareback. (I can still see the neighbors shaking their fists and threatening to call my mother.) Champ was pretty smart, and he taught me a lot.

After a year or so of this I went to a horse show, where I was surprised to see everyone using saddles and riding with two reins (pelhams) instead of only one. I figured I'd better learn how to use double reins myself—and a saddle, too—and after asking around, I learned that the best local teacher was a Mrs. Dillon.

Jane Marshall Dillon really opened my eyes, starting with the fundamentals and teaching me some of the fancier stuff also. Captain Vladimir Littauer came and gave clinics at her place that were also eye-openers, and before long I was showing in the local shows. There I met some nearby horse dealers, among them Chuck Ackerman and Tommy Jones, and they started putting me on horses. (What a thrill it was to be asked!) This was marvelous experience, and so many different horses did a lot to make riding become almost as natural as breathing, even though each day had certain awkward interruptions in the form of a fur-flying wreck.

Later on I spent a summer riding for Cappy Smith, and after that I rode a lot for Joe Green. Being a dealer's rider, with its never-ending eventfulness, was tailor-made for me. And it has the advantage that you get to jump a lot of fences. (I can never forget Greenie's voice calling, "Just one more time.") You also go to a lot of horse shows, for horse shows are the dealer's showcase. Maybe it wasn't very classical or very conservative, but it was a very practical education.

While all this was going on I did a lot of catch riding for other owners at the shows, and in particular rode a lot of ladies' and amateur classes for Mrs. A. C. Randolph, who had a marvelous stable of hunters. I finally shared my dream of making the team with her, and when the next USET trials were announced, she made it possible for me to go. Since in all her wonderful stable she didn't have a single jumper, she acquired a Palomino named High Noon whom I had been riding for Tommy Jones, and let me take him to Fairfield, Connecticut, where the trials were held.

I guess we looked a little "country"—me and my Palomino open horse. But from the trials we were invited to come and train with the team that winter. Things were sure looking up.

Kathy Kusner with her first USET mount, Mrs. A. C. Randolph's High Noon, at London during their first look at Europe in 1962.

In those days (1958) the team didn't have a permanent, year-round training center, and they were stabling at the Boulder Brook Club in Mamaroneck, New York. Joe Green had some horses there too, among them the famous Windsor Castle, whom I got to show the following summer. He had something of a reputation as a rogue, but he was really just smart—smart in the Shetland pony sense! I was riding for Joe in the afternoons, but mostly what I learned during that winter and the next were things the horse dealers *hadn't* taught me, for Bert de Nemethy took me in hand and showed me that in many ways I didn't really know what I was doing at all. There were things about riding at his level that I'd never even dreamed about. I had no illusions about how much there was to learn.

I got my first chance to ride on the team in 1961. To the surprise of many, after the 1960 fall circuit George Morris decided he wanted to study acting. (The end result was that he became a tree.) This made an opening for a new rider, and George's horse, Sinjon, would need a new jock. Unbelievably, they both turned out to be me.

Sinjon was a favorite of mine, a sort of horse hero, and getting to ride him in my first shows as a team member on the fall circuit was beyond my wildest hopes. I wanted to do everything just right, exactly in Bert's way, but instead, I did everything wrong—I got so wrapped up in my idea of flawless performance that I got to where I couldn't jump or even *canter*. Every natural instinct I had was replaced by a wooden attempt at classical correctness; I became a tree too! The harder I tried, the worse it got, and finally Sinjon, my dream horse, was forced into the only slump in his brilliant career. He sure didn't look like the horse that had been fourth in the Rome Olympics, and I sure didn't look like any Games rider.

Bert didn't give up on me, thank heavens, and he named me on the squad that went to Europe in 1962 with High Noon, but things didn't go any differently for me there. I still learned a lot, but in spite of my efforts—or more accurately, *because* of them—I wasn't exactly an asset to the team. When we got back to the States the team disbanded until the fall circuit, and I wondered if I'd ever get to ride on it again.

To say that my riding life changed shortly thereafter would be an understatement. Two big things happened, almost together. First, I went back to riding and schooling some horses on my own and found that suddenly I could apply some of the things Bert had been trying to teach me, and combine them with the old natural way I'd known before I came to the team. Secondly, I got a fancy horse to ride.

This came about as a result of another friend—"Funny" (or more formally, Mrs. Frances) Rowe. She told me about a horse named Unusual who hadn't yet had much success, but who she thought ought to be worth looking at just on the strength of his breeding: he was out of the same mare as two team Olympic horses, Miss Budweiser and Riviera Wonder.

We got together. I have never felt more empathy with a horse than I did with this one, whose talents were just as unusual as his name implied. Unusual really was unbelievable; he was as soft as a marshmallow to ride, and when he jumped, he simply ascended into the air and seemed to hang up there for minutes at a time. He was the sensation of the fall circuit in the open classes that year, winning the President's Cup at Washington and the open jumper championship at the National, and suddenly, everything turned around for me.

A lot of people told me, "You'll never get another one like him." In a certain way they were right, but as it turned out I soon encountered a very different kind of horse who was to prove even better—Ben O'Meara's (later Patrick Butler's) Untouchable.

Benny found Untouchable in the Midwest in the fall of 1962, an eleven-year-old green horse. Benny and I had been helping each other out

Kathy Kusner in her "dealer's rider" costume. The talented jumper is the green Snob Appeal, later known to USET followers as Mrs. Whitney Stone's President's Cup winner Trick Track.

at the shows and in schooling, and when he brought his horses to Florida that winter, where the team was already training for the Pan American Games, I went right on riding with him in the afternoons. Untouchable was quite a problem, being a horse with a *very* hot temperament. Trying to stay ahead of him was like trying to solve a Chinese puzzle. And I do mean trying, for I never did really solve the problems he faced me with.

His first year, Untouchable was champion at every show he went to. Though his disposition would get us into some awful problems while approaching fences, his talent and class would always jump us out. Throughout his career he sure kept me scrambling through my bit bag. (Bill Steinkraus used to tell me that if I had a bigger collection of hands I wouldn't need such a big collection of bits.)

Unusual helped us win the Pan American Games gold medal in 1963, but that fall, Untouchable won the jumper championship at the National, and the next year there wasn't any question about his being my Olympic horse. Benny came to Europe with us in 1964, and also to Tokyo for the Games, and he remained very much a team-oriented person until his death. He was so talented and so original that you could hardly believe a person could develop so fast. Benny was not only the most successful horse dealer of his time; he also really revolutionized the art of schooling and riding jumpers. He was surely the most important single influence on me as a rider, and today, from evaluating horses and schooling on through planning and riding the individual class, most of what I do is what I learned from Benny. His talent was really without parallel.

Untouchable was just that in my riding experience, but I was lucky enough to ride a number of other very high-class horses, many of them also owned by Patrick Butler. Aberali was certainly a special one, and if any horse ever jumped and moved more like a deer than a horse, it was he. He was a bad stopper when Benny and I first watched him on the Italian team, rarely finishing a course. After he was convinced that refusing wasn't profitable, he became a beautiful horse to ride; the Italians used a hackamore on him, and I did the same. His nose was just as light as his mouth.

Fire One was another exceptional horse. A registered Quarter Horse

Kathy Kusner walking the course at Tokyo in 1964 with coach Bert de Nemethy, left, and the late Benny O'Meara.

An unforgettable combination: Kathy Kusner and Mr. & Mrs. Patrick Butler's Untouchable, shown here at the Olympic Games in Mexico in 1968.

who was also a registered Thoroughbred, he had explosive strength—his jumping was so authoritative that I felt he was saying, "Just hang on, Kusner, and I'll take you for a ride." If he hadn't had such serious soundness problems, I believe his career would have been one of the great ones.

Two other special favorites of mine were two little mares, Fru and Nirvana. Though both won some bigger classes, they were really basically speed merchants rather than Nations Cup horses, and they were tremendous fun to ride against the clock. They were just like smart little Formula One racing cars—all you had to do was floor the accelerator and steer, and they'd do the rest.

Having good horses is a big factor in horse-show success, but you also have to know what to do with them, and the team experience provides marvelous opportunities to learn. The European shows give you a chance to watch the best horsemen in the world—dressage riders as well as jumper riders—and you can watch them both in schooling and in competition. (I logged so many hours watching Brazil's Nelson Pessoa that I'm sure he thought I was from the CIA.)

Supplementing such observations are the endless discussions with other riders, ranging from analyses of broad general approaches on down to tiny details of what does and what doesn't work for particular individuals. I'm an experimenter, and at times drove my teammates, and especially my coach, crazy with my "new discovery" announcements. Most of these do not survive the test of time, but a few were pretty good. However, when I see someone do something different, I can't wait to try it out, and have often jumped in headfirst. About the time that I'd painted myself into a corner, Bert or Billy would come to the rescue with a little refreshing objectivity. (I can still hear Steinkraus saying, "Why don't you try riding like everyone else—one leg on each side, one rein in each hand, facing in the right direction? Since it will be something different, you might like it.")

Mr. & Mrs. Patrick Butler's Aberali and Kathy Kusner, jumping at the National Horse Show in 1967. Aberali often showed in the hackamore he wears here instead of a regular bridle.

I'm sure that Bert and Billy saved me more than once from killing myself—they did find me pretty exasperating. I'll never forget one of Billy's lectures about my bag of bits and me being too gimmicky. It lasted at least an hour (it was one of his shorter ones), and at the end, he had the nerve to borrow my bicycle chain to put on a horse he couldn't hold. With it, he won the next four classes. We both thought that was pretty funny.

Team riders get asked a lot of questions, and two in particular are asked so often of me that I'd like to deal with them here. The first, which comes in a lot of different versions, is the "girl question"—as applied to riding jumpers, riding races, being on the team, voting or anything else. The answer is simple, for in all these things, women are just the same as men—they are not superior! Actually, it's the skill of the individual that counts, not size or sex. If weight or strength were a main factor, we'd be put into weight classes like the prizefighters and wrestlers.

The second question is a better one: "What's it really like to be a rider on the team?" The best answer I can give is to say that it's one of the greatest experiences a person can have. The chance it provides to learn, to travel, to ride good horses, to go to interesting places and meet interesting people—well, it's just a marvelous opportunity. Of course, there is another side too—to complete the picture you have to add that doing something on this level requires most of your time and efforts, which means sacrificing many other things that you would also like to be doing. And it has its frustrations. Sometimes you hit riding slumps, and sometimes your horses hit jumping slumps (generally as a result of the former); sometimes your horses go lame, sometimes they turn out to be bums and sometimes you don't even have any horses to be concerned about.

Luckily, the USET has always managed to round up a pretty interesting group of people. Between the riders, owners, grooms and Bert himself, there is always the widest possible range of nonhorse interests—things as different as golf, politics, exploration, aviation, long-hair music, country music, museums and many others. At one time or another, you get exposed to them all. There's a lot of humor, too, for the team is generally together long enough to develop some quite elaborate running jokes; but you'd have to ask "Chicken Man" Shapiro or "Bubble Boots" Ridland to explain further. The point is that even when things are going bad, they're also still pretty funny.

I've been interested in a lot of different things, and sometimes I've thought of what I might have done with the same time if I hadn't gotten involved with the USET to the extent I did. I've had a fair taste of some of the alternatives (such as race riding and flying), and though some of them are darned interesting too, I wouldn't trade the experiences I've had with the team—the trips, the Games, the whole USET life—for anything. I'm

Kathy Kusner and Untouchable after winning the Irish Trophy for the Grand Prix of Dublin for the second successive time in 1965.

lots older, unmistakably grayer and maybe not lots wiser than I was that week in Harrisburg when the team first captured my imagination. But it looks just as good to me now as it did then.

Cuttin' the Mustard

DENNIS MURPHY

People who think of the USET as drawing its riders only from Eastern show circuits get something of a surprise when they meet Dennis Murphy. At only thirty the "old man" of the 1975 Pan American gold-medal team, Murphy sounds more than somewhat like an ol' country boy from the Deep South, and he's not at all ashamed of that description. On horseback the country boy turns into a tiger: he was the leading international rider at Toronto in 1974, his freshman year with the team, and was the leading amateur point-winner in all international competitions the following year. The Murphys live in Northport, Alabama.

I FIRST STARTED RIDING at about the age of eight and soon became a member of the local pony club. For the next dozen years I rode in many of the shows in Alabama and the surrounding states in both hunter and open jumper classes, though without attaining anything more than local celebrity. Then at the age of twenty I got married, and for a few years I was only a weekend recreational rider.

It was not until I was twenty-five, and working for Gulf States Paper Corporation, that the opportunity arose for me to start serious riding again. At that time, Mr. Jack Warner, president of Gulf States Paper Corporation, was riding in shows, and I had the opportunity to accompany him there on the weekends. In this way, and by helping him exercise some of his horses, I got back into the atmosphere of equestrian competition, which I love. Eventually this all led up to one day in 1973 when Colonel John Russell and Gordon Wright were talking to Mr. Warner and asked him,

"Why not let Dennis try out in the screening trials for the team?" Mr. Warner said he would give me some time off and furnish the horses if I wanted to try, so I did. That is how it was possible for me to be at the screening trials.

Having to come all the way from Alabama, we shipped to New Jersey a day or two early so that we could let the horses rest. I watched some of the other riders arrive at Gladstone and was very much impressed; I wondered how I'd measure up against them. I took two horses with me—Blaze, the horse I wanted to ride in the screening trials, and Do Right as the extra horse—Blaze being the much older and more experienced horse and more suitable for the type of work we would have to be doing there.

It seemed that there were a great many younger riders participating in the screening trials. There were also riders with a great deal more prestige than I had, due to their lengthy show-ring records. At twenty-eight, I was considered the old man of the group; I'd literally started riding before some of my fellow candidates were born. I hoped that this was an advantage, but feared it might mean that I had even less of a chance to make the team. When I finally did become one of the riders to be picked from the group, I felt very good about it. I was very much honored to have been picked out of such a top-quality group of riders.

In the spring of 1974 I was chosen to compete as a USET member on the summer's European tour. Each rider was to take three horses to use in competition. As my number one horse I was assigned the team horse Triple Crown. He was already a seasoned, experienced horse, having been to Europe before. I used him in the Nations Cup and more important classes. My second horse would be Do Right, who had become my best horse after I lost the use of Blaze. Do Right was to be used as a speed horse, and more important than that, he was my backup horse in the event that something did happen to Triple Crown. But I still needed a third horse. Mr. Warner said to go through the barn and choose the horse I felt would be potentially the best horse to take. A little doubtful that Mr. Warner would really let me have him, as he was his own favorite horse, I chose his best hunter, Tuscaloosa. Generous man that Mr. Warner is, he immediately agreed that this was the horse to take.

About a month before the departure date, all the team riders and their horses assembled at the Gladstone training center. We spent this time in preparation for Europe, going through the intensive training program set up for each horse and rider under the watchful eye of Bert de Nemethy. One of the big problems for me in preparing my horses for the European tour or FEI competition was that I was no longer able to use the standing martingales that I had been using while competing under AHSA rules. Bert taught me some very basic training maneuvers to discipline my horses so that I was able to better control them and to make them more consistent in their willingness to work for me.

Finally the long-awaited day of our departure for Europe arrived. Everything was carefully packed. Last-minute instructions were given to all. At the airport, tension and excitement filled the air as the task of loading all the equipment was painstakingly accomplished. All the horses were carefully loaded and secured in the plane for the flight to Germany. It was a tremendous feeling when the plane finally left the ground and we knew we were on our way. Bert de Nemethy and some of the grooms knew what to expect, but for most of us, we were heading for the great unknown. Of the four initial riders, only Rob Ridland had been to Europe before. (Frank Chapot was to join us later.) Challenges were yet to be seen and to be met.

Fortunately, the flight was very easy with no problems. All the horses shipped well. We landed in at Frankfurt, Germany, and were welcomed very warmly. At Wiesbaden we started our first competition. The first class seemed very hard—not from the point of view of riding, but because I knew I was competing in international competition for the first time. I found myself a little tense, trying to be a little too careful. However, the more often I went into the ring as the show progressed, the more I began to relax, and my performance improved.

From Germany we went to Lucerne, Switzerland, where I rode in my first Nations Cup. We were only fourth in a very close class, but the horses went pretty well, and Bert was not too upset. At the end of the show, Rob Ridland won the Grand Prix with Almost Persuaded, which gave our morale

Murphy and Balalaika, donated to the team by Mr. and Mrs. Alvin Wasserman, jumping at La Baule, France, on their first trip to Europe in 1974.

Dennis Murphy and Jack W. Warner's Tuscaloosa, consistent winners both at home and abroad in their first year on the team, shown here at Hickstead.

a big boost. We had a short time between Lucerne and the next show, which was spent sight-seeing.

From Switzerland we went to La Baule, France, the site for the Ladies' World Championship. Michele McEvoy brought over two horses specially for this event and came in second behind Janou Tissot of France. Frank Chapot joined the squad as we rode in our second Nations Cup, finishing second this time.

Next we crossed the Channel to England for the Hickstead show, site of the Men's World Championship. Rodney Jenkins joined the squad here in time to participate in the championship along with Frank Chapot. After four days of demanding competition, Hartwig Steenken of Germany became the champion. Frank Chapot was equal third after the exciting finals, in which the four best-qualified riders rode both their own horses and the horses of the three other finalists. I won my first class with Do Right, and two days later I won a speed class with Tuscaloosa. I also had my first encounter with the famous Hickstead Bank. It's actually only about 7' high, and from the ground it doesn't look so big; from the top looking down, however, it looks like Mt. Everest.

From Hickstead we went to Wembley, on the outskirts of London, where we were again second in the Nations Cup. A mock World Championship Class was held here in which I placed second. Hartwig Steenken won the class and Paul Schockemöhle was third.

From Wembley we went to Cardiff, Wales, where the Professional

96

Championship and the Amateur Championship of Great Britain were held. Rodney Jenkins won the ride-off between the Amateurs and the Professionals, with Buddy Brown placing second.

Our final stop was Dublin, Ireland. It was really exciting for me because I had heard so much about the Dublin Show and all the different exhibits it had to offer. Here I won my final class in Europe.

While in Europe we felt popular and seemed well known by the people there. Horses and horse showing are followed more closely in Europe and are a very popular sport. People constantly recognized us even when we were just walking around the streets sight-seeing. Often we were asked for our autographs. In each country and at every show we were entertained and treated almost as though we were royalty. Not only did I gain a great deal of experience and knowledge through the tour, but I also have many good memories.

In the fall of 1974 I was chosen to compete with the team in Washington, New York and Toronto against teams from France, Canada and Great Britain. This was a special thrill for me because it was on my own side of the Atlantic. Riders on the North American tour are allowed only two horses

Murphy and Gulf States Paper Corporation's Do Right, winners of both the New York and Toronto puissance classes in 1974, shown here competing in the 1975 Pan American Games in Mexico.

The winning Nations Cup team at New York in 1975: (from left) Rodney Jenkins, the leading U.S. professional rider, and teammates Buddy Brown, Dennis Murphy and Michael Matz, riding Idle Dice, Sandsablaze, Tuscaloosa and Grande, respectively. The latter three riders collaborated with Joe Fargis to win the 1975 Pan American Games gold medal.

apiece, and this time my mounts were Do Right and Tuscaloosa. Do Right was the horse used in the Nations Cups, and Tuscaloosa, who had been very successful "against the clock," was my speed horse. In Washington I was on my first winning Nations Cup team, riding Do Right. Tuscaloosa also won a class.

Then we went to New York. Again we won the Nations Cup. This seemed somehow to be the more important of the two Nations Cups held in the States, perhaps because it was in Madison Square Garden and also because this show is followed so closely by so many people.

To my amazement and delight, Do Right won the puissance class, a class which is open at the Garden to both national and international riders. The final height was 7'1"—the biggest fence I'd ever ridden over. To win a class in the Garden the first time I rode there was important to me personally. But to jump 7'1" and to beat Rodney Jenkins and Idle Dice doing it was more than I'd hoped for or ever expected. The thrill of all this was over too soon.

From New York we went to Toronto for the Royal Canadian Winter Fair, which is like the National Horse Show of Canada. The week started out very slowly but got progressively better. By now I felt more confident when competing against international riders and knew that if I rode well, I had a good chance to win.

The thought of being leading rider in Toronto never really entered my mind. I was interested in each individual class and in helping my team's overall score. As I went through the show, Bert kept telling me to do the best I could, but most important, to try to be clean each time rather than have a fast round that might be marred by a knockdown and blow the whole class.

In the puissance at Toronto Do Right again jumped 7'1". This time it seemed much less like an accident and I was happier with my ride. It was not until the last day that I realized I might possibly be the leading rider. I won a speed class in the afternoon with Tuscaloosa, and coming back that evening for the Stake, I knew that if I placed fifth or better, I would be leading rider. For the first time I felt the pressure, for I realized I was very close. Waiting for the final jump-off in the warm-up area, I saw Bert coming over to give me final instructions. As he looked up, about to give me the word, I said, "I know, I know: *Just go clean!*" Luckily, I did so. The USET was champion at all three fall shows, and I learned afterward that I was the first rookie rider to become leading rider at one of the fall shows in the history of the team. It sure made me happy to show that I could cut the mustard!

Thoughts on Jumper Courses

WILLIAM STEINKRAUS

Bill Steinkraus started riding on the USET in its second year and remained active more or less continuously thereafter until his retirement from competition at the end of 1972. In the interim he was a member of six Olympic teams and winner of innumerable competitions, including the first individual Olympic gold medal ever won by a U.S. rider (at Mexico in 1968). Now president of the team's parent organization, he still often rides at home in Connecticut with his wife and three sons.

WHEN I WAS IN MY TWENTIES, I didn't think that the subject of jumper courses was either very interesting or very complicated, and on the basis of what we jumped in those days, it wasn't. Since then, things have changed a lot and so have I; some of my best friends now consider me to be fixated on the subject, and no doubt they will regard my choice of it as a topic for this book as incontrovertible proof. In any case, it is quite true that today I think of course design as an inexhaustible, vitally important yet often misunderstood subject, and I welcome this chance to deliver myself of another 2 cents' worth of my ideas about it.

Before launching into a serious discussion of course design, however, I would like to start with something a bit more personal which still has considerable relevance to the general subject: an account of what the media would call "My Biggest Thrill in Show Jumping." Surprisingly, perhaps, this was not Snowbound's performance in the Mexican Olympics. That, without question, was a marvelous moment. However, any Olympic victory presupposes, in addition to a considerable element of luck, the sustained, single-minded dedication of many people to that particular goal. As such, it may not possess the special kind of shock value that the word "thrill" usually implies.

No, for me the "sudden emotional reaction" the dictionary specifies was not so much exemplified by my most important USET win as by my very first fall-circuit blue. And what made the latter a genuinely heart-stopping thrill to me was not the fact, per se, that it was my first win, but the other circumstances that were involved. To explain, I must fill in a little background.

I first made the USET jumping squad in 1951 at the Fort Riley Olympic trials, where I rode a horse of the Don Ferraros' named Black Watch. Black Watch wasn't exactly a Thoroughbred type, and while he could jump a really big fence and was a tough customer in a small ring, he was just not the kind of mover that handles galloping courses well. Hence, as I soon realized, he was not really the Games type of horse at all. By the early spring of 1952 everyone agreed that I should return Black Watch to the Ferraros and try to find something more suitable for Europe.

At this point, the Woffords generously came to my rescue. First they lent me Hollandia, a marvelously scopy Bonne Nuit gelding they'd acquired from Hugh Wiley the previous year, and later, after the FEI ruled against women's participation in Olympic jumping, they lent me Reno Kirk, a dead-game Army Thoroughbred who would have been Carol Durand's Olympic mount. That explains how Hollandia and Kirk became my string for Europe in 1952. After the Games, however, the situation changed of course; Captain John Russell had to return to his unit (for he was still an

Bill Steinkraus and Mrs. John Wofford's Hollandia, his 1952 Olympic mount. Ridden by Warren Wofford on the 1956 USET squad, Hollandia ended his career carrying the Union Jack with great distinction, and with Warren's wife, the noted English show jumper Dawn Palethorpe Wofford, in the saddle.

officer on active duty), while Carol was eligible to rejoin the team. The logical thing to do was put Carol back on Reno Kirk for the fall circuit, and switch me to one of Russell's string. Accordingly, I was offered the ride on Democrat.

I was not at first overjoyed by this prospect. Though Democrat had been Russell's Games mount in Helsinki, and I had admired him ever since his brilliant performances at London and Dublin in 1948 (which I had witnessed), he was then nineteen years old and starting to look it. Moreover, Russell, who knew him well, had encountered some real problems with him that summer; he tended to jump to the corner of fences and sometimes stopped, and a lot of the time he didn't look very sound.

When I first tried him out at Arthur McCashin's place, a couple of weeks before Harrisburg, I found him rough-gaited and rather like a crochety old man. Schooling over little fences, I couldn't hold him at all in a plain snaffle—he'd just rush and get under his fences. When I tried him in a pelham it was better, but he made it quite clear that he didn't much care for my telling him what to do. He was sure that he knew better, and he may well have been right. Anyhow, I had no better alternative, so we decided to take him and "play it by ear," using Hollandia, in whom I had great confidence and who thrived on work, as much as possible.

Harrisburg was the first show on the circuit in those days, and it started on a strange note—the first international course was so small that almost everybody went clean, and the class ended up as a sort of team scurry, which it was not supposed to be. The riders all grumbled, and when something similar happened in the second class, word that we didn't find the courses challenging enough filtered through to the jury, headed on this occasion by none other than Major General Guy V. Henry, a former chief of cavalry and former president of the FEI itself.

General Henry was then well into his seventies and rather frail, but when he stiffened his back he was still all soldier, and all man. He knew exactly what to do with "restless natives," and he did it: he asked for the course designer's charts and jacked up the fences.

In point of fact, many of the fences planned for the later classes were pretty big even before General Henry altered the dimensions, and afterward they were huge; but if the riders wanted bigger courses, well, that was the way it was going to be. Specifically, spreads that were originally marked as 6' wide now became 7' to 8' wide, and heights that had been 4' and 4'6" were altered to 4'9" and 5'. Luckily for us, there were still not too many spread fences in the courses at that time, but when you ran into one "after the change," it was a doozer. This wasn't what we'd had in mind at all, and there was more grumbling, but General Henry was adamant; we'd wanted harder courses, and now we had them. All we had to do now was live with them.

Bill Steinkraus and Democrat at New York in 1952. To judge from the missing cap and the traditional "first fence," they are starting round again in a fault-and-out class. Democrat jumped over a hundred fences that year before incurring a fault.

Being eager to start off on the right foot, I didn't enter Democrat at all in the first few classes of the show, but when the schedule started to call for two classes a day, I had to. For his debut, we picked an easy speed class, the Pen—really a handy hunter course that was also used for jumpers. The course consisted of a 24'-square pen of sheep hurdles in the center of the ring, which you in-and-outed three different ways, and four single fences around the outside. These were nothing special originally, and only the last fence was a spread. However, this final triple bar, after the change in dimensions, became something very special indeed; it had a 4' single rail in front, a 5' single rail behind and an 8' spread in between. When we walked the course, it sure attracted a lot of attention.

As luck would have it, Democrat was drawn as the last horse to jump in this first test of our new partnership, and as I watched uneasily from the ingate area, I saw little to reassure me. By the time the gate opened for us, there had still been no clear round, nor had any horse cleared the last fence; on the contrary, the ring crew was running short of rails and there had been three or four shattering falls. I was not exactly brimming with confidence. Democrat jumped the early fences well enough, though his turns were a bit rough. Because of the handy nature of the course, you couldn't even get much of a run at the last fence, and as we came through the pen the last time and cranked up for the triple bar, I didn't see any way the fence could be jumped. In fact, there was really only one thought in my mind: *I hope we don't break anything.*

I remember clearly that we met that high first rail a bit too long, and then I must have literally shut my eyes. What happened next is what pro-

103

duced my biggest show-jumping thrill, for I found myself transported effort-
lessly aloft, as on a 747 takeoff; the old man landed just as far from the top
rail as he'd stood off, and never even laid a toe to it.

I can't swear that I even heard the crowd's roar, but I know that I wore
a stupid grin from ear to ear as I rode out of the ring, and it was some time
before I regained my senses. I simply couldn't believe what had happened.

Of course, the clear round proved that all the talk about unjumpable
fences was nonsense, and we never did get General Henry to change those
huge spreads back. Our aggregate totals of faults and falls that year must
have set a record, for there were precious few clear rounds outside of the
first two classes. But it was "the same for everyone," we were told, and
every now and then someone squeaked around clear and "showed that it
could be done." We used to hear those two expressions a lot in those days,
for many show managers really liked the idea of the "trap," or single huge
fence that practically nobody could jump. Unquestionably it focuses the
audience's attention—and competitors', too; hence its survival in the puissance class and what the British call the "bogey fence" concept even today.

Later on the circuit I learned that Democrat's jet-propelled leap was
no accident at all, but simply one of the things that he could do under pressure, like the singles hitter in baseball who can knock one completely out of
the park when he has to. Democrat went on to win every single individual
class we showed him in on that fall circuit, eight in all, and he contributed
to several team wins as well. (It wasn't an easy year competitively, either,
for the two previous Olympic champions, Mariles and d'Oriola, were both
there that year, and in good form, too.) Despite the wins, I know that my
collaboration with Democrat was pretty ragged, compared with the polished
rounds I'd seen him turn in with Fuddy Wing, and he never did get to like
that pelham. However, everyone who ever rode him agreed on one thing:
we'll never know how good Democrat really was, the war years having
wasted what should have been his prime. He was surely "something else,"
as they say these days.

I still enjoy thinking about that moment and that season, but I bring
it up not just to extol Democrat, and certainly not to imply any criticism
of General Henry, for whom I had the greatest possible admiration and
respect. My real reason for relating it is that it accurately reflects a whole
era's philosophy of courses: it's the manager's job to set them up, and the
competitors' job to jump them, right or wrong. After all, they're the same for
everyone, so quit bellyaching.

This was generally the philosophy I grew up with, and though I couldn't
really see how having it wrong for everyone made it right, I think I more
or less agreed with it—until I got a look at the European courses in 1952.
Then I started to realize that the sport of show jumping had potential dimensions that we'd never approached in the United States. Since most of us who

remember the show-jumping scene as it was during the years on either side of World War II are now getting rather long of tooth, there may be some historical interest for younger readers in an account of how things were.

In general, the standard of course design at the bigger shows used to be pretty close to what exists at the "leaky roof" shows today—and for one of the same reasons: the fact that the manager was responsible for the courses, "in addition to his other duties." Since the average manager has always had enough to do without building fancy jumper courses, most are willing to settle for a bare minimum of fences, capable of fairly quick erection even by an idiot jump crew. The traditional fare was simplicity itself: four fences and two lines. The usual set of fences consisted of a brush (with no rail), a white gate, a vertical of three rails and a stone wall. The lines were either twice around the outside or, in the bigger rings, two figure-8s.

Bigger shows offered more variety, for sometimes they owned eight fences, adding to the standard set of four such things as picket fences, road-closed signs and railroad gates. This made possible not only the "outside-inside, inside-outside" line, and the "once and a half around and down the middle," but also the occasional in-and-out (double or treble, almost always verticals) or spread fence.

Though my recollections are limited to East Coast shows, the situation

Ksar d'Esprit, Miss E. R. Sears' stellar performer, was a mainstay of the USET from 1958 to 1963, and an especially brilliant puissance specialist. He is shown winning the Bate Memorial Puissance at Toronto in 1961, one of more than a dozen victories he chalked up in such classes.

elsewhere in the country was surely very similar, aside from a few isolated pockets of progressiveness. We had a few of these on the East Coast, too, for at the top of the show-managing profession there were a couple of highly gifted people, and the very best shows sometimes offered quite challenging and attractive courses. The late Ned King, a Harvard man and a graduate architect as well as a gifted artist and a horseman, was a case in point. His courses for the National and Atlantic City horse shows were marvelously imaginative for their time, and his best—like the old Course K at the Garden and his Jumper Stake course there—came to be considered classics.

This was exceptional, however, and in general when you entered for a show you knew exactly what the courses would be, even if they were never mentioned in a prize list (as they usually were not). Not only did you know the fences and the lines, but you also knew what the distances would be (unless the jump crew messed up)—for these were either "right," or 24′. The "right" longer distances were products of guesswork or trial and error, and in practice, since the fences were mostly vertical, riders adjusted for any awkwardness by putting in an extra stride. Hence the preference, in those days, for short-striding, non-Thoroughbred open jumpers, a little hackney blood being favored by many. The main question for riders was whether to attempt that 24′ in-and-out in one stride or in two.

Mr. Walter B. Devereux's Sinjon and Steinkraus at Aachen in 1964. Winner of the George V Cup at London that year, Sinjon made the trip to Japan for the Olympics, but was prevented by injury from competing and was retired after the following season.

The only horse ever to represent the USET in Games competition in two different disciplines, William D. Haggard, III's Bold Minstrel, shown here as a show jumper with Bill Steinkraus. After participating in two Pan American and one Olympic Games as a three-day horse, Bold Minstrel won his fourth Games medal on the jumping team at Winnipeg.

What made this whole state of affairs possible, of course, was the fact that under AHSA rules, touches or rubs were scored along with knockdowns, instead of only the latter's being scored, as was (and is) done under the FEI's international rules. Dull, simple courses were practicable only in conjunction with touch scoring. However, many owners, riders and dealers passionately favored their perpetuation indefinitely. For whatever their ultimate drawbacks, simple courses have many short-term advantages.

For one thing, knowing what you were going to jump from week to week and from year to year certainly simplified schooling. The average backyard needed only that basic set of four fences, and many trainers made do with fewer than that. Preparing for the show was simplicity itself: you gave all the horses you were taking a bump with a big rail and put them on the van. Only very occasionally was it necessary to do something special, like building a practice Liverpool to prepare for Ned King's jumper stake at the Garden (and this was strictly a seasonal phenomenon, like the first frost).

I should point out that while the standard of jumping, riding and school-ing at the bottom of the spectrum was pretty crude, at the top it was darned impressive. The "big boys" became so sophisticated in their riding and sharpening-up techniques that they produced results that would be hard to duplicate under any circumstances. I can remember seeing horses jump clear over eight consecutive verticals whose top rails rested atop 6′ standards; I have seen horses jump a 6′ single rail, go through entire shows without a single rub and high-jump almost 7′ over loose rails, and these are no mean achievements.

Nonetheless, the overall implications of the prewar jumper situation are obvious, especially with the benefit of hindsight. Dull, simple courses and touch rules sheltered too many mediocre horses and too much mediocre riding; they condoned inadequate preparation of green horses, encouraged or demanded poling, often stultified public interest and in the final analysis, placed a low value on the dealers' and riders' skills. (There were always high-priced stars, but the *average* value of horses in the jumper ranks before and just after World War II was surely the lowest of any division.)

There is no need to trace in detail the long path by which our best American show-jumping standards have finally come to measure up to the best international standard. Much was accomplished by the AHSA, through legislating minimum requirements, and the USET also has surely played a role. In the end, however, it comes down to the people who got the message about better courses themselves, from whatever source, and then talked the shows into giving it a try. This usually involved not only brainwashing managers and show committees, but then planning the course, physically building it and, when it was all over, putting up with the com-plaints of the riders who didn't like it. In any case, bit by bit we've learned to recognize as a country how much good jumper courses can contribute to good sport, and hence, how important a good course designer can be to the success of the show.

Perhaps the average standard all over our big country is still not quite up to that in England (which is small enough to be serviced largely by salaried designers sent out by the national federation), or in Germany, where show jumping is more of a way of life; but it's certainly not bad, and it's improving all the time.

I hope it continues to improve, and suspect that this has the best chance of happening if there is widespread agreement about the factors involved in course design and the principles that govern it. In my view, the basic facts of life for the course designer are quite simple, and I'd like to conclude by outlining them:

1. The purpose of building any jumper course is to produce a valid result for a particular competition.
2. "Valid" means legitimate—i.e., a result primarily of skill or merit rather

than of chance; the cream should come to the top. Since the class conditions themselves vary, different kinds of cream may appropriately come to the top in different types of competitions. However, the Grand Prix, Stake or richest class should be a sufficiently balanced and searching test to preclude a fluke result.

3. The means of producing a valid result for competitors should not be dangerous for them or either boring or ugly for the spectators.

4. To achieve his result, the course designer has a minimum of four basic ingredients to play with. He can make any of them easy, hard or anything in between:

   a. The line or trace of the course.
   b. The spacing of obstacles on that line, including distances in combinations.
   c. The particular character and structure of the individual obstacles (i.e., visual perspective, solidity of construction, etc.).
   d. The actual size (height and spread) and number of the obstacles, and thus the level of physical strength and/or agility demanded, given the prevailing footing.
   e. In addition, a fifth ingredient is often available, depending on class conditions: the clock—i.e., the option of separating competitors on the basis of elapsed time in the event of equal faults.

5. The art of course design hinges on the designer's skill in orchestrating these ingredients in such a way that a fair, balanced and horsemanlike result is achieved in terms of the caliber of horses and riders he has to work with, both in the individual competitions and in the show as a whole.

There it is in a nutshell. Now let me make a few comments about the meat of this nutshell. The first thing to remember is that as a rule of thumb it is rarely desirable to use as few as one or as many as three of the above variables at once. If the course is very big indeed, it does not need to be very tricky, very long and awkwardly spaced on top of it. (In fact, *very* big alone will inevitably produce a result, though not a balanced one.) The Nations Cup at Mexico in 1968 might be used as an illustration of too many factors' being used at once: the fences were very big, yet came down very easily; the line and the distances were both awkward and the time limit was too tight. The result was a team class won with over 100 faults, which distorts the basic character of our sport.

At the other extreme, using only one ingredient, and especially that of size alone, can be just as bad a means of producing a result. Building enormous, solid fences in an easy line with good distances tests true horsepower more than anything else, and thus tends to end up as a test of owners' financial resources in buying super horses. There is only one appropriate place for this kind of course building, and that place is the puissance class.

Using the clock alone is also rather unsatisfactory. The clock will always produce a result, even if everyone goes clean, but the flat-out run over fences that don't come down belongs at the racetrack, not the show ring. Nonetheless, even this seems preferable, to me, to the final jump-off against the clock over a course that has been raised so high that nobody can go clean. For once the clock comes into play, faults need and perhaps should no longer be the prime factor in producing the result; thus the course designer can afford to be a bit generous with the severity of his course. For example, visualize ten horses coming through to the second jump-off over a big course. This is probably more than the course designer wanted, and there is a tendency to overcompensate—to raise everything, and build a jump-off course that hardly anyone can get around. It is far better, however, to raise only two or three fences, let the clock decide and save the horses for tomorrow.

The most extreme form of using a single ingredient is embodied in the idea of the "bogey fence" referred to earlier—the fence or combination on which the whole class hinges, none of the other fences counting for anything. As indicated earlier, I think it's fine for the audience to hypnotize itself on the puissance wall, but otherwise I favor an even distribution of faults except for the first fence (which should hardly ever cause a fault) and the last several, which should be somewhat harder in order to provide a natural climax for the round. I particularly dislike the kind of bogey fence that is created by a false ground line, a trick distance or abnormally flimsy construction. (One year in London a little narrow stile that fell if you breathed heavily on it was used as the "in" of a double consisting otherwise of a big oxer in a long distance. You were obliged to override the stile in order to jump the oxer, and if you rubbed it, it was down. It made a real bogey fence that hardly anyone jumped clean, and the winner, it seemed to me, was selected mostly by chance.)

In general, then, the course designer's primary goal should be to provide varied yet balanced challenges to horse and rider that test what they can achieve together. It is not necessary for each course to be completely balanced within itself; if there are two speed classes, one may well feature a running track and the other a turning track, but Grands Prix and other featured competitions should achieve an internal balance, and the classes as a whole should strike a balance also. It seems to me that if an out-of-control horse or a short-striding horse or a careless jumper wins the stake or the championship, the course designer must reckon that he's failed somewhere. I think he fails, too, if he requires riders to use up their horses unnecessarily, as will be the case if there are too many long gallops or too many lines doubling back on themselves. These invariably encourage "snatch and jerk" riding, and the same results can always be better produced in more subtle ways.

How to jump the water, as demonstrated by Bill Steinkraus and the Princess de la Tour d'Auvergne's Snowbound, the USET's first Olympic gold medalists at Mexico in 1968. Getting good height is the key to negotiating water jumps; Snowbound knows this so well that he was only once faulted at the water in his entire USET career.

One final thought: Course designers with whom I have discussed the above ideas have often retorted, "That's all well and good for you to say, but have *you* ever tried to build courses week after week without repeating yourself?"

Aside from the fact that the question is a non sequitur, I have not and do not see why it is necessary.

Indeed, I see no more reason for the courses served up by a course designer to be any more (or any less) varied than those served up by a chef. The fact that you have served roast beef before is no reason not to do it again, nor is it a reason to serve it without any seasoning, or with the wrong seasoning, or to substitute a dessert for it. I will not labor the analogy further except to acknowledge that while good food and good courses both demand sound mechanics and a lot of common sense, both will always remain more an art than a science. *Bon appetit!*

Principles of Jumper Training

BERTALAN DE NEMETHY

Perhaps no show-jumping coach of modern times has been more influential or more admired than Bert, whose twenty-year career with the jumping team neatly parallels its emergence as a major power in its field. A native of Győr, Hungary, Nemethy was a member of the Hungarian squad for the ill-fated 1940 Olympics; after the war, he immigrated to the United States via Denmark, and after several years with private stables, he was named USET coach in 1955. His record since then speaks for itself, and underlines the soundness of the methods he discusses below.

THE HISTORY OF THE HORSE goes back millions of years. There are many good books explaining its evolution from a small animal, *Hippus*, to *Equus caballus*, the true ancestor of the horse we know today. According to scientific knowledge and research, early horses were spread out all over the earth, disappeared once in America and arrived and survived in Asia and Europe. Exactly when men first became acquainted with horses nobody knows for sure, but their relationship can be traced from very early times in China. Men used horses for traveling, hunting, warfare and agriculture.

To understand the fundamental nature of the horse and the most appropriate way of handling him and dominating him took centuries, but Xenophon's treatise *On Horsemanship*, one of the first writings on the subject and dating back some twenty-three centuries, is still largely valid today. Lifelong observations by many other brilliant horsemen have served to confirm many of Xenophon's basic principles.

The natural balance of the horse does not change, and his center of

Bertalan de Nemethy, far right, in his first season as USET jumping coach in 1955, with Messrs. McCashin, Steinkraus, Russell and Wiley at Ostend, Belgium.

gravity in motion is controlled by physical laws. The skeleton of the horse, as he is now, will be the same for a long time to come. The structure of the bones and joints and their mechanical functions clearly indicate that the driving force emanates from the hindquarters, while the front legs support the long body; the neck and tail contribute to his balance. We have to accept all these facts concerning the horse, just as we must accept the basic elements of the rider's correct position and acknowledge the coordinated use of the rider's seat, weight, legs and hands as his best means of communication with the horse.

In other words, there is nothing new in the art of riding; everything has been said and done before. My training program is no more than a syste-

The winning Nations Cup team at Rome in 1959: Bert de Nemethy with Bill Steinkraus, Hugh Wiley, George Morris and Frank Chapot, who have just defeated the Italian team in a jump-off almost in the dark. The horses are Ksar d'Esprit, Nautical, Sinjon and Diamant.

matic application of basic principles. Its goals are as follows:

1. Maintaining the *balance* of the horse despite the addition of the rider's weight.
2. Developing and maintaining the proper *rhythm,* which is essential to all movements.
3. Teaching the horse to understand the rider's *aids* and to respond to them without hesitation or resistance.
4. Improving the horse's coordination and developing his joints and muscles with systematic *gymnastic exercises,* which also serve to improve his jumping style and perfect his bascule.
5. *Conditioning* the horse physically through daily, consistent and progressive exercises.
6. Developing the horse's *confidence* in himself and in the rider.

Now let us consider these factors in somewhat greater detail.

The *balance* of the horse depends on his center of gravity. With a rider on his back, his natural balance is altered, and in our basic training we must concentrate on coordinating the horse and rider's gravity lines. The proper seat must be learned, as well as the proper disposition of all parts of the rider's body. Acquiring a harmonious feeling of the horse's movement is not an overnight procedure. The rider must spend many hours in the saddle, preferably without stirrups on the longe line, with the constant correction of a dedicated instructor. Of course, the rider himself must also be determined to correct and improve his style. Exercises on the longe line to improve the influence of the seat and correct use of the rider's aids must be a constant part of the regular training program.

For improving the horse's *rhythm,* one of the most successful methods is the use of cavalletti. I like to use four or five rails, not higher than 6″ to 8″ above the ground, spaced at distances that correspond to the particular horse's trotting stride. (The distance between these rails will vary slightly, from 4′ to 5′, depending on the size, disposition and level of experience of the horse.) The horse should not change his impulsion, but should remain in balance and harmony, in full control of his body movement, as he trots over the rails. Consistent, correct use of this method will result in the horse's focusing his concentration and interest on the ground, and in his active and careful control of his movements. At the same time, his coordination, rhythm, cadence and muscle tone will improve. He will become more regulated, harmonious, flexible and relaxed.

The systematic use of cavalletti is equally significant for the rider's development. Control of balance, rhythm and coordination are basic elements of the art of riding. The rider develops "timing," an awareness of the distance to the obstacle at various speeds and a feeling for the amount of regulation necessary for the most desirable approach to the ideal takeoff point.

Bertalan de Nemethy schooling San Lucas over cavalletti at Aachen, prior to the show in 1962. Nemethy is acknowledged as a master in the systematic use of cavalletti and gymnastics.

The rider's *aids* constitute an established and logical communication system for controlling the horse's gaits and making him more flexible, obe-

A well-balanced squad: Bert de Nemethy (far right) with the riders he took to Europe in 1964: (from left) Carol Hofmann, Bill Robertson, Mary Mairs Chapot, Bill Steinkraus, Frank Chapot and Kathy Kusner. They won fifteen classes on the tour.

dient and disciplined. Training on the flat—elementary dressage—is an essential part of the jumper's and the rider's training. The rider's aids must be clear and coordinated when starting, increasing or decreasing speed, and in general when regulating or controlling the motion. Turns to all directions must be executed in balance without loss of the necessary impulsion.

A consistent and refined application of the rider's aids avoids confusion and helps to develop understanding, confidence and cooperation between horse and rider. All this cannot be explained in a few pages, and many books deal with this subject at great length. However, though they may differ slightly in detail, they rarely contradict each other in broad principle. One final goal for all remains: to produce a relaxed, lively, happy and confident horse, cooperating and accepting his rider's signals and making the optimum use of his ability.

The above work alone still will not produce a jumper. The horse's actual jumping ability must also be developed through systematic *gymnastic exercises*. The requirements for good results are using common sense, encouraging the horse's confidence with progressive and careful requirements, recognizing his weaknesses and avoiding disasters.

When employing a gymnastic system for the jumper's and rider's development, I stress the following objectives:

a. Control of impulsion prior to the takeoff point must be developed. Using the cavalletti at a trot will serve this purpose in the beginning; later the rider's judgment and skill must take over.

b. During the takeoff, when the horse is preparing to jump, the rider must be in perfect harmony with his mount. This is a most critical moment, and perfect coordination and balance between horse and rider depend entirely on the rider. The rider must neither be left behind nor anticipate the horse's movement, but go *with* it.

c. The rider must preserve a secure, balanced position, both while following the horse's body over the jump and during the landing, in coordination with the horse's changing balance.

d. Exercises must be employed to train the horse to shorten his stride in the canter. This is accomplished by a gradual shortening of the distance between obstacles. Start with exercises that require him to make one short stride, then later to make two or three.

e. Conversely, the horse must be trained to lengthen his stride by a gradual lengthening of the distances between obstacles.

f. Imaginative variations and combinations of these exercises should be used, tailored to the needs of the individual horse.

This gymnastic system has no written rules. The instructor's experience must dictate not only the type of exercises but also the progressiveness of the requirements, the amount of repetition and the systematic variations. His experience and tactfulness must suggest the limits of the requirements, when to be satisfied with temporary progress and where to start again. To underestimate the progress or overestimate the ability of the horse can result in physical and mental harm to the horse. Instead of success, the method can end in disaster.

The common opinion that horses jump better when they are "fresh"—kept in the stable with insufficient exercise—is completely contrary to my thinking. The fitness of a jumper is no different from that of a racehorse or a human athlete. Daily exercises and physical *conditioning* (of lungs and muscles) are essential parts of every training program.

Certainly, the frequency of schooling over fences must be regulated in accordance with the individual needs and condition of the horse and his competitive schedule, and must be gradually increased as the date of the performance approaches. However, the dimensions of the fences during the training period should in general be kept to a medium size—impressive enough to require some effort, but far from the limit of the horse's ability. Only toward the end of the training period for a competition do we school over fences close to the size of those in the conditions for the competitive performance. This will be important and necessary for testing the results of our training program and the form and mutual *confidence* of horse and rider. It is also known through experience with human athletes and racehorses that top form cannot be kept indefinitely. We have to prepare our horses gradually for the significant performances, and then we have to let them down. The traditional advice "Remember the date and hour of the Derby" is very sound. Being in top form on the date and hour of the Olympic Games, or other important event when we must perform at our best, is what counts.

In addition to the basic principles described above, which I would call my basic teaching philosophy, we must recognize that admirable results

Another strong Nemethy team, winners of the Nations Cup at Aachen in 1971 for the second time (shown here with President Gustav Heinemann of West Germany): Bill Steinkraus, Neal Shapiro, Joe Fargis and Conrad Homfeld, with Mr. & Mrs. W. G. Love's Fleet Apple; Patrick Butler's Sloopy; Henry, Saunders and Rowe's Bonte II and Sam Lehrman's Triple Crown.

have been achieved by different methods. There are always remarkable exceptions in all fields of endeavor, and there are also understandable shortcuts. It is no longer possible for individuals to spend years and years in cavalry schools or to devote unlimited periods of time to the training of horses. It seems to me that today's interest lies not so much in lasting high standards as in fast results; since we are living in a different world with entirely different circumstances, we may have to make compromises in the training of horses and riders, just as in many other fields of life. However, while a successful individuality should not be discouraged, it would be quite wrong to try to teach or copy the methods of those rare individuals whose success must be credited only to their exceptional talents.

The USET has had its exceptions too, but in general, the accomplishments of the jumping team during the past twenty-five years have depended heavily upon the application of the principles discussed above. Compromises are sometimes necessary, but in my experience, compromises which violate these principles are of little long-term value, and the classical traditions of the great horsemen of the past will endure long after the fashionable "gimmicks" of the day have been forgotten. In short: "All roads lead to Rome—*if* you have passed the Alps."

Gymnastic work at Gladstone: young Buddy Brown working under Nemethy in 1973, a year before he joined the team. The following summer Brown won the Grand Prix of Dublin, and in 1975 was the individual silver medalist in the Mexican Pan American Games.

COMBINED
TRAINING

The Military in Mufti

JONATHAN R. BURTON

"General Jack" first appeared on the international equestrian scene when, as a captain, he rode on the 1946 Army horse-show team, winning the individual championship class in New York. He ended his competitive career as a USET three-day rider at the Stockholm Olympics ten years later, but he remained close to the sport as judge, course designer and technical delegate, somehow combining these activities with a brilliant Army career that saw him rise to major general, commanding the Third Armored Division. After leaving the service in 1975 he succeeded George Merck as executive vice-president of the USET.

THE ORIGIN AND DEVELOPMENT of three-day eventing, or combined training, as a competitive sport was exclusively military—so much so that this phase of equestrian endeavor was long termed "The Military" in Europe, and is sometimes still referred to as such by members of the older generation. The whole conception of the event was military, and for years, so was the execution—if you ignore the sole civilian rider, the Dutch merchant Eddy Kahn, who competed in Berlin in 1936.

It was my privilege to be a member of the last Army three-day squad at the Olympic Games in 1948, albeit as a reserve rider, and to my surprise, I found myself riding in civilian dress at the Stockholm Olympics eight years later, having been given leave by the Army to compete there in the three-day event under the aegis of the USET. Before I recapitulate what happened there, it seems appropriate to review something of the background of

The U.S. Army Equestrian Team, photographed in front of Fort Riley's West Riding in 1947: (from left) Kitts, Borg, Burton, Anderson, Wright, Wing, Thomson, Tuttle, Henry, Ellis, Symroski, Frierson and Burnett. All were riders except for Ellis, who was the team veterinarian.

the event, with particular reference to our own Army participation in eventing from its inception through the London Games of 1948.

The three-day event in the modern Olympic Games was first introduced at the Stockholm Games of 1912. Its inclusion was due to the efforts of Count Clarence von Rosen, Master of the Horse to the King of Sweden. The tests were devised to test cavalry officers' chargers for their fitness and suitability. These mounts were supposed to be capable of carrying their officer/couriers long distances at top speeds to deliver dispatches across difficult terrain and obstacles. The committee formed to design a suitable Olympic equestrian competition consisted of twelve cavalry officers from various countries in Europe. They recommended a Grand Prix dressage and a Nations Cup show-jumping event, and the final proposal included a military "pentathlon on horseback." This competition was divided into five "trials," or "phases," as follows:

1. Long-distance ride of 55 kilometers (34 miles)
2. Cross-country of 5 kilometers (3 miles), this phase being included in the long-distance ride above
3. Steeplechase of 3.5 kilometers (2 miles)
4. Prize jumping
5. Prize riding (dressage)

The trials were carried out in the above order during a four-day period. The long-distance and cross-country took place on the first day, the steeplechase (speed test) on the second day, the jumping on the third day and the dressage on the fourth day. The dressage was placed last in the competition because the committee felt "the clearest obedience test could thereby be obtained."

The competition was open only to officers on active duty in the various armies, riding military horses. The minimum weight a horse was to carry

122

was 80 kilograms (176 pounds). Double bridles were compulsory for all phases except the steeplechase.

A complicated scoring system was used which included time penalties in the long-distance phase. The steeplechase phase had an optimum time. Touches were scored in the stadium jumping along with knockdowns, refusals and falls. The ten-minute dressage test utilized seven judges. This test included a collected and fast walk, collected and fast trot, rein-back, gallop, pirouette and jumping. Reins could be held in either one or both hands.

This Stockholm competition was the first modern-day horse trial. By present standards it was severe; twenty-seven competitors started and only fifteen finished. It was unbalanced because the tough first phase, which had to be accomplished in three hours and forty-five minutes, was immediately followed by a cross-country phase of 5 kilometers (3 miles) over natural obstacles with a fifteen-minute time limit. The total marks for the first four trials were less than those awarded for the dressage phase.

Sweden, in the final results, won the team gold medal; Germany came in second and won the silver medal; the United States placed third, winning the bronze medal, and France placed fourth. Other teams competing were those of Belgium, Denmark and Great Britain. The composition of the American team was as follows:

Lieutenant Ben Lear, Jr., on Poppy. (He later became a four-star general)
Lieutenant Ephraim F. Graham on Connie
Captain Guy V. Henry (later to earn two stars and become president of the FEI and Chief of Cavalry)
Lieutenant John C. Montgomery on Deceive

The test was changed for the Antwerp Games in 1920. The dressage phase was eliminated and another endurance phase added. The first phase was a 45-kilometer (28-mile) roads-and-tracks followed by a 5-kilometer (3-mile) cross-country over eighteen natural obstacles for a total time of $3\frac{1}{2}$ hours, of which $12\frac{1}{2}$ minutes was for the cross-country. Next came a day of rest, followed by another endurance test of 20 kilometers (12 miles) of roads and tracks to be ridden in an hour, followed by a 4-kilometer (2.5-mile) steeplechase at 550 meters per minute. A physical exam for the horse was conducted between the roads-and-tracks phase and the steeplechase. After another rest day, an eighteen-obstacle stadium-jumping course was ridden. The minimum weight for this second equestrian three-day event was reduced to 65 kilograms (143 pounds). Four teams finished, with Sweden first, followed by Italy, Belgium and the United States. Finland, France, Holland and Norway failed to have their teams finish.

By 1924 seventeen national teams competed in Paris, with the United States the only overseas competitor. The present pattern for the three-day event was then established, consisting of the dressage on the first day, fol-

Three-day and jumping-team riders on the last Army Olympic team in 1948: standing (from left), Lieutenant Colonel Frank Henry, Colonel F. F. Wing, Colonel Earl Thomson, Colonel A. A. Frierson, Lieutenant Colonel Harvey Ellis; kneeling, Lieutenant Colonel Charles Anderson, Lieutenant Colonel Charles Symroski, Captain John Russell and Captain Jonathan R. Burton.

lowed by speed and endurance on the second and ending with stadium jumping on the third day. The dressage included 6-meter circles, two-track movements, halts, rein-back and many transitions up and down between ordinary and extended gaits. The cross-country now covered a distance of 23 miles as follows:

1. Roads and tracks 4.9 miles
2. Steeplechase 2.5 miles
3. Roads and tracks 9 miles
4. Cross-country 5.5 miles
5. Run-in 1.25 miles

The maximum height of the fences was only 3'7"; with a spread of 11'6" for the open water. Forty-four riders started, with thirty-two completing. The team gold medal went to Holland, followed by Sweden and Italy. Individually, Major Sloan Doak of the United States placed third behind Lieutenant van Zijp of Holland.

The Games were in Amsterdam in 1928 and twenty nations competed, including Argentina for the first time. The conditions were quite similar to those at the 1924 Games except that the heights in the cross-country course were raised to 1.20 meters (3'11") and the water lengthened to 13'. The Dutch again won the team medal, followed by Norway and Poland. Individually, Lieutenant Pahud de Mortanges from Holland won first place and a German rider came in second.

The Los Angeles Games in 1932 found only six nations responding—a result of the world economic crisis. A total of 36 riders competed, with Mexico the only other entry from the Americas. The U.S. three-day team was captained by Lieutenant Colonel Harry D. Chamberlin on Pleasant Smiles. (He later became a brigadier general and wrote the two equestrian classics *Training Hunters, Jumpers and Hacks* and *Riding and Schooling Horses.*) Lieutenant (later Colonel) Earl F. Thomson on Jenny Camp won second place individually, Mortanges of Holland again winning the gold. Lieutenant Edwin Y. Argo on Honolulu was the third three-day rider. For the first time, the United States won first and second in the dressage phase. The final team standings found the United States first, with Holland second. No other country was able to finish a team.

The 1936 Games were held in Berlin, with Hitler in power. Nineteen nations responded, with fifty competitors entering the three-day event. The pattern of the event had now been formalized, and the cross-country course of thirty-five imposing obstacles included the controversial splash jump. The obstacle consisted of a small post-and-rail jump with a large pond beyond. Several team captains objected to the fence; they were overruled, however, as the organizers said several ordinary horses had been over the obstacles and found the bottom firm and the fence not as bad as it looked. It was thought that there were a shallow and a deep side, which the Germans knew about. The pond was drained the next day to prove to contestants that there were no holes or unevenness. However, the pond did slope more steeply away from the fence than the riders realized, causing many horses to lose their balance on landing. A heavy rain the night before the event raised the water level in the pond, and although Dr. Gustav Rau ordered the excess water siphoned off, it was not removed.

The result was that of the forty-six horses who reached the pond, eighteen fell, ten riders came off and only eighteen competitors went clear. Slippery Slim of the United States, ridden by Captain John H. Willems, fell at the pond, broke his upper forearm in his struggles to get out and had to be destroyed. Legeny, ridden by Stefan von Visy of Hungary (later the three-day coach of the USET, now coach for the Austrians), broke a leg while galloping on the flat on this course. In all, twenty-three horses out of fifty were eliminated.

The stadium course was made difficult with an in-and-out that had to be jumped twice. The first time, you went straight through; the second time, you had to stop after coming over an oxer and go out between the wings. Two horses were eliminated here. The gold medal in the 1936 Games was won by Germany, followed by Poland and Great Britain. Individually, the German Captain Stubbendorf on Nurmi was first, followed by Captain Earl F. Thomson on Jenny Camp, silver medalist for the second time in a row. A Dane, Captain Lunding, was third. The 1936 Games were the last Olympics before World War II.

The 1948 Games in London marked the end of participation in Olympic equestrian events by the U.S. Army Equestrian Team, as the military team was disbanded in 1949. The three-day team climaxed the competition by winning the gold medal, followed by the Swedish and Mexican teams. Individually, Captain B. M. Chevallier of France was first, followed by Lieutenant Colonel Frank S. Henry of the United States on Swing Low and Captain Selfelt of Sweden. Lieutenant Charles H. Anderson of the United States was fourth on Reno Palisade, and three-time Olympic rider Colonel Earl F. Thomson was twenty-first on Reno Rhythm.

A word about the training for the Olympic and other international events. The officer/riders, after demonstrating suitable experience, were detailed to duty with the team. Riding and training horses became their sole duty. Team captains were the coaches. The riders were products of the year-long basic and advanced horsemanship courses at the Cavalry School, Fort Riley, Kansas. Many of the riders through the years had also attended courses at Saumur in France, Tor di Quinto in Italy and the German Cavalry School at Hannover. Thus the U.S. Cavalry kept up with the "forward" philosophy of riding being developed in Europe.

At Fort Riley, every necessary training facility was available. There were two large riding halls, numerous dressage sand rings and cross-country courses with every conceivable type of obstacle. A very large stadium-jumping Hippodrome was available in which every bank, ditch, combination, water, etc. to be found in Europe could be duplicated. Horses were secured from throughout the Army. The fourteen existing regiments of horse cavalry conducted numerous horse shows, race meets, horse trials, hunts and polo events as a means of developing their horses' capabilities. Students attending the basic and advanced equitation courses also developed some outstanding horses. As soon as a horse's potential became apparent, he was turned over to the team to train and prepare for international competitions. The team also had its own permanent stable personnel, including a farrier and a veterinarian, so that superior care was available. With all this support, the Army Quartermaster General also operated a remount system which, by selective infusion of Thoroughbred bloodlines, developed outstanding replacements for the team. It was a system followed by all the armies of the world, and a splendid one, but with the passing of the horse from the battlefield, the transition to a civilian environment was inevitable.

To summarize the Cavalry era, the U.S. Army sent teams to all the modern Olympic three-day events, commencing with the first one in Stockholm in 1912. The Army team won two team gold medals (1932 and 1948) and one bronze team medal (1912). Individual Army riders won three silver medals (1932, 1936 and 1948), with the late Tommy Thomson winning the first two of these awards and Frank Henry the last.

Perhaps the principal contribution that the Army and Cavalry made

Captain Burton schooling Air Mail at Fort Riley in 1947, with the famous rimrock in the background.

to the equestrian activities of our country has been its influence on riding technique. At a time when most of the country was riding in the old-fashioned English style, sitting on the back of the saddle with legs cocked forward, the Cavalry was teaching the forward seat which had been developed in Italy. As the superior results of forward riding began to become obvious, the civilian horse world, under Cavalry tutelage, gradually changed to the Continental system, so that it is now rare to see anyone using the "old" seat. For this contribution alone American civilian horsemen must be forever grateful to our U.S. Cavalry.

The postwar transition from an Army equestrian team to a civilian one was not as smooth and easy as one would have liked, but that was probably unavoidable. Several former Army horsemen assisted in the transition and helped in various ways to diminish the trauma. Of equal importance was the fact that the horses used by the Army team in Europe from 1946 to 1950 were made available to the infant USET, to provide a cadre for the first civilian attempt to prepare an Olympic equestrian team, and the training facilities at Fort Riley were also made available.

I was ordered to bring back to the States from Germany those horses considered to have some potential for international competition. The horses had been worked and shown by the Army team riders, following the 1948 London Games, at numerous international events such as Dublin, Vichy, Wiesbaden and Paris. I brought the selected horses back by ship and turned them over to Colonel John W. Wofford at Fort Riley. The show jumpers

Major Jack Burton and Walter G. Staley's Huntingfield at the splash at the Stockholm Olympic Games in 1956.

were immediately put back into work so that they could be used on the fall circuit that year as well as in the trials.

I stayed at Fort Riley to design and construct a three-day course that could be used for the trials, and then spent my leave there too, riding in the trials myself and finishing second overall. On the strength of this I hoped to get orders to ride in Games, but it was not to be; I was assigned elsewhere and did not really catch up to the team again until 1956. By then I had six months of accrued leave to spend, and this time, when I made the team in the trials, I was able to ride in the Games as well.

The three-day team at Stockholm was coached by a teammate of mine from 1948, the dressage rider Major Robert Borg, who also competed at Stockholm in dressage. The cross-country course was very difficult, and rain

128

made it even more treacherous. I got around, and made a spectacular finish —a bit too spectacular. The thirty-third cross-country fence was a drop over a ditch of large proportions. My horse, Huntingfield, failed to extend his legs and went straight down, with me headfirst beside him. This upended picture was sent by wirephoto to the States and was the first knowledge my wife had of the event when it was flashed on the TV news. Actually, I was knocked out by the fall, but Walter Staley, Sr., who owned the horse and happened to be at the fence, threw me back into the saddle. We galloped on to complete Phase E (the run-in, no longer required), I weighed out— and only then woke up, in the ambulance!

The Pan American preparations in 1959 were first coached by Colonel Milo H. Matteson, followed by Erich Bubbel. (Bubbel, who had been the German stable manager for the old Army team in Europe, is now the coach of the Irish jumping team.) When Erich was injured, Colonel Earl F. Thomson became the final coach for the Chicago Pan American and Rome Olympic Games.

The transition from military to civilian control was not accomplished without many "growing pains," and even today, the challenge of mounting and training a fully competitive three-day team is a formidable one. Many officers played a significant role in the formative years of the USET, and I would be remiss if I did not mention the especially important contributions of the late Generals Guy V. Henry and John Tupper Cole, and two of my predecessors as USET vice-president, General F. W. Boye and F. F. Wing. Without their devotion to the cause of our nation's equestrian participation in world international competition, the USET could never have achieved the status it enjoys today.

A rough landing for Burton and Huntingfield over the last fence of the Stockholm cross-country. Despite a concussion, Burton remounted and finished the course.

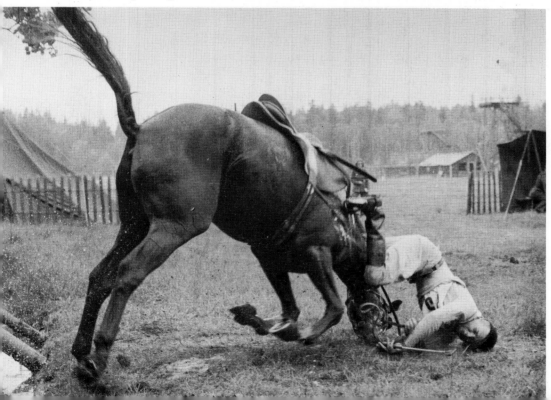

The Early Days of
USET Eventing

WALTER G. STALEY, JR.

Wally Staley tried out for the very first USET three-day squad and soon demonstrated a talent for going very fast around cross-country courses that completely belied the deliberate manner that earned him his nickname "Judge." A three-time Olympic rider and the USET's first Pan American Games gold medalist (in 1955 in Mexico), Staley retired from the team after the Rome Olympics to earn a Ph.D. and then joined the family business. However, he remains a keen recreational rider and has started an enthusiastic next generation of riders as well.

In 1951, COLONEL JOHN W. WOFFORD, a former U.S. Olympic rider and then president of the United States Equestrian Team, Inc., undertook the task of developing a three-day squad to represent the country in the 1952 Olympic Games. As no civilian riders or horses in the United States at that time possessed the necessary training or experience, his task appeared to be formidable. Fortunately, some of the facilities of the former U.S. Army Cavalry School at Fort Riley, Kansas, were made available by the Army. Fort Riley had excellent facilities for training three-day riders and horses.

In the spring and summer of 1951, Colonel Wofford assembled a group of six young students, each with some horse-show experience, but most of whom had scarcely heard of a three-day event. I was fortunate to have been invited to participate in this unforgettable program. We were all fortunate that the USET had been able to obtain the services of then-Captain Robert

130

Borg, who had placed fourth in the 1948 Olympic Grand Prix de Dressage, to assist with the coaching. Colonel Wofford coached cross-country and jumping, while Captain Borg handled the dressage training.

The Fort Riley Hippodrome contained every conceivable type of obstacle. Included were banks, ditches, walls and hedges of every size and description, and these could be negotiated in many different combinations. A horse and rider progressively and properly trained in this facility should be able to tackle a jumping course anywhere and feel confident that no major surprises were going to be encountered. By the end of the summer, we were able to negotiate most of the obstacles in the Hippodrome.

Colonel Wofford taught us pinpoint control of pace, and how to condition our horses while keeping them sound and fit. In this regard, we learned the value of slow work and of walking our horses repeatedly up and down long steep hills for building their wind and strength. Horses conditioned in this manner were not particularly taxed later by the carefully planned twice-weekly galloping sessions during which they developed that rhythm without which pace is erratic and exhaustion comes too early. An important concept in conditioning the three-day-event horse is that every step the horse is ridden, whether it be in dressage schooling or show jumping, has an effect on his condition and thereby must be calculated as part of a balanced conditioning program suited to that individual horse.

If few of us had much idea of a three-day event prior to coming to Fort Riley, none of us had any notion of what went into the rational schooling referred to as dressage. Captain Borg spent much time with each rider and, in addition, gave each of our horses a considerable amount of training. We began riding at midsummer and were scored on the Olympic Three-Day Event Dressage Test every Saturday morning for the remainder of the summer. Captain Borg's thorough critique, which followed each ride, served as an outline of the next week's areas of concentration. In addition to training the three-day riders and horses, Captain Borg was preparing his own dressage horses for the coming Olympic Games. This provided the three-day riders with many instructive and inspiring hours of observation.

A three-day event held at Fort Riley in early October was to serve as the trial for selection of the Olympic three-day-event squad. However, it was made clear that if the level of proficiency was not satisfactory, there would be no three-day team. The U.S. Olympic Equestrian Committee was on hand for evaluation of horses and riders and possible selection of a squad. Because of the inexperience of the riders and horses, there was some doubt that a squad would be chosen. However, the committee was agreeably surprised at the proficiency in dressage and sufficiently impressed with the performances on the next two days to select those who finished in the top five places. Jeb Wofford placed first, riding Benny Grimes, a tough six-year-old gelding bred and raised by Colonel Wofford. I placed second on Bari, a nice but not very dependable six-year-old gelding bred and raised by my father. Charles "Champ" Hough placed third on his own Craigwood Park, a small, elegant eight-year-old black gelding. In fourth place was Bill James, who rode his own mare Reno Prudence. She had been bred, raised and broken by the Army, but had been in civilian ownership for several years. Bob Frazer of Billings, Montana, placed fifth on his Never Trail, but elected to return to college rather than stay with the squad.

Jeb Wofford, son of Colonel Wofford, had practically grown up at Fort Riley. He was nineteen years of age. I was from Mexico, Missouri, and eighteen. Champ Hough was from Burbank, California, and seventeen. Bill James was from St. Louis and eighteen. I think each of us thought the trials held sure disaster, and only after they were all over did we realize how much had been accomplished that summer.

The rest of October and the succeeding months through January were a quiet time for the three-day squad at Fort Riley. Colonel Wofford and the jumping team were away at the fall horse-show circuit in the East, while we remained at Fort Riley with Captain Borg, resting the horses ridden in the trials for a month and working on various fundamentals of horsemanship for which there had not been time in the busy summer schedule. Two of the U.S. Army horses that had been used in the 1948 Olympic Games were added to our string. I was assigned Reno Palisades, a large brown mare who had been ridden by Colonel Charles H. Anderson to a fourth place. Jeb was assigned Reno Rhythm, the gray mare ridden by Colonel Earl F. Thomson at Aldershot in 1948. With these horses came an awareness of our awesome legacy from the great U.S. Army teams of former years.

In addition to our riding activities, Jeb, Bill James and I attended classes at nearby Kansas State College, while Champ attended high school in Junction City.

In February of 1952, the three-day squad joined the Prize of Nations squad at the steeplechase training center at Camden, South Carolina. The move was not made without tragedy. During the loading operation at Fort Riley, Reno Palisades was injured; she was left behind and subsequently was destroyed. At Camden, I was assigned Reno Rhythm, as Jeb had brought along another young horse. Also, Captain Borg lent the three-day team a promising five-year-old stallion, so that each rider had two horses to ride. Three months were spent in Camden polishing dressage and stadium jumping. We also took advantage of the steeplechase facilities to ride over brush courses in specified lengths of time. Prior to leaving Camden, we participated in screening trials, consisting mainly of dressage and stadium jumping. After these trials, my horse Bari was dropped from the three-day string.

In late April the team left Camden with the horses, traveling by ship from New York to Bremerhaven, Germany, and then by train to Munich, where the dressage, jumping and three-day squads trained and conditioned for a month prior to competing in horse shows at Wiesbaden, Düsseldorf and Hamburg. At the shows, the three-day team entered both dressage and jumping classes at the M level (1.40-meter jumps), which provided valuable experience. While negotiating a bank at Wiesbaden, Reno Prudence suffered a leg injury and had to be dropped from training.

After the show at Hamburg, the teams moved to Helsinki, arriving there in mid-June for the final six weeks of training. Bill James was then assigned Champ Hough's horse Craigwood Park, as Champ appeared to be well mounted on Cassavellanus, a six-year-old gelding belonging to Mrs. Wofford, whom he had ridden since arriving at Fort Riley.

Champ, Jeb and I were entered in the 1952 Olympic Games, as only three entries were permitted. No sooner had the entries been made than Reno Rhythm developed a persistent but undiagnosed lameness in the hindquarters. It was thought possible to amend the entries, and Bill James was entered in my place to ride Craigwood Park. We did not learn until after walking the cross-country course that the amended entry had been submitted too late, and I was committed to ride. Craigwood Park became my mount, and we had four days to get acquainted prior to the dressage test.

Dr. Gustav Rau, in the 1952 *Sankt Georg Almanach,* described the cross-country course as the most difficult to date in the Olympic Games. Many of the obstacles were high fences with ditches in front. Obstacle No. 17, a large zigzag fence in a wide ditch at the bottom of a ravine, eliminated thirteen of the contestants. The course was hard, but considered by most to be fair. Weather and footing conditions throughout the event were perfect. Thirty-six of the fifty-nine starting entries finished the event.

Cassavellanus, under Champ Hough, had a truly fine performance. They placed seventh in dressage with a beautiful ride, but fourth among those who eventually finished the whole event and only 8 points behind the best of these, Dr. W. Büsing of Germany, the eventual bronze-medal winner. Champ acquired no penalty points on the second day. He rode Cass just fast enough on Phase B (the steeplechase phase) to gain maximum bonus points—a perfect ride. On Phase D, it turned out, he was too conservative, gaining only 15 bonus points. In the third day's stadium jumping, Cass rolled one rail, costing 10 points. Champ, on Cassavellanus, placed ninth in the 1952 Olympic three-day event.

Jeb Wofford placed thirty-second in dressage, made 18 bonus points on the steeplechase and had 190 time-penalty points and 20 penalty points for a refusal on Phase D. He had one knockdown on the last day and finished thirty-first of the thirty-six riders who were not eliminated.

My dressage ride on Craigwood Park did not reflect what this horse could have done under a rider who was familiar with him. Because of his small size, I had trouble keeping contact with him, which made him some-

Presentation picture of the USET's first Olympic medal, a team bronze in the 1952 three-day event at Helsinki. At far left is the then president of the FEI, General Baron de Trannoy; the riders (from left) are: Rothe, Wagner and Büsing of Germany; Stahre, Blixen-Finecke and Fröhlen (hidden) of Sweden and Staley, Hough and Wofford of the United States.

what fidgety. We finished fiftieth in a field of fifty-nine. The second day was better. We gained 33 of a possible 36 bonus points in the steeplechase phase, and on Phase D we earned 12 bonus points for time, but also 20 penalty points for one refusal. Craigwood Park and I had one knockdown on the last day, and we finished eighteenth.

The most traumatic moment for me had been prior to the endurance phase on the second day. Being the last of our team to ride the course, I had gone out to the steeplechase area to watch Champ Hough and Cass. I arrived back at the stable area only to find that the usual bus service between there and the Olympic Village had been discontinued so that the buses could be used for transporting spectators out to the cross-country course. This necessitated grabbing the nearest bicycle and pedaling some 5 miles in order to change into my riding clothes and then pedaling 5 miles back just in time to get started on Phase A. At least, I didn't have time to become nervous.

The gold-medal winner was Captain H. von Blixen-Finecke of Sweden, riding the magnificent Jubal. His lead was so commanding going into the third day that his one knockdown was no threat to his gold medal. The silver medal went to Captain Guy Lefrant of France, and the bronze medal went to Dr. Büsing of Germany, the only rider of the top five to go clean on the third day.

The score of the Swedish team was 13½ penalty points lower than that of the German team, and they won the gold and silver medals, respectively.

Our team placed third, winning the bronze medal. To be honest, had not one rider each from France and Great Britain been eliminated for missing flags, we would have placed fifth. Regardless, Colonel Wofford and Captain Borg had, in fourteen months, started from scratch and developed a U.S. Olympic three-day team.

The Prize of Nations team of Steinkraus, McCashin and Russell also had its day in Helsinki, as it captured the bronze medal on the last day of the Games.

The following summer, Colonel Wofford assembled a group of riders at his Rimrock Farm, on the perimeter of Fort Riley, where they continued working under him and Captain Borg. Several new riders participated, including Frank Duffy, a high school student from Birmingham, Michigan.

A three-day event was held at the end of the summer, which was won by Jeb Wofford riding Benny Grimes. Others competing in the trial were Major "Jack" Burton, who had been a member of the 1948 Olympic three-day-event squad; Bill Haggard of Nashville, Tennesee, and my brother Allen. Bill and Allen had spent the summer working with Erich Bubbel in Mexico, Missouri. Erich had emigrated from Germany in 1951. He was later named coach of the U.S. three-day team for the 1959 Pan American Games.

The first Three-Day Event National Championship and trials for the 1955 Pan American Games team were held at Nashville, Tennessee, in September, 1954. The site had been chosen and the course built by Jack Burton. The most memorable feature of these trials was the intense heat. The temperature during the second-day endurance tests was in excess of 100 degrees. Many horses succumbed to heat prostration and lameness on the parched indigenous red-clay soil.

Participants included a group of riders who had spent the summer working with Colonel Wofford and Captain Borg at Rimrock Farm. These riders and horses made a grand sweep, accounting for the first five places out of the ten who completed the trial. Frank Duffy won the event riding his own half-bred gelding Drop Dead. Jeb Wofford, who had been ill with a virus a week before the event, collapsed and failed to finish the course on his five-year-old gelding Passach, but then recovered to complete the course later in even more intense heat on Benny Grimes, placing second. Third and fourth places were taken by Wofford horses, Pat's Sister and Flashmark respectively, both ridden by Jonas Irbinskas, who worked for the Woffords. Fifth place went to Mike Fields of Fort Leavenworth, Kansas. The outcome of the trials was another success for the Wofford-Borg training system.

The sixth and seventh places went to my brother Allen and me. I rode Huntingfield and Allen rode Mud Dauber. Huntingfield was a nicely proportioned five-year-old Thoroughbred gelding, who finished the course in excellent physical condition. Mud Dauber was a heavier-set six-year-old, seven-eighths-Thoroughbred mare, and she suffered some heat fatigue on the second day. Both of these horses had been bred and raised by my father and had been broken and trained by Erich Bubbel.

The Pan American Games team selected consisted of the top four eligible riders from Nashville. These were Frank Duffy, Jeb Wofford, Allen and me. Jonas Irbinskas was classified as a professional and therefore not eligible. Mike Fields was ineligible because of his young age.

Colonel Wofford was already thinking ahead to Mexico City. After the trials at Nashville, he discussed with me his plans for sending the three-day team down to Mexico City for several months of acclimatization prior to the Games, as he knew that acclimatization of horses and riders offered the only hope of being able to compete successfully in the three-day event at the 8,000-foot altitude in Mexico City. This conversation was the last one that I had with Colonel Wofford. A short time later he became seriously ill, and he died a few weeks before the start of the Pan American Games.

My brother was unable to arrange for a leave of absence from his studies at Princeton University and withdrew from the team, resulting in our sending only three three-day riders to Mexico. This was a development that had serious consequences for our chances to win a team medal.

In January of 1955, Mud Dauber, Huntingfield and Drop Dead were assembled at Junction City, Kansas, with the Wofford horses—Benny Grimes, Cassavellanus, Flashmark and Passach. The horses went by train to Mexico City, with a stable crew headed by Jonas Irbinskas. Bob Borg, now a major, and Jeb Wofford were on hand for their arrival on January 7. The horses were hand-walked or otherwise lightly exercised for three weeks until Frank Duffy and I arrived on January 28. At that time the horses were ready to begin work. At first the altitude had a noticeable effect on the horses, as they were short of breath and sweated profusely after minor exertion, but after several weeks of work they seemed, for the most part, fairly well acclimatized.

The Chilean and Argentine teams, like Colonel Wofford, had recognized the necessity for acclimatization, and both of these teams arrived shortly after we did. Thus, all four teams to participate in the three-day event—Chile, Argentina, Mexico and the United States—shared the same training facilities prior to the Games.

The horses were stabled at the Escuela Mexicana de Equitación, home of the Mexican national team headed by the famous Mexican horseman and 1948 Olympic Prize of Nations gold-medal winner, General Humberto Mariles. The general was in total command—coaching the Mexican teams, supervising the preparations for the equestrian events of the Games and attempting, when time allowed, to train himself and his horse to compete in the coming Games. He was a very cordial and accommodating host during our stay, making arrangements for anything we wished.

Much to my surprise, Major Borg spoke Spanish as fluently as he spoke English, having grown up in the Philippine Islands. Needless to say, his linguistic ability was a tremendous asset.

Mexico City at that time of year has delightful resort weather. The only rain in the two months that we were there was a freak thunderstorm one afternoon during the first week. The afternoon temperatures were generally about 80 degrees, but at night it was close to freezing. This temperature extreme presented a distinct hazard to the health of the horses.

During the early part of our stay, we received considerable assistance from the Mexican and Argentine team veterinarians. Later, Lieutenant Colonel Wilson Osteen, a U.S. Army veterinarian, was in Mexico City and attended our horses. In spite of this care, a distemper epidemic, apparently aggravated by the altitude, affected our horses. Cassavellanus contracted distemper early in the period and recovered in time to resume training. For Benny Grimes, Flashmark and Drop Dead, however, the illness came too late in the period for them to resume training in time to be ready for the Games. Passach, Huntingfield and Mud Dauber avoided catching distemper. The horses from Argentina and Chile stabled near ours also suffered from a considerable amount of distemper, and unfortunately, one of the South American horses died of pneumonia.

Another hazard was the ground, which was either rock or hard-baked adobe soil. Major Borg made a rule that except in the prepared training areas, the horses would not be ridden faster than a walk. Consequently, no lameness developed among our horses due to the ground, while the horses of the other teams, including those of the Mexicans, had a considerable amount of lameness and foot soreness prior to the Games.

Near the Escuela was the major racetrack of Mexico City. Arrangements were made, and we utilized this facility for two mornings each week for the last four or five weeks of the training period.

During the first few days after our arrival, Major Borg arranged for Major Eduardo Pérez of the Mexican three-day team to take us on a mounted tour of the surrounding countryside. Later we returned to an area with high steep hills which became the main device for conditioning our horses. Major Borg laid out the program, and twice weekly each horse was ridden to this area and then up and down the steep hills an increasing number of times each week. As a result, the horses developed the necessary large lung capacity, and also exceptional muscular development, particularly in the back and hindquarters.

In the mornings the horses were either ridden to the hill area, galloped or schooled over jumps. During the mornings, Major Borg worked his two dressage horses in one sand ring, but would take time out to supervise schooling over the jumps, which were in the same vicinity. In the afternoons, the three-day horses were schooled in dressage for twenty or thirty minutes.

Under Major Borg, Huntingfield and I progressed nicely in dressage and by the end of the period could consistently ride a good test. Huntingfield was a capable jumper and in fine condition. The final gallop, consisting of 2 miles in six minutes and 1 mile in two minutes twenty seconds, was no effort for him. Having ridden him in the Nashville trials, I was confident of his ability, and he was my intended mount for the coming event. After being cooled following the final gallop, Huntingfield was tied to a post while being groomed by one of the stable crew. A piece of paper blew in front of him, causing him to pull back, uprooting the post from the ground. He became frightened and ran around the stable area with the post dragging between his legs. As a result, he was lame from cuts and bruises and could not be used.

Mud Dauber was a recalcitrant dressage pupil, and Major Borg had done most of the schooling on her himself. There had been some rough sessions, but she seemed to be coming around. I was able to get along with her for short periods of time, just long enough to get through the test. In jumping she was strong, but not as consistent as Huntingfield. About a month before the Games she tested one of the local unforgiving parallel rail-cactus oxers with me aboard, and we executed a spectacular somersault. Fortunately, Mud Dauber's only injury was a slightly puffed knee, which cleared up in a day or two; however, it made such a great impression on her that she jumped everything with room to spare from then on.

For the Games, Cassavellanus became Jeb's mount because of the sickness of Benny Grimes. Passach, the greenest horse on the squad, became Frank's mount because of the illness of both Drop Dead and Flashmark, while Mud Dauber was nominated as my horse because of the injury to Huntingfield.

Argentina, Chile and Mexico each entered a three-day team of four riders and horses. Except for our team, all were army officers. Four riders were to compete, with the three best scores added for the team score. We were the only team with three riders.

The cross-country course was walked on Saturday, March 19. Phase A started at the Escuela and traversed paved streets and then rocky roads, climbing some 400 feet to a plateau area, where the steeplechase course was laid out on a plowed field. This course was a figure-8 over seven brush fences which had to be taken twice, and it caused, I understand, a few traffic problems. Phase C went through a number of *arroyaderos* which separated the steeplechase-area plateau from the hilly plateau area on which the cross-country course was built. The roads of Phase C were rocky and ascended out of one *arroyadero* in switchback fashion.

Phase D could be described as treacherous. The ground was, in various places, hard, rocky, loose soil or dry grassland. The course had many, many turns and crossed itself in a number of places. The jumps were large and mostly made of natural logs. Many were filled with brush or had cactus growing underneath, while others appeared as poles suspended in air. There were large spread fences, but not many ditches. Several jumps were set on the precipices of hills or slides. The obstacles were generally narrow across

Mud Dauber and Staley en route to an individual gold medal in the 1955 Pan American Games in Mexico City. Assorted cacti gave the riders a powerful incentive to stay mounted that year!

the front, more like show-ring jumps rather than Olympic-quality cross-country fences.

After walking the course, the team captains of Argentina and Chile, along with Major Borg, protested the fairness of several of the obstacles. One of particular concern was a fence near the end of the course situated on the edge of a slide into a gravel quarry. After jumping the fence, a horse would probably land some 10' or 15' below the point of takeoff. It would be a sure fall for a tired animal. The Mexicans reluctantly agreed to make the requested changes.

On Sunday, March 20, the individual dressage was held in the large sand ring at the Escuela. Major Borg on Bill Biddle placed a close second behind Captain Héctor Clavel of Chile riding Frontalera.

The three-day-event dressage was held on Monday and Tuesday evenings, also in the large sand ring. The judges were Colonel Pierre Cavaillé of France, Colonel Baron Sirtema von Grovestins of Holland and Major Henri St. Cyr of Sweden. A beautiful ride by Mexico's Lieutenant Héctor Zataraín on Monterrey earned him the best dressage score. Mud Dauber and I got along well for the duration of the test, and we had the next-best score, but some 40 points inferior to Zataraín. I was followed closely in score by several other contestants. Jeb Wofford placed fifth on Cassavellanus, and Frank Duffy placed fourteenth on Passach.

The cross-country tests took place on Wednesday morning, March 23. Three of the fifteen starting horses and riders accomplished the notable feat of completing the second day without incurring penalties at obstacles. The riders were Lieutenant Ramírez and Major Pérez of Mexico, and Lieutenant Cano of Argentina. Lieutenant Ramírez incurred time penalties on Phases A, B and D; Major Pérez on B and D, and Lieutenant Cano on B, D and E. On Phase D, the cross-country, four horses and riders were eliminated for refusals, and no rider earned fewer than 110 time-penalty points. The twisting, turning and hilly nature of the Phase D course, in addition to the altitude and the steep ascents of the trails of the previous Phase C, accounted for the slow times. Five horses were penalized for slow times on Phase E, the 2-kilometer gallop in on the flat, for which six minutes was allowed. At Mexico, Phase E involved galloping 1½ times around a field. Some of the time penalties for this phase appeared excessive and evidently in error. This was the cause of more protests, and the discrepancies were settled by negotiation.

Frank Duffy on Passach had the fastest time on the steeplechase, gaining 21 bonus points. On the cross-country course, he had two hard falls and a refusal, costing him 140 points, and the time required to recover from the falls gave him 680 penalty points for being overtime. He was assessed another 20 penalty points for being slow on Phase E.

Cassavellanus, with Jeb Wofford, fell on Obstacle 19, with Jeb suffering a mild concussion. Dazed, he remounted and took Jump 27 out of sequence, resulting in elimination. Jeb had made the mistake of wearing a soft-crown cap. Had he been wearing a hard cap with a chin strap, the fall would probably have cost him only 60 points instead of elimination. However, it should also be remembered that Cassavellanus was not in top condition, having been ill and consequently having missed part of the training period. Jeb too had missed a week or more of training, as he had returned to Kansas to attend the funeral of his father.

Mud Dauber and I picked up 12 bonus points on the steeplechase, and she finished this phase strong. I traversed as much of Phase C dismounted as time would allow. She was in good shape to start Phase D. At the narrow second obstacle, she refused twice, and then she refused once more at the jump before the slide, for a total of 80 jumping faults. However, our time penalties on Phase D were 110, the lowest of the day. On Phase E we were originally penalized 123 points, indicating overtime of two minutes three seconds.

Mud Dauber finished the second day in the best apparent physical condition of all the horses, and several observers indicated that she had traversed Phase E at a normal pace. Our score on Phase E was negotiated

A proud moment for the USET—its first individual Games gold medal. From left, the medalists in the 1955 Pan American Games Three-Day event: Lieutenant Octavio Ramírez Juárez of Mexico, the silver medalist; Walter Staley, Jr., winner of the gold for the United States, and Major Eduardo Pérez Hernández of Mexico, the bronze medalist.

to 23 penalty points prior to the stadium jumping. After the Phase E scores had been adjusted, Mud Dauber and I stood in first place by 43 points ahead of Lieutenant Ramírez of Mexico. Major Pérez of Mexico was in third, 4.6 points behind Lieutenant Ramírez.

Lieutenant Héctor Zataraín of Mexico, who had the best dressage ride, was one of the four on Phase D eliminated for refusals. Two Chileans and one Argentinean were also eliminated, leaving only Mexico and Argentina in the running for team awards.

The stadium jumping was held the next evening in the large sand ring at the Escuela. Mud Dauber had two knockdowns costing 20 points, but not enough to yield the lead to either Lieutenant Ramírez or Major Pérez, who both went clean but had minor time penalties. Frank Duffy on Passach had two knockdowns and finished eighth.

Lieutenant Ortíz of Argentina was eliminated for getting off course, resulting in the Mexican team's being the only team to finish three riders.

The medals were awarded in ceremonies held in the University Stadium on Sunday. First the individual medals. I received the gold, Lieutenant Ramírez the silver, and the bronze went to Major Pérez. The Mexican team members were awarded gold medals for being the only team to finish.

Mud Dauber's and my success was due to several factors. Her surprising great endurance was, of course, an inbred quality, but greatly enhanced, I believe, by the conditioning program in Mexico City prior to the Games. This would not have been so effective had she not been sound and healthy during the eleven-week period. Schooling over the jumps at the Escuela had probably been the best preparation possible for negotiating the Phase D obstacles. Major Borg's tireless and patient work with her and me was responsible for our good dressage ride. Finally, all of this was built on four years of training under Erich Bubbel, and horse-show and trial experience under my brother Allen.

Not winning a team award was a great disappointment. In making his plans for Mexico, Colonel Wofford had allowed sufficient time to acclimatize and train the horses. Then, in Colonel Wofford's absence in Mexico City, Major Borg had done an outstanding job of coaching the team. I believe our training program was superior to that of the other teams. Two primary factors played a part in the failure of the team. If ever a particular horse seemed destined for a particular event, Jeb Wofford's agile and tough horse Benny Grimes was well suited for Mexico City. Therefore, distemper, by making Benny Grimes unavailable, and also by causing Cassavellanus to miss part of the training program, had been one major factor. Also, since each team had at least one elimination, starting only three riders instead of four had certainly reduced our chances of finishing three riders.

Added to our disappointment was our sadness on the death of Colonel Wofford.

I remained an active participant for another five years after Mexico and had the honor of riding in three more games, the 1959 Pan American Games in Chicago and the 1956 and 1960 Olympics. However, the gold medal in Mexico stubbornly remained the high point of my competitive career, despite my best efforts and some tantalizing "might have beens."

My association with the three-day team in the early years of the USET has left me with many memories of rich and rewarding experiences. First was an education in horsemanship which at that time was not available anywhere else in this country. Then there was forming friendships with many people here and abroad. Most meaningful of all was having the honor and responsibility of representing my country.

To complete a challenging cross-country course on a strong and willing horse must certainly be among the most satisfying accomplishments in all of sports. Since the cross-country course of the Olympic Games is generally designed to be the most difficult and demanding test in the world, one can really never know, as a certainty, if he and his horse are up to the task until it is completed.

The greatest thrill of my career was having the opportunity, in a foreign country, of hearing my national anthem played, once for my team's accomplishments and once for my own. It was a shame that my horses, who had so generously given such supreme efforts, could not share this elation.

Finally, all of this has left me with a great debt of gratitude which I can never adequately repay. Had it not been for Colonel Wofford, there probably would not have been a three-day team in those years. Then, his

Mud Dauber and Staley warm up at Stockholm, prior to entering the ring for the dressage phase in the 1956 Olympic Three-Day Event. Staley says that though both horse and rider appear quite composed in this picture, the situation did not endure very long inside the stadium.

and Major Borg's tireless efforts developed the team, and were responsible for its success. The U.S. Army made the facilities at Fort Riley and former Olympic horses available. The U.S. Equestrian Team, which came into being in 1950, made it all possible for me and the others who were privileged to ride on the various teams. The USET, then, as now, received the dedicated service and support of many who believed the United States should be well represented in the equestrian events of the Olympic Games and other international riding competitions. I earnestly hope that the United States Equestrian Team will continue to prosper and be successful in these endeavors.

The Education of a
Three-Day Rider

MICHAEL O. PAGE

Mike Page's career as a USET three-day rider started with a pair of medals, the individual gold and a team silver, at the Chicago Pan American Games, and ended with a pair at the Mexico City Olympics in 1968, a team silver and the individual bronze. In between, he successfully defended his Pan American title at São Paulo and barely missed an individual medal at the Tokyo Olympics while leading his teammates to the team silver. As this consistency reflects, Page knew something about eventing, and he tells below how he learned it. These days he is mostly a New York businessman, but still stays active as a show jumper, and coached the 1976 Canadian Olympic Three-Day team.

Tʜᴇ ᴘʜɪʟᴏsᴏᴘʜᴇʀ Bʀᴀɴᴄʜ Rɪᴄᴋᴇʏ once said, "Luck is the residue of design," and as I look back on my career as a three-day rider I see the unalterable truth of his words. Hard work and determination go into the formation of every successful man, yet if you take away all the calculations and study he puts into his life, what is left over is the instances of luck that allowed him to stride forward while others lagged behind.

I attribute my great good fortune as a competitive-event rider to two underlying factors, for neither of which I was in any way responsible. First, I always had an obsession for riding, and second, I had the understanding of my father, who guided my ambitions with the mature practical judgment I often lacked. For only one contribution do I give myself credit. When I was about fifteen, I decided that my father truly had my basic interests at

Michael Page at the age of fifteen, working under the keen eye of Captain F. E. Goldman at Cheshire, England, in 1955.

heart, and therefore, when I went to him for advice and counsel, I determined to listen to him carefully and stick faithfully to any decision we made. Now as then, I believe that you should go to someone for instruction or advice only if you respect him enough to give 110 percent of what he asks. Every time. All the time.

When I was fifteen my father and I were reading *The Light Horse,* a British monthly publication containing ads for various teaching establishments in England. He suggested, "Why don't you write three or four places and see what they have to offer? You can spend the summer, travel and get background in a more classical equitation. It probably would cost a lot less than camp here." It sounded like a good idea, and so it proved. After inquiring and comparing several prospectuses, we decided on Captain Edy Goldman in Cheshire, England. It was a wise choice indeed, for today Edy Goldman is universally acknowledged as one of the top event trainers in Great Britain. He was a hard taskmaster and a strict disciplinarian, but I enjoyed my summer immensely. I lived through my first experiences of having "a horse on the bit," establishing a truly independent seat and learning the correct use of my "aids," and had the added benefit of watching Sheila Willcox being polished under Edy Goldman's instruction. She subsequently went on to win three Badminton titles and with her horse High and Mighty became part of one of the world's leading event combinations.

When I returned to the States, my good friend Herb Wiesenthal offered me the use of his former cavalry mount Candlestick, whom he had shown locally in small jumping events. For the next two years I used the background I had gained in England, showing and polishing in the horsemanship division. This period terminated in 1956 when I won the AHSA Medal Finals at the old Madison Square Garden in New York.

145

Not only did I win the medal in 1956; I also graduated from high school. The time came for my father and me to discuss the direction my interest should take from a practical point of view. He felt at the time that the possibility of my making the jumping team depended primarily on our ability to acquire quality horses, for which the competition was great. In the late 1950s, fewer riders specialized in eventing than in show jumping, and there he felt greater possibilities existed directly related to the development of my technical proficiency and experience.

Event riding it was to be, and once more England seemed the place to go for training. Two days after my win at the Garden, I sailed on the *Liberté,* my saddle under my arm. Before me lay three or four years of riding, as far as I could or would be able to go.

My first stop was back to Edy Goldman, who was doubly pleased to see me, rightly feeling he had made a major contribution to my horsemanship successes at home. I had no plans beyond England when I left home, and only an indistinct picture of what the future held. My allowance was about $300 a month, from which I saved what I could. (College at that time ran about $3,500 a year.)

Edy Goldman suggested I move on to Neuchâtel, Switzerland, in the French sector. My father agreed to the idea with the stipulation that I study the language of any country in which I rode. I therefore lived in Neuchâtel and took courses at L'École de Commerce, riding or hitching to the Manège de Colombier about 6 kilometers away. From approximately the first of January through the spring I got to ride and show and spend some additional time as a groom, shipping horses by train to various events throughout Switzerland. The head groom of the manège, Philippe Maheu, was the first to mention Saumur, the French cavalry school, to me. He suggested one of the two-week summer courses open to civilians of all countries, and the possibility of the nine-month intensive course. This he felt to be the most fantastic experience in the world for the truly dedicated horseman.

In the spring I left Neuchâtel and made my way to the school of Paul Stecken in Münster, Westphalia. I traveled via Paris, stopping at the French Fédération des Sports Équestres, similar in many respects to the AHSA office in New York. With my French under control, I was accepted for a two-week course in July. In the meantime, I spent several very interesting and fruitful months in Westphalia. Reiner Klimke, later to become dressage world champion, was riding with Paul Stecken and at that time was an ardent three-day rider. Even then Reiner was convinced he would become a world-champion dressage rider, but felt the background of jumping, conditioning and competitive event riding could only make him a better specialist in the future. A sign on the stable wall read, *"Reiten lernt man nur durch reiten,"* which translates as "You learn to ride only by riding." I found this to be true as I rode with Reiner Klimke and competed in my first three-day event, yet the chance to observe the dedication and determination of this future champion considerably broadened my outlook and background as a whole.

As a young man in Europe I was truly grateful for the opportunities to ride and learn, and paradoxically, this became a benefit in itself. If you are truly appreciative of the chance to learn from people you respect, they in turn are much freer with their time and knowledge.

After spending a fruitful three months in Westphalia, where I had lived in the *Kaserne,* or military barracks, I returned to France for my two-week course at Saumur. Here remained a symbol of what had once been the greatest equestrian educational institution in an age when horse cavalry was the paramount machine of war. The huge stables, once the home of three thousand horses, now housed three hundred and continued as the home of the famous Cadre Noir.

The two-week course was only a superficial exploration of the various phases of horsemanship, but I felt that here was perhaps the last place on earth where one could spend time completely immersed in riding and think of nothing else. It was.

At the end of the two weeks my instructor advised me that civilians would be accepted for the first time in the nine-month noncommissioned officers' course starting in October. On my way back to Germany to spend another month with Paul Stecken, I stopped at the French federation in Paris and I spoke to General Boucoud about the possibility of my being accepted. Aside from being surprised by the request and asking if I indeed had the time, he told me to cable our national federation, the AHSA, for a

The team medal awards at Avandaro, site of the three-day at the 1968 Mexican Olympics. Mike Page, fourth from left, with silver-medalist teammates Plumb, Freeman and Wofford and the winning British and third-place Australian teams. Page wears two medals, having also won the individual bronze. Wofford's unlucky fall on the flat robbed him of another individual medal.

Eventing in France: Mike Page, right, talks things over during the French Three-Day championship at Fontainebleau in 1958 with Major Pierre Durand, now head of the Cadre Noir, and Adjutant Chef Jack Le Goff, now coach of the USET three-day team.

recommendation. Two days later the reply had been received, and I was told the course started on October 15. I sent my saddle and suitcase to Saumur by rail and hitchhiked from Paris to Barcelona, along the Côte d'Azur and back again, skipping a second stay in Germany.

The experience of Saumur would require a book in itself. Jack Le Goff, the present coach of the U.S. three-day team, initially took charge of me and oversaw my participation in the numerous events in which the French government sponsored me. As a civilian, I was a member of both the officers' mess and the NCO mess, and had a room in the NCO barracks. My *piquet* consisted of two young horses, two event horses, one jumper and a dressage horse, Grand Prix level. All this cost $65 a month. At this time Major Henri St. Cyr, the two-time Olympic dressage champion, spent his winters training at Saumur. That year he had with him a working student named Lars Seder-holm, a man who became my lifelong friend as well as the leading event trainer in England.

Eventually Colonel Margot, the *écuyer en chef,* transferred the other civilian and me to the officers' course that was running at the same time. Until then, we awoke every day at 6:30 for eight solid hours of riding, and spent three months literally wearing out the seats of our pants (as well as several layers underneath) until finally the only agony was getting off the horse and trying to walk.

The transfer to the officers' course was fortunate for me, as it was more oriented toward the technical aspects of riding and competition. Although I had the additional option of riding steeplechase and tried it, the greatly increased likelihood of injury persuaded me to devote myself to the event area. The specialized experience I had gained served as valuable background for the steeplechase phase of three-day cross-country runs.

I stayed a full fourteen months at Saumur, for one of the event horses I was given, Gabelon, qualified for the French National Championships at Fontainebleau. I was quite successful in all phases except for the roads-and-tracks, where I became confused over the time allowed and almost doubled it, which would have eliminated me. The course was sufficiently difficult, however, so that not too many finished the event, and I placed sixth in the military section.

During this period my old friend Herb Wiesenthal had kept the USET officials informed of my progress. As a result, I received a telegram from Mr. Whitney Stone advising me that John Galvin in California had several event horses he was placing at the disposition of the U.S. team. If I found one satisfactory as a possible team mount, would I be available? I was!

Because I am quite light, I usually wind up with the smaller type of horse, if and when there is a selection. In this case Mr. Galvin had purchased from Ian Dudgeon the fantastic Copper Coin. He stood barely 15 hands high, but was a freak of nature because of his incredible speed and stamina. After the 22-mile Rome Olympic Games, with my having fallen off twice, he had the third-fastest time and finished up by running away with me on the run-in, so that I almost got eliminated for not stopping at weigh-out!

Grasshopper, as he was renamed, was a winner, yet the first few weeks of our collaboration were rough. Fresh from my stay in Saumur, I rather prided myself on staying on anything that stood on legs. Grasshopper tried his best to take me down a peg. In mutual exhaustion we finally learned to respect each other. At least, I certainly respected him. He could maintain a speed over a furlong that was about two seconds slower than the rest of the team horses went when breezing. In dressage, when he was good, he was able to win that phase, as he did in the Chicago Pan Am Games in 1959.

Grasshopper competed in three Olympic Games, one with Ian Dudgeon and two with me, and was retired after Tokyo, having only just missed the bronze individual medal by one-fifth of a point while being part of our

Mrs. John Galvin's indomitable little Grasshopper, Page's mount in the 1960 and 1964 Olympic Games. This formidable combination accounted for five Games medals, including two Pan American individual golds at Chicago and São Paulo.

silver-medal team. In Pan Am competition he won two gold individual medals, one in Chicago in 1959 and the other in São Paulo, Brazil, in 1963.

After Tokyo in 1964 and helping win the three-day silver team medal—the only U.S. equestrian medal of the Games—I returned to the family printing business in New York and kept up my association with horses by judging. By 1966 I really missed actual competition, and when the opportunity arose to ride again with the USET and train for the Pan Am Games in Winnipeg, I took it.

Stefan von Visy, then the three-day coach, had several horses for me to ride, one of whom was Foster, lent to the team by Meg Plum. I had once seen him compete while judging at the Gladstone Trials. I remembered seeing him come crashing home with a tremendous burst of power and stamina, and had noted his scope as a jumper, a necessary attribute for an international-event horse. Although while at Gladstone Foster had not had the success expected of him, I could not forget the positive impression he'd made upon me. The girl who was taking care of him believed in his potential too. (Since she was later to become my wife, I guess there were more good reasons for teaming up with Foster than I then suspected.)

Foster presented a problem. Since he and I both needed competitive experience in a hurry, the team and Mrs. Plum consented to my idea of going to England and training with Lars Sederholm, my old friend from cavalry-school days. He was truly a professional event trainer, one of the few in the world capable of advising and assisting in a way that improved and complemented my ability as a rider.

With Foster's problems basically solved, as demonstrated by a successful Badminton in the spring, we went well in the trials and became members of the Pan Am team in Winnipeg and subsequently the Mexico Olympics. My career as an event rider ended there on a high note, with an individual bronze and a team silver medal. I regretted no step that had brought me to that point in my life nor any that carried me on to new and different goals. I enjoyed my development as a three-day rider and find that it continues to influence every aspect of my life.

Each rider interested in specializing in eventing must find his own way, and this brief account of my training can serve only as one particular example. The one thing that I can state is that the rider must be aware of his relatively minor athletic contribution in the combination of horse and man. Maximizing the role of the animal, as the major physical component of competitive success, represents the first step to achievement. Successful event riding depends not so much on the extraordinary athletic capabilities of the rider as on his knowledge and understanding of the capabilities of his horse and his ability to prepare and use them.

Learning to do so isn't easy. As one of the famous d'Inzeo brothers, riders on the Italian jumping team at the Rome Olympics, was quoted as saying: "The mastery of a perfect technique takes a lifetime. Technical mastery is merely sufficient for you to become good; it is not enough to make you great. From excellence to greatness, a man is alone. He must count on imponderables—his own instinctive resources, his character and his secret gifts. These are never the same for two people, not even for brothers."

If you look at your chances realistically and still decide to try for the top, I wish you luck. Maybe you will be the uncommon man who can do more than anyone else. In any case, if you keep your perspective, you should derive a lot of benefit—and have a lot of fun doing it.

A real powerhouse: Mr. and Mrs. Matthias Plum's Foster, Mike Page's mount at the 1968 Olympics in Mexico, shows the form that carried them to individual bronze medals there and at the 1967 Pan American Games in Winnipeg.

"Ice-Breaking" in Japan

LANA duPONT WRIGHT

In contrast to Europe, where women were traditionally excluded from many riding activities, they have long played a major role in U.S. equestrian affairs, and were prominent in the USET from the very beginning. However, despite strong U.S. and British pressure, women remained ineligible for Olympic jumping until 1956 and for the three-day until 1964. There was only a single lady competitor on the latter occasion, the honor falling to a member of a famous American racing family, Lana duPont. After her gritty performance in Japan, nobody ever questioned the presence of "the weaker sex" in Olympic eventing again.

UNTIL THE 1964 OLYMPIC GAMES in Tokyo, women had never been permitted by the FEI to participate in an Olympic three-day event. The dressage and jumping teams had long benefited from women Olympic competitors, and they had frequently distinguished themselves, but the three-day sport remained an exclusively male domain.

In view of the origins of the competition, this was not entirely unreasonable, for eventing had begun among the European cavalries as a test of strength, versatility and endurance for officers and their mounts. As the sport evolved, the physical demands made by the speed-and-endurance phase on the second day became extremely rigorous, especially on the Olympic level, and the FEI long pondered whether women were equipped physically to endure the demands and dangers of competing on an Olympic cross-country course.

In the post–World War II era, however, as the military hold on eques-

152

trian sport diminished, an increasingly heterogeneous field of competitors developed, including many women, in every level of eventing except the Olympic Games. By 1964, women riders had demonstrated their ability to compete on even terms with men almost everywhere; three different women had won Badminton, and Sheila Willcox had taken the European Championship. The change in FEI policy that finally made women's participation in the Olympic three-day event possible recognized the outstanding achievements of those many women eventers whose skill and fierce determination had overcome the disadvantage of inexperience our late entry into eventing had created.

I was fortunate to have had that same intensity of determination myself, as well as an excellent event horse at a most advantageous time. Thus it fell to me to be the first woman to "break the ice" in the Olympic Games three-day event.

Mr. Wister, by Occupy out of Panamerica, was a gift to me from my mother, Mrs. Richard C. duPont. Foaled in 1953, Mr. Wister spent his second and third years in training as a racehorse. I received him as a four-year-old—a big, rawboned Thoroughbred, anxious for activity and challenge. Wister accepted the change in his training with eager determination to excel as an event horse. He proved to be a natural jumper, never once refusing a fence. His natural ability, honesty and courage destined him to be a successful event horse.

I must admit that Wister was not a good dressage horse, and at first our combined inexperience and lack of understanding presented a handicap. At that time, America had little dressage instruction available, especially in comparison with the number and availability of competent dressage instructors in Europe. I was fortunate to find a good instructor in the late Richard Wätjen, a distinguished German dressage rider and coach then teaching in New York. I began studying with him in 1959 and found him to be of impeccable character, both as a coach and as a person. Since then I have never lost the conviction that dressage is critically important for both rider and horse. Jumping is a natural ability, and stamina and courage are inborn characteristics that must be present for you even to consider a horse for eventing. Dressage is different, for it can be taught to any horse. Not only will it enhance his jumping ability, by developing smoother, more controlled movements, but by improving the discipline of both horse and rider, it increases their coordination as a team. At every level of competition it requires constant practice, for with the tremendous competition that exists in eventing today, a low dressage score is often the decisive factor in the final result.

While I was studying dressage with Mr. Wätjen, Wister and I found an increasing challenge in eventing. Eventing was not then as popular in America as it is now. International experience was to be gained only in

The splash on the Gladstone course during the 1964 trials, negotiated by Lana duPont and Escanoba, her intermediate horse.

Europe, and so in the winter of 1961, Wister and I departed for England. We participated in three or four events before Badminton, where we confronted our biggest challenge. There were endless crowds, pressing around the dressage and stadium jumping arenas and forming a solid line along the cross-country course. Wister was undaunted by the crowds, having survived the racetrack indoctrination of his early life. He performed with ease, placing tenth overall out of sixty or so competitors.

Returning to the States, I resumed dressage with Mr. Wätjen, relocating at the USET's then newly established training center in Gladstone, New Jersey. We continued our work there through the following winter. While the three-day team for the 1963 Pan American Games trained in Camden, South Carolina. Women were not yet allowed to compete in the three-day event at the Pan American Games, but as I continued working on my dressage at Gladstone, my hope was that the policy might be changed in time to allow women to ride in the Olympic Games in Tokyo the following year.

As 1964 unfolded, the controversy over women's eligibility for three-day eventing was resolved, and we were informed that women would not be excluded from the 1964 Olympic three-day event. I began training with the team at Camden, where they had returned, early in 1964. A screening test was held in August for all equestrian competitors, and this proved an unfortunate time for me, as Wister was recovering from a tendon injury.

However, I rode Ferdinand, a second horse I had purchased in England, and did well enough to qualify as a possible competitor for the Olympic three-day team. Three of the four team members were definitely named at that time—Michael Plumb, Kevin Freeman and Michael Page. I was one of two to be chosen to complete the team.

Wister's tendon injury left us in precarious circumstances. Wister's veterinarian, Dr. William H. Wright, feared a possible bowing and advised a temporary adjustment in training. Less strenuous interval training was begun, balanced by a strict dietary program. Wister's physical condition did not deteriorate, and when his leg had healed sufficiently, we resumed training with the team. By the end of the summer, Wister was fit.

The decision as to who would accompany the team to Tokyo as the fourth competitor was not finally made until seventy-two hours before departure. Then at last I was notified that Wister and I would complete the team. The coach and trainer, Major Stefan von Visy, had finalized his decision, and to him I owe a debt of gratitude.

Wister's groom, Rosemary Wollard, was not permitted to accompany Wister on the plane to Japan, since there was not enough room for all our personnel. Despite the good care Wister received during the trip to Karuizawa, where the three-day event was to be held, he arrived with a temperature of 105 degrees. René Williams, our stable manager, and Rosemary spent the next twenty-four hours nursing Wister back to health. Luckily, we lost only two days of training.

Wister and I trained diligently for the next ten days. To improve my own physical condition, I ran 2 miles each day through the Japanese coun-

Mr. Wister and Lana duPont on the cross-country at Karuizawa, site of the 1964 Olympic three-day event. They finished gamely despite two hard falls.

tryside. Karuizawa is a beautiful town surrounded by mountains and one "puffing" volcano. Our Japanese hosts were very gracious and agreeable, eager to understand and comply with our needs. (The greatest test of their patience and hospitality resulted from our attempt to purchase beet pulp from the feed vendors. There was a good deal of gesturing, nodding and "*A so!*" but we eventually agreed on every aspect and description of beet pulp!)

The three-day competition began on October 17. My dressage ride was the first of the American team and was scored somewhat better than average. Though I still felt there was much room for improvement, I was certainly grateful for the years spent studying under Mr. Wätjen.

That night it began raining, and the rain continued on into the next day, which proved bitterly cold and foggy as well. It almost seemed as if I would have to do some ice-breaking literally as well as figuratively! The cross-country course had been bulldozed through 22 miles of Karuizawa countryside. It was not a particularly difficult course, but it became extremely slippery and hazardous in the prevailing weather conditions. The lack of ground covering on the course inhibited traction and compounded the slippery conditions. Heavy rains plagued many of the competitors who had the misfortune of being scheduled to ride during a downpour. There were numerous falls that day caused by the poor visibility and flooding trail.

With the usual sagacity that hindsight affords, I later regretted that I had not been better prepared strategically for the arduous course. There was one official walking of the course and a second short period available for individual study of the course. The individual study was less fruitful than I anticipated, and in retrospect, the discussion among the team members was not adequate for my needs.

There were two big spreads that I misjudged during my ride, the first

Mr. Wister and Lana duPont jumping in the final phase of the 1964 Olympic three-day. The sun came out too late to help.

being the third jump of the course. Eager to collect Wister for a smooth jump, I gave him insufficient momentum for it, particularly considering the slipperiness of the takeoff ground. It would have been wiser to let airspace carry us over the jump; instead, we found ourselves caught on it. We fell hard, Wister breaking several bones in his jaw. We were badly disheveled and shaken, but Wister was nonetheless eager to continue. We fell a second time near the end of the course, tripping over another spread. When we finished, we were a collection of bruises, broken bones and mud. Anyway, we proved that a woman *could* get around an Olympic cross-country course, and nobody could have said that we looked feminine at the finish.

Wister recovered to do well in the stadium jumping, considering his broken jaw and various other aches and pains. However, we incurred 30 penalty points, which put us in thirty-third place overall.

The U.S. three-day team won the silver medal, 19.94 points behind the winning Italians. Michael Page placed fourth individually, Kevin Freeman twelfth and Mike Plumb fifteenth. It was quite an honor to have been part of such a successful team, particularly since it opened the avenues for many other women participants in the Olympic three-day event thereafter.

Women today are strong competitors at every level of eventing. The Pan American and Olympic three-day events are providing many women with the challenge to participate at the height of sporting competitiveness.

I was not unique in eventing among women when I was chosen to ride on the Olympic team, but I had the advantages of an excellent horse and years of devotion to learning dressage and increasing my eventing experience. I will always be indebted to Mr. Wätjen and Major von Visy for the excellent instruction I received, and even more, I will always be thankful to my mother for her gift of Mr. Wister and her quiet, enthusiastic support of my endeavors.

The 1964 Olympic three-day silver-medal winners:
Lana duPont, Michael Page, Kevin Freeman and
Michael Plumb share the podium with the winning Italian
team and the third-place Germans.

Steeplechasing and Eventing

KEVIN FREEMAN

Though a native of Portland, Oregon, Kevin Freeman was for several years almost as well known in East Coast hunt-racing circles as he is among eventers, and he can speak with authority on both activities. A member of three consecutive silver-medal-winning Olympic three-day teams, Freeman was also the individual silver medalist at the São Paulo Pan American Games in 1963. His trips to the winner's circle as a race rider included such major victories as the New Jersey and Pennsylvania hunt cups and the Cheshire Bowl.

THROUGH THE YEARS, a number of the USET riders have also raced over timber under National Steeplechase and Hunt rules. Arthur McCashin of the jumping team rode races long before the USET even existed, and since then, Frank Chapot, Jimmy Wofford, Bruce Davidson, Mike Plumb and Kathy Kusner, to name only a few, have taken everything from a crack at it to a full swing. Because I love both 'chasing and eventing and have been quite active in both, I've often been asked to discuss how they relate to each other. My answer is a personal one, and no doubt others would answer the same question differently. (Surely they would do so more comfortably, for I am no writer.) But for better or worse, here are my views.

When it comes to sheer excitement per second, I think steeplechasing leads all other equestrian sports.

Certainly there is a lot of excitement connected with a three-day event too, but when the action is spread out over three days, it's hard to develop the same emotional pitch that can be generated in the four to five minutes it takes to run a jumping race. Also, it is hard to equal the thrill of rolling down to a solid timber fence late in a race with one or more other horses at your side, everyone's effort let out to the last notch, knowing that the outcome of the race can be decided right there. In the end, it is a fortunate person who has the chance to both race and event. Such people have it the best of all.

The question is sometimes asked if racing helps you develop as a three-day rider. I don't personally think it makes much difference either way. Steeplechasing is another type of riding, and it asks different questions. To some degree it can help you by making you more comfortable at speed, by improving your balance and by teaching you to "listen" to your horse more effectively. But conversely, it can hurt you if you get into the habit of riding too short, or start seeing too many long distances to fences. On balance, I would always encourage an event rider to ride races if he asked me, because it's another kind of riding experience, and it's so much fun. The USET three-day coach, Jack Le Goff, rode a lot of races in France both on the flat and over jumps before his successful eventing career, and I think he feels the same way.

In considering the advantages to be gained from racing, the most important is what I call "listening" to your horse. By this I mean being very conscious of what is happening to your horse as he's going along. You must become sensitive to such things as how he's breathing, and learn to constantly ask yourself the right questions: Is he moving as relaxed as he can? Did the last fence scare him and drain some of his confidence? Is his balance changing? These and other factors are important to recognize as a race unfolds. They can dictate your pace, your position in a race, when you make your move and how much liberty you dare to take with fences toward the end of a race.

USET riders on vacation: Kevin Freeman (foreground) and Frank Chapot, tin-canning over timber at the Piedmont Point-to-Point races in Virginia.

Though this kind of communication with your horse is easier to learn in racing because there are fewer changes of direction and terrain, it obviously has great relevance around a cross-country course. It helps you to get your horse galloping smoothly and quietly, and thus economically, between fences. You learn, for instance, to let a horse breathe for a few strides after you've topped a hill before asking him to run again. It can also be a signal late in the course to jump a fence another way, to give up some time, to take the easier alternative and preserve a clear round. A good example of this was Bruce Davidson's effort at the Stolen S fence at Ledyard '75 on Mr. and Mrs. Ray Firestone's Golden Griffin. Because his horse was tired, Bruce chose to avoid all the shorter no-stride alternatives at the fence, pulled down to a trot and popped over the three single rails. He was rewarded with a clear round and, in fact, first place in a very important international competition.

The main thing to remember is that racing and eventing really ask different questions of the rider. In an event, you're alone on the cross-country course, and you're really riding against the clock and against the difficulty of the course. You also must come back the next day with your horse, pass a vet inspection and jump a stadium round. In racing, your only concern is beating the other horses in the race; the clock has little relevance, and except for the two big courses in Maryland and perhaps the Pennsylvania Hunt Cup, the difficulty of the fences doesn't come much into play either.

This difference even colors your attitude toward a fall. Obviously, nobody likes to fall, but in the cold light of analysis, you must try at all costs to avoid a fall in eventing, or even the chance of one, if you can—the penalty, pointwise, will usually put you right out of the competition. It's generally too hard to anticipate how the second you might save by deliberately chancing a fall will pay off in your final placement, after your dressage score and the stadium round are added in. Prudence tells you to avoid the big penalty if you possibly can, especially where team competition is concerned.

In racing, however, it often gets down to the point, late in a race, when everyone is making his final move and you just have to take a chance if you want to win—not a foolhardy chance, but a calculated one. Of course, if you're riding what is obviously the fastest horse, you can afford to steady a bit, be a little safer over the last fence and trust that you can outrun the other horses at the finish. But having what is obviously the fastest horse is a rare occurrence, especially at that stage of a race. Usually it's a case of having to stay with the pace, using your best efforts to get there as right as you can, but mainly jumping the last fence with as much speed as you can muster.

All the good timber riders who compete a lot, such as Paddy Neilson, Buzz Hannum and Turney McKnight, expect to hit the deck once in a while.

Paddy Neilson had an outstanding year not long ago in which he rode thirty races and won fifteen of them. Though that's an exceptional percentage, in the process he also had six falls, four of them in a row. Some of these came early in the race and may have been bad luck. The others were an accepted risk by one of the most competitive and certainly most successful amateur riders in the United States.

For event riders going into racing, the hardest element to master is the strategy of a race—in other words, a racing sense. As event riders, they're used to making detailed plans on how they're going to ride the cross-country course, with most of the emphasis on the safe negotiation of the fences and taking the shortest route. In racing you must evaluate the other horses and riders and try to predict how they'll run their race. You must weigh these factors along with the characteristics of your own horse and, very importantly, the lie of the land over which the course is to be run. Some courses—Fair Hill, for instance—have an uphill finish. Novice riders have a tendency to wait until near the end to make their move, only to find that most of the smart riders in the field have left them behind on the down-hill run before the finish. By pouring it on as they start downhill, they make their horses run where they can run the fastest with the least energy. The novice rider then must run to them on the uphill pull for the finish, which is more difficult and certainly more discouraging for the horse.

Using the terrain of a course as part of your strategy is important in steeplechasing, because hunt races are seldom run over level ground. Generally the fastest horse that jumps well wins the race, but seldom does a horse come along that wins every start. The smart rider can often influence the result, especially when the race is composed of horses of near-equal ability. Crompton "Tommy" Smith was always considered one of the smart-

Mrs. Nelson Slater's Stutter Start and Kevin Freeman, en route to winning the Pennsyl-vania Hunt Cup at Unionville in 1969. Hunt racing, Freeman believes, develops the event rider's feeling for how much horse he's got left.

est riders, and you can see from his description of his trip around the Grand National how much prerace planning figured in his victory.

Knowing what to expect of the other horses and other riders and learning to use the course to your advantage take some time and experience. But I also think that the converted eventer can save a lot of time by giving proper weight to this aspect of racing and by trying to study it as you would anything else. I was lucky to have two owners, Mrs. Nancy Hannum and Mrs. Jill Slater, who had a great deal of experience in point-to-point and timber racing. They placed a lot of emphasis, when I was riding for them, on the tactical element in racing, and their concern helped me develop respect for this aspect of a race and, hopefully, improved my performance as a rider.

If there is a common denominator among event riders and race riders, it is their attitude toward riding down to solid fences. You have to like to do that—in fact, you have to love the thrill and challenge of it—to be good at either sport. Of course, everyone gets a little spooked once in a while facing a rough cross-country fence, and if you think riding at the thirteenth fence in the Maryland Hunt Cup doesn't claim your undivided attention, you're kidding yourself. But those who do well in eventing and racing are generally comfortable with this type of challenge and are able to keep the spooks in the closet during the difficult moments.

Earlier I mentioned the number of USET jumping and event riders who have tried hunt racing, some with considerable success. Though there's no reason why it couldn't also happen in reverse, to date there have been no race riders in this country who have taken up eventing. This is probably due to the time and patience it requires to become proficient in dressage, and the long behind-the-scenes training and conditioning process the event horse requires. For riders accustomed to the almost constant thrills of racing, such careful preparation may seem tiresome.

Abroad, however, it has by no means been unusual for top amateur race riders to become interested in eventing. Eddie Harty rode for Ireland at Rome before going on to win the Aintree Grand National; Alessandro Argenton of Italy won a silver medal at Munich; Laurie Morgan and Bill Roycroft of Australia, gold medalists at Rome, both had outstanding racing careers at home and in England; many of the French military riders, among them "our own" Jack Le Goff, raced extensively in France. Countless English eventers have done some racing, and currently Chris Collins, one of the most successful English amateur riders ever, is making a determined bid for his country's Olympic team. One could go on and on.

I hope it's just a matter of time until some of our better amateur steeplechase riders try their hand at eventing. It might not provide a thrill a minute, but it's still quite a challenge to produce a good dressage test with

Kevin Freeman and his 1972 Olympic mount, Miss Geraldine Pearson's Good Mixture, competing at Eridge in England prior to the Games. A few weeks later they led the USET to a silver team medal at Munich, and they were fifth overall, only one unlucky fence away from an individual medal.

the same horse that can cope with tricky combinations, gaping spreads and heart-stopping drops on the cross-country and turn in a clear round over a stadium course the next day. And once they got lured by the challenge, I'm sure it wouldn't take them long to experience that wonderful satisfaction of putting together a winning effort that seems to keep the rest of us coming back.

163

Getting the Most from the Three-Day Horse

J. MICHAEL PLUMB

Veteran of four Olympic three-day teams and twice captain, Mike Plumb is not only a four-time national champion, but son of a national champion, too: his father, Charley, the famous former steeplechase rider and Meadowbrook huntsman, was the winner in 1963–1964. In addition, Mike has won no fewer than eight Games medals, including the Pan American individual gold in 1967, and was barely nosed out by teammate Bruce Davidson in the 1974 World Championships. Mike and his dressage-rider wife, Donnan (his teammate on the 1964 Olympic team), live on a horse farm in Chesapeake City, Delaware.

ACTUALLY COMPETING in a three-day event is only the final episode in a very complicated process that starts with the selection, training and conditioning of the other half of the competitive partnership—the horse. So many things can and do go wrong during these earlier stages that it sometimes seems to me that the actual competition is also the easiest thing, for during the "countdown," one wonders if the competition will ever come.

When you pick up your horse in the spring you can just visualize yourself a few months later, performing a smooth dressage test on the first day to place in the top five; then breezing around the cross-country in beautiful weather to go comfortably into the lead; and finally jumping a safe, clear round to a gold medal on the third day. That's my dream, and I haven't yet been able to experience it in real life.

164

GETTING THE MOST FROM THE THREE-DAY HORSE

Real life goes more like this: First, you miss ten days' work because your horse incurs a big knee while schooling; second, another week is lost to an ankle grab from working on the flat; next, a fortnight goes down the drain because of a suspicious-looking tendon, and another few days are lost when you yourself pull a groin muscle schooling over the drop jump. When you finally get to the competition, you wonder how. Now all you have to do is "put it all together." But anyhow, most of your earlier worries and anxieties are history at last.

The culmination of all this preliminary effort really begins not with the dressage ride but with the first veterinary inspection that precedes it. Ideally, one wants an impressive showing for the vets and the judges. Johnny O was perhaps my most impressive horse to jog—just a chirp and a cluck, and you had an extended trot in stride with your own. A little bit showy, but why not? The difficult types are the lazy ones whom you have to pull along, or those with a stone bruise which requires you to hold up their head at each stride. The Russians often create a different kind of stir at the inspection, for they invariably ride stallions, and there are always a few event mares present who have poor "timing."

For some event riders, the dressage day is an emotional one, but for me it has always proved to be a big effort. As I look back, I wish I'd known as much about coping with it when I started as I do now. Preparing for the dressage phase probably gives you more alternatives than the other two phases, and a lot depends on the individual horse's temperament. Since I want a strong, fit, slightly "hyper" horse for the second day, I have often had problems to contend with on the first. Prior to 1975, the FEI test called

Mike Plumb and Plain Sailing, donated to the USET by Mr. and Mrs. Raymond Firestone, the individual gold medalists in the Winnipeg Pan American Games in 1967 and team silver medalists in Mexico the following year. Here they are shown preparing for the Olympics at Badminton in the spring of 1968.

for two extended walks and two extended canters. With a "bearcat" whom you can't hold anyway, such movements get a little scary in an enclosure that's only 20 to 60 meters, surrounded by an 18″ fence! Longeing, I find, can be a very good therapy for the horse that's wound up a bit too tight—I've used three or four sessions of up to twenty minutes each. In addition, an hour's hack that morning is beneficial. I've known real problem cases that spent as much as several hours on the longe line on the day; this may not be what the book says, but it has been done with success.

I think of the actual dressage test as a game between you, your horse and the judge. For all 7½ minutes a smile is essential, regardless of whether you break at the extended trot, or blow a canter depart. Once I rode an excellent mare named Frolicsome. When she was not in season and I could concentrate on my posture, we could burn up the dressage area, as we did on a certain day at Essex in 1974. She was doing her thing—a brilliant extended trot across the diagonal—and I became so excited with her extension that I came around the corner and proceeded down the long side, omitting one entire movement. Luckily, the judges never noticed the mistake and we won with a very low score. I may have lost some games in the ring, but we won that one!

Perhaps the most frustrating dressage tests I've ever ridden were on possibly the best event horse I've ever ridden, Good Mixture. Mixture would never let you get close to him—with leg, with seat or, for that matter, in the stall. I'll never forget Burghley in 1974. It was the first time we had worn pink coats for competition that season, and when I arrived all dressed up to warm him up, he took one look at me and ran to the rear of the stall. He was a very sensitive little guy!

For the last few years in eventing there has been a great emphasis on riding your horse *forward* on the first day, which is difficult to do with a spooky kind of horse. He will often be a good jumper on the second and third days, but you sure have to watch out for the lurking monsters in the judges' tent, or near B or K. Johnny O was one of these. If the centerline was limed, then there was no way to stay on it, despite days of practice beforehand. Only at the end of the test would he step over (instead of jumping) the centerline.

It is a blessing when you occasionally get a horse on whom you can sit down and ride the test without worrying about anything. Bold Minstrel was such a type. What a disposition! Whether it was a local hunter trial or the Olympic Games, he gave you 150 percent.

The second day is the real heart of the contest, with its spills and thrills, drama, excitement and, sometimes, pain. It all begins with the inspection of the course. You hopefully know your horse, and now you must apply your knowledge to 15-plus miles of roads-and-tracks, steeplechase and cross-country courses. Sometimes the initial shock of course-walking is almost

Mike Plumb and his own Free and Easy, his Games mount at Munich in 1972, where the USET won its third consecutive Olympic silver medal. The picture shows them at the Army Horse Trials at Tidworth, just before the Olympics.

more than one can handle. In 1960 at Rome, the fences seemed so impossible the first time we saw them that I felt like a child. I just kept walking the course until it finally got a little lower. On the first walk around at Burghley in 1974 there were also a few fences where we just shook our heads and walked to the next obstacle. Fortunately, it too was better the next time around.

It is through the course inspection that you make your game plan. Are there any shortcuts on Phase A? Is there a stretch where you can give your horse a canter before the steeplechase? Where is the halfway point on the steeplechase course, and what is the maximum time at that point?

At one of my first competitions in Colorado in 1958, I was beginning the steeplechase course with a secondhand, runaway hunter belonging to a friend. I had studied the maximum time and the course. My horse got away from me right at the start, and ran away until the final fence, where he fell exhausted. He lay there for minutes, it seemed, but finally got his breath and regained his feet. I jumped on and we still finished with some bonus points!

Until lately I thought the steeplechase phase was simple: try to reach 690 meters per minute, check your watch at the halfway and don't get jumped off or run off with. Then one day in the spring of 1974 on a windy

167

course at Gladstone, New Jersey, I jumped an extra fence. Now it is a rule with me to review the steeplechase course in my mind while riding Phase A.

In some cases the steeplechase course will make a horse blow, particularly if you make a bad fence or two. After finishing Phase B it is best to get off, loosen the girth, check for missing shoes and, if all is well, hand-walk for a few minutes. Be sure not to lose track of the time!

Phase C can sometimes be a very long way, with many obligatory turns and numerous kilometer signs to reckon with. Often you're tempted to start thinking about that big oxer or that tricky combination on Phase D when you should be looking at your watch or checking red and white flags.

In the old days, some of us heavy jocks jogged beside our horses on Phase C for as long as we could stand it, or until we couldn't keep up with our horses. I stopped that practice after an incident in the early 1960s. I was riding an unfit horse at the annual Pebble Beach event. I had planned to run beside him the entire Phase C, and accomplished about three-quarters of this. When we got to the start of Phase D he was well rested, but I was all in. My mount took advantage of this by refusing three times at the third fence, to get us eliminated. On Phase D, I was on the short end of that game!

Dull as Phases A and C may seem, they play an important part in second-day strategy. If you are riding a horse with a big, freewheeling trot and he doesn't pull, A and C can be a very pleasant journey. On the other hand, if you have a bearcat on your hands, you can both be worn out by the time you reach the ten-minute break.

If all has gone well on Phase C, you arrive with three minutes to spare in addition to the ten-minute required break. The most exciting part of the second day now lies before you. Before the start you may change caulks, depending on ground conditions; give your horse a washdown, if it is hot, and make any necessary tack changes. Once or twice I have forgotten, in the rush, to change saddles, thereby finding myself in the starting box riding a four-pound steeplechase saddle. This is not a comforting feeling if you are riding a chickenhearted horse.

You have long since walked the course—hopefully, four or five times, including once or twice by yourself. I think it is alone that you can come closest to how it will be on the day. Ideally, you also have a cool, not-too-bright day; a fit, sound, safe jumper and lots of good luck. I think the nearest I've come to these ideal conditions was in the 1974 World Championship on Good Mixture. I'll always remember the rhythm with which Mixture negotiated that big course. You learn to remember and appreciate that kind of ride, for you may not get another one like it for a long time. You'd better remember the Good Mixtures and the Bold Minstrels, to make up for those less gifted or less brave performers who require a good bit of attention on the cross-country phase. I've certainly had my share of that kind.

One can get terribly involved in analyzing the many facets of riding a cross-country course. I think the job might best be broken down into two parts: the game plan and the actual game on the day.

The game plan includes certain variables. The footing is most important. Is it a fast track or are there boggy places? What are the most suitable caulks? Where can you make up for the time lost at the twisty combination? If you dare to jump the corner of fence 6, will he try to run out on that side? Is the landing deeper on the right or left in the splash? Will he try to fly the entire bullfinch? One must be reasonably sure of each approach, as well as the designated speed, the track of the course and all alternative routes to fences.

The game itself will invariably present certain discrepancies with your plan. For instance, there will be throngs of people before and between the fences. Particularly in England, the crowds can be tremendous, and they always know where the difficult fences are. It's quite a shock to come around the corner at the Trout Hatchery at Burghley, for example, to find two thousand spectators awaiting you, and it may take your horse four strides to look at the obstacle, having been stunned by all those faces. Then there is the problem of the sun and where it will be when you approach certain fences; horses are very much concerned about jumping from light into darkness. When you add a few thousand spectators to the darkness, you can have a problem.

Another hazard on the day is bad weather. Rain has made the difference in many a competition. Both in 1964 at Tokyo and in 1968 at Mexico there was torrential rain. Since both courses had been constructed recently, the

Plumb and Free and Easy on the steeplechase course at the Munich Olympic Games in 1972.

footing around the obstacles became dangerously deep. You must carefully consider the fitness of your horse and the position of your team when riding in such poor conditions. In Mexico, the rain was so severe that one straight-forward one-stride combination into the stream became almost entirely submerged. Many riders came to grief there.

Because of such discrepancies with the game plan, while riding the course you must learn to make decisions. The approach to a big oxer may have become deep because of previous traffic; you must be sharp to see this, and jump instead to one side or the other. Perhaps there's a combination where you had decided to take the long way through, because you didn't trust your horse over the corner. Recently such a decision confronted me in a two-day competition in New Jersey. When I studied the fence in question, I decided not to risk the corner. However, by the time I approached the combination my horse was jumping straight and confidently, but getting slightly tired. Since any tired horse is difficult to turn, I changed my plan and aimed at the corner. Fortunately, it worked out.

As in almost every sport, rhythm is vitally important to the good three-day performance, and perhaps the most important rule in cross-country riding is to try to maintain a good rhythm while jumping fences. Everything will tend to flow if you can "hit a lick," so to speak. Your timing is also simplified if you can relate it to the cadence of the gallop. By developing a feeling for the rhythm of your horse's gallop, you can start to acquire confidence in judging the various stipulated speeds. This too is very important.

For those whose horse goes clean and fast, the cross-country day is a short one, but for those who are less fortunate, the day often seems as if it will never end, particularly if there are injuries to deal with afterward. At best, the hours between the second day and the vet inspection prior to the stadium jumping on the third are long ones for all competitors. The cooling-out process, watering off, treatment of wounds and bandaging are all important parts of the second day. Not infrequently one finds oneself spending the night with a big knee or a big tendon. I'll never forget a long night in Munich, 1972, with Free and Easy. He had injured his tendon on the cross-country and required ice applications through the night. Thanks to good veterinary care and his great courage, he passed the vet and had only two rails down in the stadium jumping.

The final challenge in eventing is posed by the stadium jumping on the third day. Although the maximum height is only 3'11" and the fences are not very imposing to someone who does a lot of show jumping, they can still be a considerable problem to the event rider. The course must be evaluated partly in terms of the two preceding days' exertions, and it would be a lot simpler if you only had to jump it by itself; on average, speed and endurance on Saturday don't always go together with a smooth, well-calculated stadium trip on Sunday.

GETTING THE MOST FROM THE THREE-DAY HORSE

Since poling is not permitted at three-day events, it may occasionally be necessary to let your mount "accidentally" run through a schooling fence, if he thinks he's still on the steeplechase course. You can overdo this "sharpening up," of course, and I can remember seeing a fall or two in the warm-up ring—though the last one I recall did produce a very careful, clean stadium round.

Part of the problem is that the average stadium course is so well within the good performer's scope that it's hard to make him try, and this, I suspect, will change as the standard of competition continues to improve. Few international stadium courses today set enough fences at or near the maximum height and spread, but at the rate at which the sport is evolving, they should and probably will. In eventing, as in everything else, the challenges must always be adjusted to the level of accomplishment of the athletes—and the standards of eventing have improved strikingly during the period in which I've been riding in them. Long may they continue to!

Mike Plumb and Good Mixture at Burghley, England, in 1974, where they won the silver individual and gold team medals in the World Championships. Good Mixture was purchased for the USET team after the 1972 Olympics by a syndicate headed by Neil Ayer.

The Road to Burghley

BRUCE DAVIDSON

The only U.S. rider ever to win an individual World Championship title, Bruce Davidson first came to the USET's attention in the 1969 regional screening trials. Only three years later he was a member of the silver-medal team at Munich, and he won the individual silver medal in the Mexico Pan American Games in 1975 behind teammate Tad Coffin. Married to a keen eventer/foxhunter, Bruce lives in the heart of the Chester County hunt country in Pennsylvania when he's not off eventing.

WHAT IN PARTICULAR made me want to become an event rider? I think back to my childhood, and more specifically, to the ponies and horses that brought me along. There was nothing unusual about my background. Growing up near Millbrook, New York, I pony-clubbed, fox-hunted and went to as many horse shows as possible, though that was not a great many, since I was the only one in my family interested in riding.

However, I distinctly remember going to Madison Square Garden with the pony club one fall and seeing the American team for my first time. Then and there, at age eight, I recall promising myself that I would learn to ride at the highest level I could—hoping it would be international, but never daring to tell anyone. I kept this ambition a secret—partly because I didn't really understand what it was going to take, and also because it was my personal goal and I knew only I could make it come true.

It wasn't until I attended the McDonogh School in Maryland that my competitive interest with horses was given a more consistent chance, for riding was a varsity sport at McDonogh and I became team captain. After

Mr. and Mrs. Raymond Firestone's Golden Griffin and Bruce Davidson, winners of the Ledyard Horse Trials in 1975 and the silver individual medal at the Mexico Pan American Games later that year.

that, at nineteen, I went to Burton Hall in Ireland, and got my first taste of what riding a made horse was really like. I still remember the frustration of returning home and not knowing how to make my horse give and respond the way the horses at the riding school had!

Even before going to Ireland, I had undergone screening by Captain de Nemethy in consideration for the U.S. Equestrian Team. When I got back, in May of 1970, I was asked if I would like to come for a three-week training session with Jack Le Goff. It all seemed too fantastic. It represented a chance to really study riding with someone who could perform all phases at the highest level. To be able to do so myself became my goal, and still is.

The challenging thing about combined training is that it demands precision and a complete understanding between horse and rider in each phase. It isn't enough to be proficient in one or two aspects of the three-day and hope those good results will carry one's weaker points.

At the end of the initial three weeks I was fortunate to be asked to stay at Gladstone for an additional three weeks. The deeper we went into each problem, the more intrigued I became. I had to work hard, because I didn't want to be sent home and lose my chance to learn more about those things of which I was so obviously ignorant. In September of 1970 I returned to Gladstone to work with Mr. Le Goff "through the winter," as the invitation read. That same month my family purchased Irish Cap, who at that point was six years old, but only just broken.

As spring came and the competitions started, I really came to appreciate those months of criticism. My results were by no means impressive, but each outing helped me evaluate my progress and, even more important, kept reminding me how much more I had to learn. In September of 1971 came my first competitive success. I was lucky enough to ride Plain Sailing and win the Eastern Canadian Championship. At this point Irish Cap still had not been in any competitions.

Later that fall I returned to the team for another winter of training. Each day we worked on what one calls "the basics." Some of the older team horses were used to help us gain experience on some of the more advanced movements. All this time I realized how much improvement I had to accomplish if I was to be permitted to remain at the team and work with Jack Le Goff. As 1972 came, along with it came the pressure of an Olympics. Rather than struggle with it, I resolved not to worry about making the team for the games, but to concentrate simply on learning to ride each phase as efficiently as possible. My fear lay in being sent home and not attaining the standard I wanted.

The winter months of work again brought us to the spring events. Five riders and twelve horses were selected to train in England from April 1 through the Munich Olympic Games in mid-September, and I was named to the squad. As September approached, the horses that seemed capable of doing the Olympics became more obvious. I knew that Irish Cap was too inexperienced, so I started to plan his career for 1974, which would be the World Championships at Burghley, England.

In late August the six horses not considered for the Olympics flew home from Orly Airport, in France. The remaining six—Free and Easy, Good Mixture, Kilkenny, Foster, Plain Sailing and Johnny O—went by van to Munich. All had competed throughout the spring in England, and now needed only to be maintained in condition, and kept relaxed and sound, so as to be ready to compete when the time finally came.

What a marvelous opportunity it was just to watch all the various teams in training—not just the three-day, but the dressage and jumping teams as well. The team blacksmith back in Gladstone had told me, "It won't be until after your first Olympics that you realize how little you know." How right he was—except that I realized it as soon as I saw the top riders preparing themselves and their horses.

Although the three-day event at the Olympic level offers both team and individual medals, we have always regarded the team awards as far more important. Riding to orders, Jim Wofford on Kilkenny was first to go. He was told not to take any unnecessary chances, but to get around safely so as to help the rest of our team evaluate the course and the possible trouble areas. Kevin Freeman and Good Mixture went second. They were told to set as good a pace as possible while taking no chances with any fences, because Kilkenny had run into some trouble. Thus getting around clean was still Kevin's first consideration. When they encountered no trouble and made a fairly fast time, my orders were just to go. Since I was riding third and we

Bruce Davidson and Plain Sailing, donated to the USET by Mr. and Mrs. Firestone, on their way to a silver team medal in the Munich Olympics in 1972. They were eighth out of seventy-three starters individually.

already had two horses at least completing the course, Jack felt that Plain Sailing should go ahead and take a cut. If anything went wrong, Mike Plumb and Free and Easy could still ensure that we finished a team.

Plain Sailing finished with one stop and a fairly fast time, so Jack told Mike he could ride to win. Unfortunately, the measure of luck needed in a competition of this caliber wasn't with us, for Free and Easy had one stop and one fall. Munich closed with a team gold medal for Great Britain, and the individual gold as well. The Americans were once again silver medalists, having also placed second in Mexico in 1968 and Tokyo in 1964.

Once the games were over, I couldn't wait to get home and start to work with Irish Cap. From the two years of concentrated work with Jack Le Goff, I had enough of a foundation to know what I wanted; now all I had to do was make it happen. Though this was my first attempt at training my own horses, I had carefully kept track of our daily schedule while training under Jack, and I used those guidelines in training my horses at home. The season ended with an advanced three-day at Ledyard Farms. It was both my first effort at conditioning a horse to that level and Irish Cap's first start in an advanced three-day. Cappy did not finish in the top five because of a slow cross-country time, but he gave me hope for the coming season.

Shortly thereafter, I decided to take him to England and compete at Badminton. The idea was to gain experience for myself and to try to qualify both of us for the World Championships in September. The entire plan worked out perfectly. To top it off, that January I married Carol Hannum, an event rider herself who had always been intrigued by the idea of competing at Badminton. Thus we were able to combine our honeymoon with an attempt at Badminton.

175

Again Jack's conditioning program proved its merits. Both our horses were extremely ready and fit, and best of all, they were very sound. As it turned out, Carol didn't have much luck, but the competition proved successful for me. Irish Cap placed third, which was good enough to get him selected for the team for Burghley. Better still, this proved to me our ability in international competition. There was plenty to be improved (and there always is), yet for the first time I was convinced of Irish Cap's chances in the World Championships.

One must believe in what one sets out to do. Badminton paved the way for our attempt at Burghley. I did not want to start with the idea that I would be happy just to get around, or to get around clear; if we were to go, I wanted to try to win. The team planned to enter two smaller events before Burghley as part of our tightening-up process. Since Cap had been so fit in the spring, his condition came back quickly—at times too quickly—and we had to give him an easy week, here and there, of just quiet long walks and trots in the country to keep him from peaking too early. His wind was the major consideration, since the course was both long and relatively rolling. Toward the last stages of his conditioning we gave him some shorter but faster gallops, using hills to make him expand his lungs. Our purpose in the

Bruce Davidson and his own Irish Cap, competing in the last day's stadium jumping at Burghley in 1974.

two events prior to Burghley was not to try to win the preparatory competitions, but to let the horses gain a little more condition and to keep the riders tuned to riding a cross-country course.

Naturally, the more one competes the sharper one gets. For that reason, the horses that were not intended for Burghley competed on off weekends. Two weeks prior to Burghley the second horses did the Bramham three-day event, primarily for the benefit of the riders.

By the time we shipped to Burghley, we had all competed regularly during the previous month and our horses were all fit and fine. During our first look at the course we were somewhat overwhelmed by its enormous size, but the more we walked it and then considered our horses, the more realistic it began to appear.

As the final days approached, we all anxiously awaited our team selection and order of start. We were also anxious to know which English horses were to be nominated, as they were the obvious threat. Right from the first vet inspection, American hopes were high. All the U.S. horses seemed ready for the test—certainly as ready and capable as any of the others, if not more so. Of course, one hears rumors of this great horse or that, but no country could have been more hopeful for its entries than we were.

Our strategy in the dressage is always the same: Do the best possible test; put all problems and worries aside; try to both relax and concentrate, so you can start the second day with every possible point. When cross-country day came, the American team was very much in the competition, having placed second after the dressage.

Plain Sailing set out first with Don Sachey. Because of his team position, Don's orders were again to ride conservatively and try to go clear, not worrying too much about his time, so that his teammates could benefit from his report on the course. Don's steeplechase was clear with no penalties. Late in the cross-country he had a stop and a fall, but he completed the course and finished strongly. Victor Dakin went second with Denny Emerson. Again his instructions were to ride more or less conservatively and do his best to get around clear. Although he had time faults in both the steeplechase and the cross-country, he had no jumping penalties, giving the United States two horses that had completed the test.

By now we could evaluate our team position. Great Britain's first horse, Cornish Gold, had one refusal at the Bull Pen. Chris Collins' Smokey had had two falls. All the other countries had been having problems here and there also. My orders were to go clear if possible, to try to be right on time in the steeplechase but not over and to let Cappy gallop easily in the cross-country, provided I could do so without taking chances.

We did just that. Cappy went easily in the steeplechase, and jumped clean and well cross-country with a reasonably fast time. The English horse Columbus under Captain Mark Phillips also went clear, and with a very

Sitting on top of the world: World Three-Day Champion Bruce Davidson and Irish Cap, followed by teammate Michael Plumb and Good Mixture, receiving their individual awards at Burghley in 1974.

fast time. Now the heat was on. With Richard Meade left to go for Great Britain on Wayfarer, who had a good chance to go clear, Mike Plumb on Good Mixture was told to go! Three American horses were already around, so Mike's round, hopefully, would put us in a better position still. It did just that. Wayfarer also went clear, but nowhere near as fast as Good Mixture.

The third day brought little change. The Americans were well in the lead, and the forced withdrawal of Columbus, due to an injured hock, substantially increased our lead. Plain Sailing had one rail down and Victor Dakin with Denny Emerson had three down, which was very unusual for them, but the American team position was still reasonably secure. This was not the case for the individual standings; Irish Cap was less than one point ahead of Good Mixture, and only 1½ points ahead of Playamar and Hugh Thomas, who were competing as individuals for Great Britain. As it turned out, all three of us negotiated the course with no jumping or time penalties, leaving the standings unchanged. The United States had not only the first two individual placings, but most important of all, that long-awaited major team victory. The 1974 World Three-Day Championship was ours!

178

Eventing and the Spectator

NEIL R. AYER

Neil R. Ayer, a former competitor in three-day events, is MFH of the Myopia Hunt, director and organizer of the famed Ledyard Farm Horse Trials in Wenham, Massachusetts, and president of the United States Combined Training Association. He is also chairman of the AHSA Combined Training Committee and a member of both the Three-Day Selection and Advisory committees of the USET.

THE MILITARY ORIGINS of eventing and our own military participation in it have been discussed elsewhere in this volume, as well as have some of the major exploits of our USET three-day teams in more recent years. These achievements are extremely gratifying, and reflect how far the eventing movement has progressed in this country during the past quarter-century. I hope the USET will share at least a little of the credit for this improvement with the USCTA, which has accomplished a great deal in a short time with respect to the actual conduct of combined training competitions. (And nobody who has not actually staged a full-scale three-day event can possibly know how many details this involves.) In addition, the USCTA has played an important role in educating people about combined training, for this rather complex and technical sport probably requires the most explanation of any of the three disciplines.

The basic concept of combined training originated in the cavalries of the Old World as an exercise for the military horse. In fact, in many European countries the three-day event is still known as The Military, while the

French term for it is *Le Concours Complet*—the complete test. For the cavalry officer, dressage showed that the horse was calm, obedient and precise on the parade ground; cross-country, that the horse was fit enough and bold enough to cover miles and miles of difficult terrain at speed, and stadium jumping, that the horse, after a grueling day under battle conditions, was still sound enough to continue performing the duties expected of him.

How has the United States done in this demanding event?

The sport first appeared in the 1912 Olympics at Stockholm, where our team of cavalry officers won a bronze medal. In 1932 in Los Angeles we took our first team gold, with Colonel Earl Thomson accounting for the individual silver on the famous mare Jenny Camp. The principal U.S. achievements since then include a gold team medal in London in 1948, a bronze team medal for our first civilian team in Helsinki in 1952 and silver team medals in each of the last three Olympics: Tokyo (1964), Mexico City (1968) and Munich (1972). In September of 1974 the USET squad of Bruce Davidson, Mike Plumb, Denny Emerson and Don Sachey won the World Championship at Burghley, England, with Bruce and Irish Cap taking the individual gold, and Mike and Good Mixture the individual silver.

In addition, the USET has made an outstanding record in Pan American Games competitions: In 1955, Wally Staley won the individual gold medal in Mexico City; in 1959 at Chicago, Mike Page and Grasshopper won the individual gold medal while the team won the silver; in 1963 at São Paulo, Page nosed out Kevin Freeman for his second gold and the team won its gold medal also. The team victory was repeated in 1967 at Winnipeg and again in 1975 at Mexico City, Mike Plumb winning the individual gold at Winnipeg and Tad Coffin squeaking past Bruce Davidson to win the Mexico City individual gold.

Although the full-scale three-day event, as presented in Games and championship competitions, requires the full three days that the name implies, several abbreviated forms of eventing are offered at lower levels.

For qualification as a combined-training event, at least two of the three tests must be offered: either dressage and cross-country, dressage and stadium jumping or cross-country and stadium jumping. Since two-phase events of this sort are relatively few, it is the Games form of horse trials, encompassing all three phases, that we will be talking about in this chapter.

Horse trials can be scheduled with all three tests on one day, or with the three tests spread over two days (two tests on one day and one on the other). However, in major events one test usually takes place on each of three consecutive days, with dressage on the first day, cross-country on the second and stadium jumping on the third. When a horse trial is run off in either one or two days, the endurance factor is virtually removed and therefore the order of the tests is often reversed for convenience. A horse trial scheduled over a three-day period and offering both a steeplechase phase and a roads-and-tracks phase (in addition to the cross-country phase) on the second day is known as a full three-day event. In practice, most major three-day events actually involve four days of competition. This is because the dressage test takes some ten minutes to complete, and if you have many more than thirty entries, there just isn't time in one day to have all of them perform before one set of judges.

(This might be a good point at which to explain that horse trials are conducted at various levels from the Pre-Training Level, intended for either green horses or novice riders, to the Advanced Level [Olympic Games, Pan American Games, National Championships, etc.], for which both the horse and the rider must have a wealth of experience. The levels start with pre-training and progress to training, preliminary, intermediate and advanced in that order. With each level of competition the various tests become increasingly demanding. The dressage test goes from the very simplest movements to those requiring more and more training and coordination. The required speeds for the cross-country test get faster, the length of the courses longer and the size of the obstacles bigger. A steeplechase is not included below the Preliminary Level, because the physical development and training of the horse have not reached a point where it is beneficial to jump obstacles at speed.)

Horse trials are a superb spectator sport, enabling the spectator to be close to the action in each of its various phases. Now let us talk about these various phases from the time the horses and the competitors arrive on the scene until those in the "victory gallop" leave the field.

Four important happenings take place on the day before the competition actually starts. First, either riders or owners (or the *chef d'équipe,* in the case of a team) must "declare" their horses. In other words, they must notify the horse-trials secretary that they do in fact intend to compete. (Entries are often made as much as six weeks ahead of time, and a lot can happen to both horse and rider in that span of time.)

Second, all competitors must attend a briefing at which the members of the Ground Jury (dressage judges) and the Jury of Appeal and other officials are introduced and during which both general and special instructions and ground rules are gone over carefully.

Third, all competitors are conducted on an Official Inspection, or "Walking," of the cross-country course. Phase A (roads and tracks) is usually traversed by jeep or truck, Phase B (steeplechase) on foot, Phase C (roads and tracks) by vehicle and Phase D (cross-country) by foot. Fourth, each horse must be tested for soundness and condition by the Ground Jury and a Veterinarian Adviser. At this inspection temperature, pulse and respiration are taken so that at subsequent vet checks there will be a norm with which to compare.

Both the competitors' briefing and the official course walk are ordinarily limited to competitors and officials, but the first vet check is open to interested spectators, and this affords an excellent opportunity to see close up the horses that will be performing over the next three days. Spectators should take advantage of the time available on this opening day to walk and examine both the steeplechase and cross-country courses. Maps of these courses, with drawings and descriptions of the obstacles, are usually included in the official program. Study the program thoroughly before the competition begins. So doing will enable you to follow the trials much more intelligently and will provide you with a great deal of interesting information about the horses, the riders and the course.

THE FIRST DAY—DRESSAGE

The dressage phase, which can be likened to the school figures in a skating competition, is probably the least understood of the three phases. As an equitation term, it is defined as "the gradual harmonious development of the horse's physical and mental condition with the aim of achieving the improvement of its natural gaits under the rider and a perfect understanding with its rider." The natural movement of a horse is, of course, altered by the weight and influence of the rider, and dressage serves to give back to the ridden horse the grace of attitude and movement that he enjoyed in the open fields.

A typical dressage test is made up of some twenty separate movements, each one of which is worth from 0 to 6 points (or 0 to 10, depending on the scale being used). Each movement is judged simultaneously by each of the three judges (one or two judges may be used at the lower levels of competition) according to the following scale:

6 Very good
5 Good
4 Fairly good
3 Passable
2 Bad
1 Very bad
0 Not executed, or fall of horse and rider

In addition to the 120 points that can be earned for the twenty movements, another 24 points can be earned for the general overall impression of the test. Such qualities as freedom and regularity of paces, impulsion on the part of the horse, attention and obedience, lightness and ease of movement, acceptance of the bit, position and seat of the rider, correct use of the aids, etc., are taken into consideration.

There is a time limit within which the test must be performed, and

The dressage phase: Beth Perkins and Read Perkins' Furtive, who finished a solid sixth individually in the 1974 World Championships at Burghley, despite Beth's handicap of a broken foot!

one-half penalty point is deducted for every second in excess of this time limit.

If a rider makes an error of course—forgets a movement or performs one out of sequence—he is penalized 2 points for the first error, 4 points for the second, 8 points for the third, and is eliminated on the fourth.

Horse trials are scored on a penalty-point basis. To arrive at a score for a particular rider, the good marks awarded by each judge are added together and any error of course or time penalties are deducted. The final totals of all three judges are then added together and averaged, and the resulting number is subtracted from a perfect score in order to convert good marks into penalty points. Thus, the better the test the lower the score, and vice versa.

Theoretically, the relative influence on the whole competition exerted by the dressage test should be slightly more than that exerted by the jumping test but considerably less than that exerted by the cross-country phase. In order to preserve this balance, a multiplying factor of from 0.5 to 1.5 may be applied to the dressage scores.

A copy of the dressage test is usually printed in the program so that you can follow the ride movement by movement. The expert will probably vie with the judges, scoring the ride movement by movement. The novice will know whether or not the ride is a good one by simply observing whether or not it is pleasant and smooth and flowing and happy to watch.

As a dressage spectator you should be aware: that each competitor must undergo a tack inspection before entering the ring; that the judge will either blow a whistle or ring a bell as a signal for the rider to enter the ring, the rider being required to enter within a minute of this signal; that most riders use a different saddle for dressage than they do for cross-country; that spurs are compulsory above the preliminary level, and that the carrying of a whip is forbidden, except for ladies riding sidesaddle. A calm and quiet test is a great tribute to the tact and patience and skill and training of the rider, because, you see, the horse has to be super fit and is fully aware that he is going to be asked to cover some 15 miles or more, much of it at top speed, on the following day.

THE SECOND DAY—CROSS-COUNTRY*

The heart of a three-day event takes place on cross-country day with the Speed and Endurance Test. This test is made up of four phases, and the horses are now required to carry a minimum of 165 pounds, including the rider, saddle and, if necessary, a weight pad containing lead. Every contestant's weight is verified both before the start of Phase A and at the end of the course.

Phase A, the first roads-and-tracks, is designed to warm up the horse and rider for the more demanding tests which are to follow. It is usually from 2 to 4 miles in length and must be accomplished at an average speed of 240 meters per minute, which works out to about 9 miles an hour. The route is marked by sets of red and white flags between which the horse and rider must pass (red to the right, white to the left); by large yellow disks with the letter "A" painted on them placed at intervals to help keep the rider on course; by yellow arrows which aid in the same function and by kilometer signs (every thousand meters) so that the rider can better judge his pace.

Riders work out in advance a detailed time schedule as to just when they should be at what point and write all of this information on adhesive tape strapped to their forearms. For example, they know they should be at the second kilometer mark about eight minutes after starting. If they are behind schedule they know that they must speed up. If they are ahead of schedule they know that they will have time to spare at the end of Phase A—and most riders will calculate their pace on this first roads-and-tracks so that they will finish it with a minute or so to spare.

Phase B, the steeplechase, is designed to test the horse's ability to jump at speed over a course approximately 2 miles in length, incorporating some

*Note: In the discussion of both the second and third days, the speeds, distances and other measurements are those applicable to the Advanced (International) level; at lower levels of competition the requirements are less demanding.

This rather unusual steeplechase fence was in the Mexican Pan American Games in 1975, where the individual gold medal was won by the pair you see negotiating it: Tad Coffin and Bally Cor, lent to the team by Dr. Charles Reid and Mr. and Mrs. Harden Crawford.

ten steeplechase-type obstacles. Having completed Phase A, each competitor enters the starting box a few seconds before his predetermined time of start for Phase B and is "counted down" until the word "Go" sends him through the flags. He must finish the two-mile course within an Optimum Time (based on a speed of 690 meters per minute, or 26 miles per hour) or be penalized by 0.8 of a penalty point for each elapsed second in excess of this Optimum Time. If he does not complete the course within the Time Limit (twice the Optimum Time) he is eliminated. He can incur additional penalty points from disobediences at the obstacles to be jumped. A first refusal or runout, by way of example, costs 20 penalty points, a second refusal at the same obstacle 40 points, a fall of horse and rider 60 points and a third disobedience at any one obstacle, elimination.

As soon as the horse and rider pass through the finish flags of Phase B, automatically start on Phase C, the second roads-and-tracks. Phase C can be anywhere from 6 to 10 miles in length and must be negotiated, like Phase A, at an average speed of 240 meters per minute. Most horses when they finish a conventional steeplechase are led back to their stable, not to run again until yet another day. Here they must keep right on going—8 or more miles at a trot, moving on, and then an additional 4 or more at over 20 miles per hour over varied terrain and formidable obstacles of every description.

At the end of the second roads-and-tracks there is a mandatory break of ten minutes in the timetable of each horse. During this interval a committee of officials including the trials veterinary surgeon examines each horse to determine whether it is fit enough to continue. Should the committee decide that any horse is in fact unfit to continue, it is their responsibility to order immediate withdrawal. During this second vet check the riders dismount, readjust saddlery, wash their horse down a bit, apply ice if the temperature so demands and in general do whatever they can in the time allowed to ready their horse for the cross-country proper, by far the most demanding test of all.

Phase D, or the cross-country proper, is what horse trials are all about. At the advanced level of competition this phase measures from 4 to 5 miles in length and requires the horse and rider to clear some thirty or more obstacles of various design—vertical fences, spread fences, ditches, banks, drops, brush jumps, bullfinches and combinations of these. An average speed of 570 meters per minute (or 21 miles per hour) must be maintained, as 0.4 of a penalty point is incurred for each second in excess of this speed. As on the steeplechase phase, penalty points are also assessed for disobediences at the obstacles—20 points for the first refusal or runout, 40 points for the second (at the same obstacle), elimination for the third, 60 points for a fall of horse and/or rider, etc. Faults at obstacles are penalized only if they occur within the penalty zone, which is an area extending to 11 yards each side, 11 yards in front and 22 yards beyond each obstacle.

Spectators should, if at all possible, walk both the steeplechase course and the cross-country course prior to the second day of the competition. By so doing they will become familiar with the layout of the courses and will have an opportunity to determine which obstacles will be the most interesting ones to observe. As Phase C (second roads-and-tracks) is usually some forty minutes in duration, it is often possible to watch the first two or three horses go on the steeplechase course and still get to the first obstacle on the cross-country in time to see the first horse jump it.

There are many ways to go about seeing the most of Phase D. One is to pick out the most interesting jumps and spend all your time at one or more of them. Another is to see horse No. 1 over obstacle No. 1, horse No. 2 over obstacle No. 2, and so forth. Another is to start at the final obstacle and work your way around the course backward. This has the advantage of allowing you to face the oncoming horse, to anticipate the line the rider will take (to keep well clear) and to shorten the waiting interval between horses. Whatever plan you choose, do so with a schedule of starting times before you so that you can know just where you will be to see the particular horses you are most interested in. These schedules of starting times can usually be picked up at the secretary's tent shortly after all of the dressage tests have been ridden.

Spectators should be particularly careful not to interfere with the rider on course in any way whatsoever. Fence judges and patrol stewards, either

Sometimes it hardly seems fair! Denny Emerson and Victor Dakin suggest what can happen on the cross-country if you don't remember where the ditches are—a quick 20 penalty points. But guess what: they didn't come down! The incident occurred at Burghley, during the 1974 World Championships.

mounted or on foot, are responsible for keeping the galloping lanes clear, and their every signal and instruction must be scrupulously observed. Spectator ropes and barriers must be honored at all times. No other equestrian sport permits such active spectator participation—and yet this freedom of movement does depend in the long run on the enthusiastic cooperation of all who come to watch. A loose dog can mar an otherwise faultless round, so do obey the signs that ask you to keep your dog on leash, not only during cross-country but during the other phases as well.

Riders while on course are not allowed any outside assistance. For example, shouting directions to a rider would, if it were learned of, mean elimination, whether the rider had asked for help or not. Should a rider fall, however, it is perfectly permissible for a spectator to catch his horse, help him back into the saddle and in general give him whatever assistance is necessary to enable him to resume the course. A good rule to keep in mind is that you must not render assistance to a rider unless he has fallen.

Just as the rider weighed in at the very beginning of the speed-and-endurance test, he must weigh out at the very end. If through the heat of the day the rider has lost weight, he may include in this final weighing the bridle worn by his horse. If he is still below the minimum weight of 165 pounds, he is eliminated—as he is if he in any way communicates with or has access to any unauthorized person until after he has been weighed.

THE THIRD DAY—STADIUM JUMPING

On the morning of the third day of the competition, all of the horses less those that have been either eliminated or withdrawn must undergo yet another vet check—this one to ensure that they are sound enough and fit enough to tackle a stadium-jumping course later in the day. This test is neither an ordinary show-jumping competition nor is it a test of style. Rather, it is a test to determine whether after a severe test of speed and endurance horses have retained the suppleness, energy and obedience necessary to continue in service.

The course for the stadium jumping is approximately 700 meters in length with from ten to twelve obstacles. An average speed of 400 meters per minute must be maintained in order to achieve the Optimum Time. Completing the course in less than Optimum Time is not rewarded, but exceeding the Optimum Time is penalized at the rate of a quarter of a point for each second up to the Time Limit (which is twice the Optimum Time). In addition, penalties are assessed as they are in cross-country for disobediences at obstacles, but at half the value. In other words, a first refusal in stadium is penalized by only 10 points, whereas in cross-country it is penalized by 20. In cross-country the obstacles are designed and built so that they will not knock down, but in the stadium they are set up so that they will, as in ordinary show jumping. Each knockdown is penalized by 10 points.

With the three competitive phases over and done with, each competitor's marks for all three tests are now added together, and the rider with the lowest total penalty score is the winner. There can never be a tie, for if there are two or more competitors with the same final score, first the best score on the cross-country is taken as the deciding factor; then the best on the steeplechase; then, if necessary, the rider with the closest to Optimum Time on the cross-country is declared the winner.

The final act of any horse trial is the presentation of awards and the victory gallop, in which those in the ribbons circle the field at a high rate of speed and then leave through the outgate with their victories and their accomplishments behind them. For the spectator it has been three full days of participation—three full days to be remembered and to be looked forward to at the time of yet another horse trial.

Mike Plumb and Good Mixture give a splendid example of show-jumping form, clearing the water handsomely on the last day of Burghley, 1974. They finished less than a point behind the winner, teammate Bruce Davidson, and less than a point in front of third-place Hugh Thomas of England.

Selecting and Conditioning the Event Horse

JACK LE GOFF

A member of the bronze medal-winning French three-day team at Rome in 1960, wearing the black tenue of the Cadre Noir, Jack Le Goff went on to coach France's 1968 Olympic team (including the eventual individual gold medalist) before joining the USET in 1970. A fine all-around horseman who has proved himself equally at home on the racecourse, across country and in the dressage arena, Le Goff is versatile in other ways as well: he cooks a splendid Algerian couscous and is, like many of his fellow Bretons, a dedicated angler and wildfowler.

PERHAPS THE MOST BASIC FACTOR OF ALL in the sport of eventing is the initial selection of the three-day horse. Obviously, he must be versatile—he must have a sufficiency of all of the qualities needed to perform satisfactorily all three tests of this three-phase competition. However, an objective analysis of recent international three-day events reveals that the endurance test is by far the most important aspect, from a scoring point of view, of the three phases, and that there has been a definite revolution in the way horses negotiate cross-country courses today in comparison with twenty years ago. At the end of World War II, a good jumper who had no jumping penalties but was not fast would still place quite well in the results. Today not only is it necessary to go without jumping penalties, but a horse must also be fast if he is going to place well. Therefore, adequate speed is a vital factor in selecting a horse.

189

The cross-country courses are also becoming more and more technical. The horse we select has to be a good natural jumper and must be bold and willing as he faces all different types of fences. He must be athletic enough to handle combinations with very short distances as well as longer distances. Although a three-day horse does not require as much jumping ability as an international show jumper, he certainly needs to be a good enough jumper to handle the average intermediate show-jumping course, and be comfortable over a single well-constructed 5½′ show fence.

Speed and jumping ability are the two essential requirements to win, but these qualities must be complemented by stamina and endurance. With stamina and endurance the horse is able to preserve his speed and jumping abilities for the cross-country course. This is especially important when one considers that in competition, the event horse must complete the first roads-and-tracks phase, proceed to the steeplechase, then complete the second roads-and-tracks phase and finish up with the cross-country phase.

In considering the specialized qualities the event horse requires, it must be remembered that any competitive horse should, as much as possible, have both good conformation and a good disposition. However, the disposition of a three-day horse has special importance. When the horse is becoming fit he should still remain quiet enough to do dressage, and he should not waste energy in fighting against the rider during the endurance test.

Lastly, I would like to emphasize the importance of soundness. No matter what kind of competition a horse is being trained for, he *should* be sound, but in eventing the soundness factor is essential, for the event horse must work harder and longer over all types of ground than any other.

When we think we have found a good horse who has speed, can jump, has stamina, has good conformation and disposition and has three good gaits, we should look for a well-qualified, event-oriented veterinarian to examine and vet the horse. A good event horse is hard to find. Essentially you are

Three-day coach Jack Le Goff looks on with pardonable pride as the president of the FEI, Prince Philip, congratulates the members of the winning U.S. team at the 1974 World Championships. The riders are Mike Plumb, Bruce Davidson, Denny Emerson and Don Sachey.

looking for a dressage horse, a show jumper and a point-to-point horse all in one. Although the horse does not have to be of international caliber in each of the above, he must certainly be above average in each.

The quality of animal the international rider has today for eventing purposes has improved tremendously in recent years. Many horses, after retirement from eventing, now become first-class show jumpers or point-to-point horses. This confirms the fact that one must start with a high-quality young horse to compete successfully at the international level. The mediocre horse is just as expensive as the good one to support. It behooves an event rider who is going to invest several years developing a three-day horse to pay a sufficient initial cost to get a quality mount.

TRAINING THE EVENT HORSE

Let us say that you are going to start with a four-year-old, well-broken horse, commencing in the fall of his fourth year. Begin by working the horse in basic dressage to improve your control, for control must be established before you start to work over fences. You can take all winter to teach him to respond to the aids.

Dressage is often a misunderstood word. Basically, it means training— i.e., schooling—a horse on the flat. All horses—jumpers, hunters, dressage horses (which should really be called high-school horses when doing FEI-level tests), eventers and horses racing over jumps—should be given a good base of flat work. Often, horses are schooled over fences before they have even learned to go forward, turn or halt without resisting the rider's aids. If the horse with no foundation of dressage refuses a jump, the rider cannot possibly control him and the result is a catastrophe. It is like driving a car on a mountain road with a loose steering wheel and no brakes. If you watch the best show-jumping riders and the best trainers, you will note that their horses are thoroughly schooled on the flat, including the flying change of leads at the canter. This good foundation is a necessity for consistent success at the big shows. Let me add that better control is not the only advantage of dressage, for as the horse's training progresses on the flat, he will also become more supple, respond more quickly to our aids and develop strength and muscle. The basic goal of dressage must be borne in mind at all stages of the horse's training: the horse should remain *quiet, forward* and *straight*.

Once the horse is under fair control at the walk, trot and canter, preparation for work over fences may begin. Of course, the length of time spent on developing a good foundation on the flat will vary with each horse and the experience of the rider. Two to three months' time is about average. Schooling the event horse over fences is accomplished the same way you start a show jumper: by teaching the horse to trot over cavalletti. From there you

Maréchal de Logis Jack Le Goff, in the black uniform of the French Cadre Noir, riding for France in the Rome Olympics of 1960. He finished sixth individually.

can progress to doing gymnastics over small oxers at variable distances (one stride, two strides, three strides, etc.). The procedure of jumping cavalletti and gymnastics is explained elsewhere in this book by Bertalan de Nemethy, so I will not go into further detail here. However, I cannot stress too much that cavalletti and gymnastic exercises are as necessary to the event horse as basic dressage is to the show jumper. When the horse begins to be confident and regular over his cavalletti, you may start to trot him over small fences of different types. This will help him get accustomed to bright colors and different rail fences, small walls, brush fences, etc. This work should be done two to three times a week, always in short sessions.

By now the horse should be ready to jump single fences from a canter. After this he can jump part of a course, then, finally, a whole course. Aside from mounted work, it can help to longe the horse over cavalletti and oxers, if it's done well, and also to let him jump at liberty in a corral once in a while. These exercises provide a chance for the horse to find his own balance while jumping from a canter.

Our horse now has had basic jumping training. As soon as he gains confidence over the usual variety of small show-ring fences, it is time to introduce him to the different cross-country jumps. There are five basic types of cross-country fences: banks, drops, ditches, water splashes and bullfinches. For schooling purposes, approach these types of fences just as you did the small show-ring fences. Use small natural fences and slowly trot or canter the horse over them. If possible, begin this new aspect of instruction in the company of another, experienced horse who can give you a lead if needed.

Once your horse is able to jump boldly and with no hesitation over small cross-country fences, you are ready to progress to the next step, schooling over a small course of varied obstacles at a canter. Do not jump more than ten or twelve fences to a mile. A good principle to follow is always to

192

school over fences that are easier than those you expect to confront in competition, in order to build the horse's confidence.

After about six months, when your horse has a good foundation in all three disciplines, he will be ready to appear in public. Most horse trials are one-day competitions. This exerts much pressure on our young horse, as he will be asked to do dressage, cross-country and show jumping all in one day. Therefore, I personally prefer to take a young horse to dressage shows and horse shows of appropriate difficulty separately. Traveling to different horse shows will also give the horse experience in riding in a van and facing fences and a different atmosphere from home. When the horse becomes confident at dressage and horse shows (this may take about three to four outings), and he is sufficiently fit, he is ready to begin eventing in a training division.

One must prepare a logical play of competition for the horse. This following example starts with our four-year-old in the fall and leads toward progression up to the international level.

I. The Four-Year-Old Horse

October–December: School in basic dressage.

II. The Five-Year-Old Horse

January–March: Continue horse's dressage and introduce him to jumping by cavalletti and gymnastic exercises over show-jumping and cross-country fences.

April–May: Participation at dressage and horse shows.

June–October: Participation at one-day trials. If the horse does not present any particular problem, he should be able to go to about four events, the first three being at training level. If all goes well, horse can compete in an easy preliminary at the end of the season.

October–January 1: Rest horse and turn out.

III. The Six-Year-Old Horse

January–March: Gradually bring horse back into training. Participate in horse shows and dressage shows toward end of winter before eventing season starts.

April–June: Ideally, try to take horse to two or three one-day preliminary horse trials, ending in late June with a two-day preliminary horse trial.

July: Rest horse and turn out.

August–October: Take horse to one one-day preliminary and one two-day preliminary. End the season with the first three-day event at preliminary level.

October–January 1: Rest horse and turn out.

IV. The Seven-Year-Old Horse

January–March: Same procedure as at six.

April–June: One one-day preliminary, one or two intermediate one-day events. If the schedule of competition permits, take horse to a two-day or three-day event at the intermediate level.

July: Rest horse and turn out.

The team medal awards at Rome: Jack Le Goff, at far right, as a member of the bronze-medal-winning French team in the 1960 Olympic Games, behind the second-place Swiss riders, at left, and the winning Australians.

> *August–October:* One one-day intermediate, one two-day intermediate and one three-day intermediate event.
> *October–January 1:* Rest horse and turn out.

V. The Eight-Year-Old Horse

> *January–March:* Same procedure as previous years.
> *April–June:* One one-day intermediate event and one or two one-day advanced events. If schedule of competition permits, enter into a two-day or three-day at the advanced level.
> *July:* Rest horse and turn out.
> *August–October:* One one-day advanced competition and one two-day advanced competition. Horse should now be ready to go to his first international three-day event.

This training plan for your three-day horse is to serve only as a guide for his progression; every horse's particular circumstances are different. However, one certainly can observe from this schedule that it takes much time and work to make an international three-day horse. Therefore, invest wisely at the beginning and purchase a good horse. Another point to remember is to try to schedule events two to three weeks apart. This helps in getting the horse fit for the two- and three-day events.

CONDITIONING THE EVENT HORSE

The conditioning of the event horse must be adjusted (a) according to conditions of the endurance test of the event considered and (b) to the horse.

(a) The distances, the speed required and the nature of the terrain (which can be flat or rolling hills) are the factors you must consider to plan a good conditioning program.

194

(b) The basic conditioning program planned according to (a) must then be adjusted to your specific horse, taking into consideration the following factors:

1. The date of his last competition. Obviously a horse who has competed recently in several events two to three weeks apart will not need as much galloping exercises as a horse who is competing for the first time in a long while.

2. The horse's temperament. With a hot horse, you must use a lot of long distances at slow speeds. With a horse of easygoing temperament, you use shorter distances at higher speeds.

3. The soundness of the horse. Some older horses do not have very good legs. With them you must replace the speed work on the flat with slower work uphill.

In taking into consideration all the above information, one can realize that conditioning programs can vary considerably. It is the experienced eye of the trainer and the feel of the rider that will make a conditioning program work. Using a "gallop" program as an example, let's assume that we are training for a three-day event at the advanced level. There will be a steeplechase of 3600 meters, speed required 690 meters per minute, and a cross-country of 7500 meters, speed required 570 meters per minute. The cross-country will take place over gently rolling terrain. Let's say that the horse has been turned out for three months, and therefore is starting from scratch.

First, the horse has to be legged up gradually. Start by walking him under saddle, alternating every other day with longeing in order to give his back a chance to get in shape. After two weeks of alternate longeing and riding, the horse should be able to work under saddle six days a week. He then should start short trotting periods of three to four minutes. Gradu-

Adjutant Chef Le Goff and Monclos, winners of the Three-Day Championship of France at Barbizon in 1963.

ally increase the number of trotting periods to about four or five four-minute sessions over a period of about three weeks.

At this point the horse is ready to start on a light training program. Although this chapter is devoted to conditioning the three-day horse, a "galloping" program must be inserted in the general training schedule. A typical schedule is shown on the accompanying chart.

Weekly schedule

> *Monday:* Hack outside and dressage
> *Tuesday:* Gallop
> *Wednesday:* Dressage
> *Thursday:* Schooling over jumps
> *Friday:* Dressage
> *Saturday:* Gallop
> *Sunday:* Day off

Remarks: If the horse is schooled cross-country or over a steeplechase course, this should substitute for a gallop. If the horse is having a strong gallop on Saturday, he should go out for a short session on Sunday. After the fifth or sixth week of legging up, the horse can start galloping in the following progression:

1st gallop	1600 meters at 375–400 meters per minute.
2nd gallop	2400 meters at 375–400 meters per minute.
3rd gallop	Same.
4th gallop	1600 meters at 375–400 meters per minute twice, with a three-minute break.
5th gallop	Same.
6th gallop	1600 meters at 375–400 meters per minute; three-minute break; 2400 meters at 375–400 meters per minute.
7th gallop	Same.
8th gallop	2400 meters at 375–400 meters per minute twice, with a three-minute break.
9th gallop	Same.
10th gallop	1600 meters at 375–400 meters per minute; three-minute break; 2400 meters at 375–400 meters per minute twice, with a three-minute break.
11th gallop	2400 meters at 375–400 meters per minute; three-minute break; 3200 meters at 375–400 meters per minute, lengthening to 520 meters per minute for the last 500 meters.
12th gallop	2400 meters at 375–400 meters per minute; three-minute break; 3200 meters at 375–400 meters per minute, lengthening twice during the gallop—first time up to 520 meters per minute for 500 meters, second time up to 600 meters per minute for the last 500 meters.
13th gallop	Participation at a one-day-event horse trial: cross-country 3800 meters, speed required 520 meters per minute. Easy week after the event; first gallop seven days after event.
14th gallop	2000 meters at 375–400 meters per minute; three-minute break; 2800

meters at 375–400 meters per minute, finishing at 550 meters per minute for the last 800 meters.

15th gallop 2400 meters at 375–400 meters per minute; two-minute break; 3500 meters starting at 400 meters per minute, building up gradually to 600 meters per minute.

16th gallop 2400 meters at 375–400 meters per minute; three-minute break; 2400 meters starting at 400 meters per minute, finishing at 520 meters per minute; two-minute break; 3200 meters starting at 500 meters per minute, building up to 650 meters per minute for the last 1600 meters.

17th gallop 3500 meters at 400 meters per minute, finishing at 570 meters per minute for the last 500 meters; two-minute break; 3200 meters starting at 550 meters per minute and building up gradually to finish at 700 meters per minute.

18th gallop Participation at a two-day event: steeplechase of 3000 meters, speed required 690 meters per minute; cross-country 5500 meters, speed required 570 meters per minute. Easy week after the event; first gallop nine days after event.

19th gallop 2400 meters at 375–400 meters per minute; three-minute break; 3200 meters at 375–400 meters per minute, finishing at 550 meters per minute for the last 500 meters.

20th gallop 2800 meters at 375–400 meters per minute; two-minute break; 3600 meters starting at 400 meters per minute, building up gradually to 650 meters per minute.

21st gallop 3500 meters at 400 meters per minute, finishing at 550 meters per minute for the last 800 meters; two-minute break; 3200 meters starting at 550 meters per minute, building up to 700 meters per minute for the last 1600 meters.

22nd gallop 2400 meters at 400 meters per minute; two-minute break; 2400 meters starting at 500 meters per minute, finishing at 600 meters per minute; one-minute break; 1600 meters at three-quarter speed, which is 75 percent of the horse's full speed.

Jack Le Goff with his 1975 Pan American Games champions: (from left) Tad Coffin on Bally Cor, Beth Perkins on Furtive, Bruce Davidson on Golden Griffen, and Mary Anne Tauskey on Marcus Aurelius. Coffin and Davidson won the individual gold and silver medals as well.

A horse completing this three-month galloping program with no set-backs should be fit to run his three-day event. The day before the endurance test and after the dressage, he should get a "pipe opener."

The principle used here in conditioning the horse is, first, to build up the muscles. This is done by increasing the distance gradually at a basic "working conditioning speed," which varies from horse to horse at between 375 and 400 meters per minute. When the horse has a good "bottom," or base, his muscles being hard, the speed is increased. The two competitions included in this plan are a very important part of the conditioning program. The principle of breaking up the galloping sessions with short periods of rest is the same principle used in interval training with human athletes, adapted to horses.

One final warning: Horses are not machines! They do not work like automobiles, which is why this plan is just an example or guideline, which should be adjusted for every horse and to the training facilities available. However, it will serve to provide a concrete illustration of the kind of program that has proved, in my experience, to be most valuable.

DRESSAGE
&
GENERAL
CONSIDERATIONS

Dressage in America

ROBERT J. BORG

Some people might consider Bob Borg's career with horses an ill-fated one: in his Olympic debut in 1948, a single unaccountably low score deprived him of an individual medal, and a dozen years later, a freak accident ended his competitive career and left him partially paralyzed. Bob himself would be the last to agree, for he has shown an equal contempt for fate and for self-pity by continuing his active career as a horseman and trainer, working horses in hand from a special platform he has devised at Red Bob Farm in Michigan. The riders Bob worked with when he trained the USET three-day squads from 1951 to 1956 regarded him with a certain awe and thought him bigger than life-size. They knew their man.

As a practical matter, dressage was unknown in this country forty-five years ago. Admittedly, we had a few Army officers who had been given some dressage instruction, and a handful of civilians who had practiced it or seen it abroad. But in general, only those who were connected with military equitation or were confirmed dressage enthusiasts were even aware that this branch of equestrian sport existed prior to the Olympic Games of 1932, held in Los Angeles.

Our Army team in Los Angeles consisted of Colonel Hiram Tuttle, Colonel Isaac Kitts and Major Alvin Moore. Though the field was small—there were only eleven competitors in toto—we did fairly well, the team winning a bronze medal behind France and Sweden, and Colonel Tuttle winning the individual bronze. Four years later we had an Army team in Berlin, too, consisting of Colonels Tuttle and Kitts and Captain Conrad

201

Babcock, Jr. The competition was a lot tougher this time, and we finished last of nine teams. Once again, hardly anyone at home even knew that we had a team.

My own interest in dressage came directly from the Los Angeles games, while I was still very young. I couldn't get tickets to see the actual competitions, but I watched some of the schooling, and I was fascinated. Later on I hunted up some books on the subject, among them Beudant's *Horse Training*, which became my virtual Bible, and with its help I undertook to train a horse of my own.

You can imagine my excitement when in October, 1940, the great Colonel Tuttle visited my home state of Oregon to give some exhibitions of Grand Prix dressage! I wasted no time in introducing myself to him after his first performance, and told him about my own dressage efforts. He was gracious enough to let me sit on one of his horses, and perhaps all three of us were amazed to find that I could operate him a little bit. In any case, when his exhibitions were over, Colonel Tuttle accepted my invitation to visit my home and evaluate the stage of training my horse had reached.

By today's standards, my horse was a very coarse type, but considering that I had no outside instruction, I had reached quite an advanced degree of training with him. Colonel Tuttle was surprised to find that an animal who did not possess desirable qualities could perform so well, and he gave me some help and encouragement, which was most kind of him and greatly appreciated. I continued working on my own with renewed enthusiasm.

At that point, World War II entered my life, and needless to say, I wanted to be sent to Fort Riley, Kansas, where the U.S. Cavalry School was located. In 1943 I was instructed to report there, and hoped that somehow I would be able to advance my knowledge of dressage, even with a war going on. I assumed that a number of officers there would have some interest in and knowledge of dressage, but I was wrong; at that time, only Colonel Tuttle was engaged in this field at all. We renewed our acquaintanceship and soon became great friends. Needless to say, strictly military duties soon preempted most of my waking hours, but I still managed to learn a lot from Colonel Tuttle, and he did a great deal to help me.

Almost as soon as the war was over I started to train a new dressage horse in my off-duty hours. And thanks to this demonstration of interest, in March of 1947 I was fortunate enough to be assigned to the Army Equestrian Team, to start training for the 1948 Olympic Games to be held in London.

Our immediate objective was the Olympic trials to be held in the fall of 1947. Trials for all military personnel were to be held at Fort Riley, while open trials for anybody else who wanted to compete were scheduled for Hinsdale, Illinois. These trials were to be held in all three equestrian disciplines—dressage, three-day and jumping.

First Lieutenant Robert J. Borg and Reno Overdo, the eventual dressage mount of Colonel Frank Henry in the 1948 Olympic Games.

There were only two dressage competitors in the Fort Riley trials, Colonel Tuttle and me. I was selected to represent the Army in the open trials at Hinsdale. When I got there I found that there were no civilian entrants at all, and I gave an exhibition of the test instead. The idea was that the public could then get an idea of what the requirements were, and would be able to determine more accurately whether there were any civilian horses that had the capability or potential of attaining this level. We learned of none.

In October of 1947 the Army Equestrian Team traveled to Europe by ship to commence its Olympic training proper, and I was assigned to accompany the shipment of the horses. Upon arrival in Europe they were transported by rail to Munich-Riem, the site that was later chosen for the equestrian events of the 1972 Olympic Games, and we set up our training quarters there.

The Army was anxious to field a full team (which at that time meant three riders) in each of the equestrian events. Fortunately, there were several officers already in Germany who had horses that could be considered dressage prospects. I selected three of them, hoping that with proper training they might be able to reach the necessary level in time for the Games. If the horses made the grade, we would then try to find riders for them, somehow.

In January, 1948, with four horses in one boxcar and three other boxcars loaded with forage and bedding, I started on the trip to the famous Vornholz stud in Warendorf, Westphalia, the property of the Baron Clemens von Nagel, a very well-known and enthusiastic horseman. At that time, he had Hans Brinckmann to handle his jumping horses while Otto Löhrke was in charge of the dressage horses. There I set up my training operation, the

203

Borg with Pancraft at the extended trot. Trained by Borg, Pancraft was ridden by Colonel Earl Thomson on the Army's silver-medal-winning dressage team in 1948.

baron supplying not only the stable facilities, but also living quarters for me and my groom. The Nagels treated me as a member of the family, and they were most kind and helpful.

At Vornholz, I had the opportunity to work with Mr. Löhrke, who was a very talented and skillful horseman, especially in the preparation and training of horses for the Grand Prix levels. He was a hard worker, and nothing was impossible as far as he was concerned. His favorite theme, repeated innumerable times, was *"Schülter herein, halbe parade, immer wieder, jeden tag,"* which meant "shoulder-in and half-halts, over and over again, every day." His theory was that *any* horse was capable of performing the Grand Prix movements, although the quality of performance would differ. For him, it was not a question of *whether* the horse could perform the movements, but a question of *how.*

Otto Löhrke was at this time in his late sixties, but he still trained four to seven horses a day. Each horse was ridden for thirty minutes only, and as each successive horse was brought to him, he leaped directly to its back from that of its predecessor, thereby saving precious minutes.

I rode the Olympic test ride every Thursday, using only the part of the ride that the horses could do. The rest of the week was spent on the parts that were faulty. The following Thursday a little more was added to the test ride, and in a few months considerable progress had been made. My best horse, Klingsor, needed only the ability to perform under pressure in a calm and sure manner. Löhrke and I developed a very friendly relationship over the years. In my opinion he was truly outstanding in his field—certainly the best that I have ever had the opportunity to observe at work.

In June, 1948, our dressage horses were back in Munich, preparing for the show in Aachen. I competed only in the Olympic test there, and was fortunate enough to win the amateur division and place second in the open, beaten by Mr. Löhrke by only a few points.

After Aachen we crossed the channel to England and stabled at Aldershot during the final stages of our training. In order to have a complete dressage team, two of our three-day riders, Colonel Earl F. Thomson and Colonel Frank Henry, had agreed to ride in the Grand Prix dressage as well. Since both horses and riders had to be prepared to meet the requirements of the tests, and since the riders' time was extremely limited because of their three-day preparation, this was not an easy matter, to say the least. Nonetheless, it was worth the effort, for in contrast to the disappointing dressage placings at Berlin in 1936, in London we won the silver team medal behind the victorious French, Sweden having been disqualified for using an ineligible rider.

[Editor's note: Bob Borg is too modest to mention his own contribution to this fine result, an individual fourth-place finish that, in most qualified opinions, should have been even higher. The three judges—none from our continent—placed him first, second and ninth, respectively, and the judge who could see him as no better than ninth placed his own countrymen first, second and third. In all fairness, Borg should have won a medal.]

After the London Olympic Games, the U.S. Army Equestrian Team was deactivated and its members were reassigned to new duties. I was assigned to a horse troop that was patrolling the border of the Russian zone near Hof, Germany, on the Saal River.

Upon returning to the United States in the fall of 1950, I heard the rumor that a civilian group was being formed to take over our Olympic equestrian effort from the Army, and that the Army team would be no more. Soon rumor was replaced by fact, and through Colonel John Wofford I made contact with the new organization. By the summer of 1951, Olympic train-

Pancraft and Borg in training for the 1948 Olympic Games.

ing was under way at Fort Riley again, but this time it was civilian Olympic training.

The Army turned over to the new USET everything it had in the way of horses that was still potentially usable, either for training or for competition. Civilians also lent or donated horses, and the organization started to roll. From the beginning, the jumping team had both the largest quantity and the best quality to work with. The three-day picture was much less promising, as both the horses and riders were pretty green, especially in the dressage phase. Colonel Wofford put me in charge of the three-day dressage training, and it was quite a challenge to try to develop both horses and riders simultaneously.

In addition, I was working on Grand Prix dressage as well, and here the picture was even bleaker. We had only two horses who had been in competition at all, and one who needed a lot of work to even reach that standard. Individuals who could train a Grand Prix horse were almost nonexistent in those days, and even now they are far from plentiful.

I would love to be able to recite that a series of successes followed this rather unpromising start, but that's not exactly what happened. Our three-day team did surprisingly well at Helsinki, considering its inexperience, and accounted for the bronze team medal, but our dressage squad, consisting of Marjorie Haines, Hartmann Pauly and me, could beat only two of the seven other teams in Helsinki. In the 1955 Pan American Games I had the pleasure of seeing Wally Staley win the individual gold medal in the three-day event, but took no satisfaction from the fact that I was our only representative in dressage. I was awarded a silver medal, but the field was so small that it didn't amount to much.

The Stockholm Olympic Games the following year merely confirmed that our infant USET was going to have to get into a different gear if it hoped to stay abreast of the resurgent Europeans. None of the squads produced a medal this time, and in dressage we couldn't even field a complete team, Elaine Shirley Watt and I competing as two individuals. By the end of Stockholm, morale was pretty low all around, but in retrospect, that was also the turning point. In 1959, Patricia Galvin won the first of her two Pan American Games gold medals at Chicago, and the all-girl team of Galvin, Newberry and McIntosh won the team gold. In Rome the following year there were no team medals, but Irish Galvin placed sixth and Jessica Newberry twelfth, individually. By then, my own direct participation in the USET's dressage was over, and the detailed story of this and subsequent developments is for others to tell. Instead, let me make a few general observations.

From that low point in 1956 to date, tremendous strides have been made in the field of dressage. In 1956, the word "dressage" had for most Americans a strange foreign sound, and only for a few did it have any real meaning or significance. To find a dressage class included in a horse show was a rare occurrence, and it usually required a great deal of persuasion to prevail on the show committee to risk it. But gradually, thanks to the efforts of a few key individuals and the enthusiasm of a few others, progress was being made. Each year, a few more classes were added and improvements were made with respect to the quality of the training and the instruction that was being presented.

Soon dressage organizations were being formed to assist in improving the overall standards and to try to obtain qualified personnel to give lectures and clinics to groups interested in improving their knowledge. Slowly but steadily, more and more individuals were taking an interest in this form of equitation, which, in turn, caused shows to start adding a few dressage classes to their prize lists.

At the Detroit Horse Show in 1975, there were over one hundred entries, compared with ten just a few years before. The classes offered included the training level, fourth level, Prix St. George, intermediate and Grand Prix. To include the FEI Grand Prix, and actually have some entries for it, was quite a step forward. After so many years in which the dressage was associated primarily with Olympic competitions every four years, it is now familiar to everyone connected with horses.

This is extremely important, because, in the end, the only way to get good Grand Prix horses is to have all the other levels first. Buying made horses abroad is at best a temporary expedient, for the horses sold will obviously never be the best ones. Establishing a broad base of horses and riders on the lower levels is the only sure way of achieving quality

Major Robert Borg, at left, the Pan American dressage silver medalist in Mexico in 1955, with gold-medal winner Captain Héctor Clavel and the bronze medalist, Major José Larraín, both of Chile.

at the top, and this is now happening. Horses and riders who can achieve the Olympic Grand Prix level will never be plentiful, anywhere in the world, but as more horses and riders move to higher levels, the quality of performance will steadily improve. I believe that at our present rate of progress, the United States will be a strong adversary in international dressage within the next dozen years, and in dressage, this is a short time.

In 1948, one man rode in our open Olympic trials, and one man prepared all of the horses who competed in the Games. In 1975, twenty competitors performed the Grand Prix dressage test in the Pan American Games trials at Gladstone. This is progress!

The Green Armband

JESSICA NEWBERRY RANSEHOUSEN

Though most riders gravitate to dressage from some other form of riding, Jessica Newberry was drawn in that direction almost from the start of her riding career. She demonstrated the value of this singleness of purpose by becoming one of the very few Americans ever to win a major dressage honor at Germany's most prestigious show when she headed the dressage classification at Aachen in 1958, as related below. Twice an Olympic rider, Jessica now lives in Au Sable Forks, New York, and remains an active competitor, teacher and judge.

LEGEND HAS IT in our family that at the age of three or four I would cajole any susceptible soul into driving me down nearby country lanes in search of horses.

I had a Scotland Yard technique. We would drive along until I spotted a heap of manure. I would then call, "Stop, stop!" My indulgent driver would comply and open the car door for me. I'd hop out and inspect the manure. If I found it still steaming I knew I was hot on the trail. And we would continue until we found the horse.

As far as my family was concerned, this was not according to Hoyle. They should have produced a malacologist, an ornithologist, a botanist or an ichthyologist. All would have been acceptable to them. But a horse-crazy offspring, never!

And so it was that just before I turned six I began demanding "When *are* you going to buy me my horse?"

My mother snapped back, "Never. If you want a horse, buy it yourself!"

Puzzled, I asked, "How can I get the money?"

"By making all sorts of little sacrifices. If the other children are having treats—candy or the comics, a movie or an outing—and you'd prefer to have your horse, just pass up the treat and put the money into your piggy bank."

The family legend continues that I was quite undaunted by the magnitude of my task. I developed a stockbroker's sensitivity to the going rate of the commodities around me. A midmorning snack, 15 cents; small candy bar, 5 cents; a stick of gum, 1 penny; a comic, 15 cents (borrowed comics are just as funny)—the list was long, and I kept it in my five-year-old head for constant use.

Just before I was about to enter the first grade, I remembered that my mother (who made all my clothes) had made me a "first day in kindergarten dress." I sounded her out. Was she planning to make me a "first day in first grade dress"? And when she said yes, I asked her to find out at the store just how much everything would cost. She did. One and a half yards of flowered cotton, $1.30. Zipper and seam binding, 65 cents. Pattern, 45 cents. And to my joy, she let me have the $2.40 for my piggy bank. But when I suggested we might add the cost of her labor for the sewing, she flatly refused.

There followed five long years of skimping and saving, and although the money outgrew my piggy bank and was placed in a savings account, it was still painfully around $75.

Then, in the autumn of my eleventh year, business took a definite turn for the good. The year before, Mother had made me a handsome bright red Forstmann wool coat and hat, and had, at my urging, bought an extra half yard of the wool for future alterations. Just before cold weather, we tried the coat on and found the sleeves so short she would have to add false cuffs, and the hem so far above my knees that she would have to add a 2-inch band. So she added. But to her horror, she found that the coat now had three colors: the weathered red of the coat itself, a slightly deeper red of the turned-down strip and a very much deeper red of the added material.

She said I couldn't wear the coat like that. I jumped at the idea of having it dyed and told her to phone and ask if it could be done and what it would cost. Mother fell into the trap. The dyeing would come to about $16. I smiled as I put the money into my savings account and wore the coat to school the next day.

Mother had a drawn, unhappy face when she picked me up that afternoon at school. As she drove home silently, I could feel her eyeing my coat, cuff and hem. I thought the coat of many colors was an accepted fact. But Mother, poor soul, thought otherwise. She slipped off to New York City and brought back three beautiful winter coats for me to choose from. They all fitted perfectly. I asked her how much they cost. All were around $90. Ninety dollars, praise be! That would bring my grand total to $181. So I continued to wear the old rag, and it looked beautiful to me because my father decided to match my $181, and I got my horse—Patches.

To me she was a 15.2-hand bundle of glamour. Gray with lovely large dark eyes. Two dark patches over her rump. To the rest of the world she was a rather long, short-legged, heavyset, thick-necked model. But everyone agreed she had a wonderful temperament—was safe in any company, in any situation, anywhere. And that fitted in with my parents' plans too. Both of them had had unhappy riding experiences as children, and they were determined that I start on a suitable, safe horse and under careful supervision. We went instructor shopping. We sampled a few of the establishments in the area and found them unsuitable.

Then, one day, a close riding friend asked us to go with her and watch a newly arrived German instructor. As we sat and watched Fritz Stecken exercise his finished, trained horse, I edged up to my parents and whispered, "He knows how to ride. I'll take lessons with him."

With Patches dawned a whole era of delight . . . and riding without stirrups.

The period of riding without stirrups was a succession of riding stages that lasted about four years, carefully planned by Fritz Stecken.

Stage one was simply the crossing of the stirrups over Patches' withers and trying to keep my shoulders, hips and heels in the straight classical line. In a walk, it was not so impossible. Straight ahead in the trot wasn't so bad, either. But the torture came at the corners of the indoor ring; every corner! I felt I was going to slip off at every corner. I fought to stay on at every corner. I made myself tense and rigid. Then it took half the long side of the

A time for concentration: Jessica Newberry and Forstrat, just before entering the arena in Tokyo in the 1964 Olympic Games.

ring to make me relax again. And then another corner appeared . . . and another and another. . . .

By riding without stirrups until I was tired I began to relax and absorb the rhythm of the horse through my seat. Then keeping my balance was not so difficult. And as the months went on, the time of tenseness in riding without stirrups grew shorter and shorter.

And then came stage two. The stage in which I became so at home without stirrups that when the work moved into more difficult areas, I preferred to deal with the situation without stirrups! At that point I didn't ever want to ride with stirrups.

And then came stage three. A much more balanced era. Riding with and without stirrups became equally comfortable. Those stages of advancement in strengthening my seat by riding without stirrups were paralleled by my learning the art of riding.

In the first stage, I was only able to cope with easy transitions—walk-to-trot, trot-halt and the ordinary gaits. I did these over and over again. I had plenty of time to perfect these basic movements. I wasn't in a hurry. And I didn't do any showing at all during those four years.

A certain independence of the uses of parts of the body evolved through this work. It was a pleasure to be able to use one leg more than the other, as in leg-yielding or turning on the forehand. Or to use both legs to push Patches forward and yet not hang on her mouth with my hands. These independent aids made my riding more effective and the riding aids themselves more subtle, more nearly invisible.

Patches too profited from this harmonious interworking of the aids. She found me to be more supportive of her efforts at shoulder-in, haunches-in. I was able to correct her balance sooner because I grew more and more sensitive to its shifting.

When Patches had been in our family for about two years, my dad fell in love with, and secretly bought, a funny, friendly little horse, hardly a streamlined, elegant mover. This funny little Lipizzaner proved to be a steady, reliable performer with an interesting future.

Pluto took over where Patches left off. Patches, after all, was a beginner's horse—her conformation made anything beyond shoulder-in a poet's dream. But with Pluto, figures that had only been explained to me were now within my reach. Turns on the haunches, travers, collected canter, collected trot—I wanted to try them all. But there was a hang-up. Pluto was as young and green as I was. And so the learning and the mastery of these figures was a slow and sometimes frustrating process.

I remember to this day the very first stumbling block. Fritz Stecken would warm Pluto up for me. Get on. Squeeze his legs. And then the horse would obediently go on the bit. What a picture! Up until this time, I had always ridden Pluto with side reins because my seat was not steady

212

Jessica Newberry and her first "serious" dressage horse, the Lipizzaner Pluto, competing at Ludwigsburg, Germany, in 1958.

enough and Pluto's training was not far enough advanced for me to keep him in a consistent frame without their help.

At this point, Fritz decided that the side-rein crutch should go. I was thrilled. I got on. Squeezed my legs, steadied my hands. Nothing happened. Pluto's head was straight up in the air. An hour later, he was still stargazing!

It took weeks for me to learn just how much pressure of the leg and how much steadying of the hand I had to do to get Pluto on the bit. Each stage with Pluto had its frustrations and its joys. I had to learn the feeling of a correct movement while I was still trying to ride that movement correctly . . . there were no buttons to press. It was the most difficut method of training for both me and Pluto.

In the late 1950s, the standards for world competition in dressage were set in Europe, just as they are today. I was so eager to see the best and to learn more that I prevailed on my parents to take me to Germany—to Aachen and Hamburg. And day after day, for ten days, the three of us would troop out in the fog, in the cold and in the drizzle at 5 A.M. to be sure to catch all the international riders warming up. It was cold in Aachen that July! My father took a firm stand early in the game. He said he didn't know what the hell he was doing there anyway. And he'd be damned if he'd face that 5 A.M. freeze without proper long woolen underwear. So we bought the underwear.

We made many friends among the top riders, and I brought home copious notes on their performances and their horses. And all of them encouraged me to return the next summer and compete.

When I returned home after Hamburg, a definite plan to enter European competition began to take shape. And we concentrated our efforts on the tests that I would have to ride in Europe. While working on some of the figures, I mentioned to Fritz Stecken that the international riders rode some of them differently. He assured me that the way he taught them was the only proper way, but I was still puzzled.

I arrived in Aachen a very inexperienced, idealistic eighteen-year-old. As in all sports, fashions in dressage changed and fluctuated. And a rider who may have been doing well at home can find, as he rides before international judges, that he is executing some of the figures in an outmoded way.

For instance, in my case, I was blissfully doing the two tracks with horse's shoulders leading instead of its being a parallel figure. This automatically lowers the score to 4. And no matter how beautifully my horse did the two tracks with shoulder leading, the figure was "insufficient" as far as the judges were concerned.

After a disastrous week in Aachen, there was only one shining light: the unanimous praise for my seat from judges and sports critics alike. Those long, tedious hours and days and years of work without stirrups had paid off.

Also in Aachen I found that my Pluto, who had struggled faithfully to learn dressage at the same time that I was learning it, was considered an unsuitable type for top international competition. He was a Lipizzaner. What a blow!

A blow, in fact, that might well have daunted the most ambitious person. But I wasn't ambitious; rather, I was fascinated, consumed by dressage. I was fascinated by the way dressage was interpreted in Germany, in Switzerland, in Denmark. And so I stayed on in Europe.

I had the unique privilege of living with the Linsenhoff family—of watching Liselott's daily training and having Herbert Kuckluk, her talented trainer, as my trainer too. Both Liselott and Kuckluk had worked for years with one of the world's supreme dressage trainers, Otto Löhrke. And the Linsenhoffs owned two of the famous horses trained entirely by Löhrke: Adular and Famos. This was all heady stuff for an eighteen-year-old. Generously, the Linsenhoffs became interested in introducing me into the German riding scene and national competition.

I settled in for a wonderful year. I continued to ride Pluto, and our first

A lighter moment: Jessica Newberry and two fellow competitors, both Olympic gold-medal winners—Henri Chammartin of Switzerland, the 1964 winner, and the Russian Sergei Filatov, the winner in 1960.

Jessica Newberry and Forstrat, her Olympic dressage mount in 1960 and 1964, competing at Wiesbaden, where they won the S Kür.

task was to pull apart the various tests and decide what points of the tests Pluto did well. Good collected trot, good collected canter, good flying changes, pirouettes and travers. So we perfected those things and practiced the German National Tests until the movements were fluid and smooth. Then we started off on some of the national shows.

The exactness of the figures that we produced in these national shows helped the judges to do some forgetting that Pluto was a little Würstchen. Like a happy graph, the success line rose and rose. Ulm, fourth in S. Herborn, tied for second with Liselott Linsenhoff on Monarchist (until the judges asked for two consecutive extended trots, alas!—why didn't they ask for two pirouettes instead?) Next Wiesbaden, Pluto second in S Kür and third in Grand Prix. And with this, Pluto's colorful and sometimes amusing career ended and he returned very happily to our farm in the States.

In the meantime, Forstrat had entered my life. He came without passage, with flying changes every stride—on the place, with a piaffe-in-a-hurry and with a cyclonic pirouette. He had a beautiful golden-bronze coat and was a luscious Rubens-type stallion. Before buying him, we went to a small show to see him perform. It was difficult to judge his degree of accomplishment, because he was naughty in the ring through most of the test. He just shied and bucked! But when I tried him, I liked the way he went. He was springy and eager. And so, while Pluto's star was rapidly setting, Forstrat's star was rising.

Much strong and steady work went into completing Forstrat's training.

The easiest fault to correct was the flying changes every stride on the place. First of all we made him move forward at an ordinary canter and make a single flying change. And still going at an ordinary canter, we tried a series of three changes at every stride, not allowing him to hesitate or slow down. When he learned that he couldn't hesitate, we began doing the flying changes at the collected canter, with me always pushing him a little more forward to remind him that the forward impulsion during the change was most important.

His piaffe and passage came along slowly. We worked on them for many months, improving them but never making the vital transitions between piaffe and passage as good or as brilliant as they should be. And that cyclonic pirouette became slower and smoother, but never one of Forstrat's excellent features.

And while all this work was going on, we entered a number of national and international shows. And Forstrat started to place well consistently. In Wiesbaden, we were first in the S Kür and second in the Grand Prix. In Aachen we won the S Kür again, and again placed second in the Grand Prix. This time there was a special bonus, for the second in the Grand Prix gave me enough points to lead the riders' classification, and I could proudly wear the Green Armband as the most successful dressage rider in the Aachen show. It was a far cry from those first rides on Patches!

Dressage for Girls
and Grandmothers

PRINCESS PATRICIA GALVIN
DE LA TOUR D'AUVERGNE

Trish Galvin, as the USET first knew her, started off to be a three-day rider but switched to dressage when the FEI ruled against women's participation in the 1960 Olympics. Fourth overall and leading woman in the 1957 National Three-Day Open, Trish won the individual dressage gold medal at São Paulo two years later, and the next year won the Grand Prix of Aachen and placed sixth in the Rome Olympics. It is safe to say that no one *else ever progressed so far so fast in this most demanding art; but then, the Galvin family does not know the meaning of "can't." To say that the USET would never have been the same without their many and varied contributions would be an understatement.*

I THINK THE MOST IMPORTANT THING for a dressage rider to do at the beginning is walk right in where angels fear to tread. Get a nice sound horse and a good dressage book, ride every day and practice, practice, practice. Patience is the highest virtue, to be developed at all costs, regardless of nerves, crossness, bad humor and other natural inclinations.

I have watched the masters and they all seem to have a sort of Buddhistic detachment, an intense concentration on things like walking in a straight line, endlessly playing with the horse's mouth until he gives just as he should or monotonously stopping and starting *exactly* at X until the

Trish Galvin (now the Princess de la Tour d'Auvergne) and Rath Patrick at the extended trot. Her 1960 victory in the Dressage Grand Prix at Aachen was part of a unique double for the Galvin family, the jumping Grand Prix that year having been won by Night Owl, her mother's horse, and George Morris.

watcher is bored to death. Dressage's magic formula is the overpowering force of a combination of gentleness and repetition.

I began serious dressage with a French-Canadian Californian, Captain Léonard Lafond. He was the kindest person on earth. He was almost entirely self-taught, and dressage was his passion. He managed to transform Rath Patrick from a spoiled and nasty hunter into a dressage model. When I came to him with the problems of my three-day hunter and its dressage training, he told me to get on Patrick, who would "explain it better."

It was an incredible sensation to be on a horse that responded to a finger-tip, a minute shift of weight or the brush of a heel—and yet it is possible for all horses with the same simple formula: gentleness and repetition. Of course, there has to be a lot of good free galloping in between, to build up muscles and develop the lungs of the horse and of the rider. But to put up with a horse trained by force that has to be ridden with force is as exhausting as it is unpleasant.

As for the dressage competitions—everything is turned upside down. The gentle, patient master becomes an ambitious, domineering victim, for now the horse has the last word. A movement has to be performed whether

218

The Pan American dressage gold medalist for the second time, Trish Galvin hears our anthem played in São Paulo, Brazil, following her 1963 victory. Silver medalist Francisco d'Alessandri of Argentina and bronze medalist Héctor Clavel of Chile share the podium.

the horse is ready or not, and either he does it or he does not. It is hard to recover once things go wrong. I have always admired the imperturbable Major Henri Saint-Cyr: no matter what happened, he always had such presence that one almost forgot the horse. I find the tests themselves are rather

Rath Patrick and Trish Galvin, competing in Rio de Janeiro shortly after their Pan American Games victory in 1963.

wearisome to look at unless it is a Grand Prix test, but I love the free movements of the French school of dressage. A horse is capable of such wonderful things that I only wish the competitions were more imaginative.

To carry on beyond the good-book stage, in the absence of a cavalry school, it is very important to have someone on the ground to look on occasionally. Movements have to be seen as well as felt. Another good thing is to go into as many competitions as possible. Not being used to pots of flowers and fluttering papers can cost as many points as a terrible piaffe. Also, there one has a standard of comparison. I came to Europe and competed in the spring shows in Germany and France. It is very exhilarating and most instructive; there are so many people full of help—especially after a particularly bad go.

A last word of encouragement to those with an inclination to take up dressage is my father's advice: "Remember, Trish, you can still be doing this as a grandmother." Not, perhaps, a very exciting prospect for a teen-ager, yet I cannot think of another Olympic sport that can boast as much. In fact, one improves with age, especially as far as patience goes.

There are many unusual sights in an Olympic village, but one of the most unusual is the presence, mixed in with the cream of athletic perfection, of some wrinkled sexagenarian (or even septua-) limping along in a track suit—and quite possibly destined to win an Olympic gold medal in dressage!

Dressage as a Creative Art

Kyra (Mrs. Franklyn) Downton was hardly a younster when she first presented herself to the USET as a dressage candidate for the 1959 Pan American Games, and the story of how she got from eastern Russia to California via Shanghai reads like a novel. No USET rider has ever shown more unquenchable determination, however, or demonstrated more clearly that youth can be more a question of spirit than of chronology. The individual Pan American gold-medal winner in dressage at Winnipeg in 1967 and a member of the 1968 Olympic team, Mrs. Downton is currently working a new horse with an eye to renewed participation on the team.

TWO STRONG INTERESTS have been a continuous influence throughout my life—artistic creativity and horses. The earliest recollections of my childhood involve both. In later years they were merged into the sometimes satisfying, sometimes frustrating, but always fascinating creative art form with horses—dressage.

Picture a little three-year-old girl in a white party dress placed on a big white horse by some Russian cavalry officers. Then visualize a fast gallop along a narrow mountainous road with soldiers dashing madly after the runaway. That is my first recollection of riding.

Ever since that time, horses have held a great fascination for me. I remember running alongside the horse of my older brother, who was allowed to ride alone. On his more generous days, my brother would pull me up onto the saddle with him. It was his job to go to the post office each day for the mail. This was a big thing, and as I got old enough, I would bribe him to let me take his turn to go for the mail—because it involved a horse.

My father, being a cavalry officer, understood the attraction of children to the equine family. So one Easter, my brother and I were told that there were two rabbits in the stable for us. Rabbits, indeed! There were two donkeys, with the longest ears imaginable.

Father was correct. The donkeys occupied us completely, though I think we chased after them more than we rode. The animals seemed to plan just how and where they would buck us off. The gorgeous mountain country of eastern Russia where I was born provided many steep slopes where these devious beasts could unload their riders. Their constant tricks did not dull our interest, and we were mounted and riding again as soon as we caught them.

About this time, art entered my life in a very real way. My father, being a so-called "White" Russian, suddenly found that he was no longer a cavalry officer. To support and feed his family he tried farming literally "by the book," for he had no background other than his officer's schooling. Farming was a disaster, for everything that could go wrong did, and usually was not covered by his book. Fortunately, Father had natural artistic talents. He was good with his hands and did some wood carving. In the course of the wood carving, he would turn small tasks over to me. (Little did he know that I would develop a latent talent as a wood sculptor.) He could also paint, and devoted more and more of his time to paintings. If it were not for the sale of these paintings to Japan, I do not know how our family could have eaten.

Involved in the farming effort were two gray draft horses, purchased for work, but with so little inclination in that direction that I was allowed to do with them as I wished. What a thrill that was, and what a change from a narrow donkey to a huge draft horse! I am sure that they did not know we had legs at all, since we could just barely straddle them, but what fun!

Finally Father was able to arrange a visa for my mother to take me out of the country to go to school. Although it was planned otherwise, my brother and father were never able to follow us. Mother and I went to Shanghai, China, where I was placed in a convent. As it turned out, I was to be educated and raised in Shanghai, and I soon considered it my home.

Schooling occupied my life completely for a number of years. I was dropped into a culture that spoke either French or English. My native language was of little use except to communicate with the many other Russians who had migrated to Shanghai.

Horses had to be sidetracked while I was making this tremendous adjustment. I was a hard worker and got along well with the nuns. I suppose I was always given extra tasks because of my willingness, and it was not too long before I was a teacher's helper. (If the nuns could only know, though I am writing this article, I cannot spell English words to this day! Perhaps because as a child I learned Russian, which is wholly phonetic in its spelling, the gymnastics and contradictions of English spelling have never made any sense to me.)

My artistic inclinations were soon discovered by the nuns, and they proceeded to make maximum use of me. Whenever there was a drawing to make or a picture to paint or draw, the nuns would give me the job. In those days, you did as you were told without question. I would never have dreamed of saying no, consequently, the art work piled up. It seemed that there were frequent visits by high dignitaries of the church, and I had to paint religious pictures for presentation to them.

I continued in art work after I graduated from the convent. The nuns found me a job with an American company as a designer of Venetian lace. The detail and fineness of that work was not only difficult and tedious but also very hard on the eyes. Perhaps that period of working with excessive detail accounts for my preference for more smooth and sweeping lines in my art work of today.

Shanghai in those days was a busy, fascinating "Paris of the East." As time went on, we met many interesting people. Inevitably, an acquaintance asked if I would like to ride one of his horses, and somehow I gained almost immediate acceptance into the riding group because of my "ability." This amazing "ability" was not a matter of skill or evidence of any training, but depended entirely on my willingness to ride anywhere, to try anything and mainly to hang on and go faster than all others.

Before long I joined the hunt, which was a "paper hunt." This meant that the "fox" went ahead dropping or placing pieces of paper which the hunt followed. Obviously, it became a steeplechase of sorts. The first rider to finish was considered to have brought the fox to ground. We did not have jumps as they are known in this country and in Europe, but we jumped many broad ditches (probably 10′ to 16′ in width) used for irrigation and an occasional Chinese grave.

I continued with pleasure riding and hunting and graduated to having several saddle horses of my own. These were mostly imported, as the only local horses available were the Chinese ponies which were herded down from the north-central plains of China when they were seven or eight years old. By that age, the ponies were set in their ways and had mouths of steel. I also had several horses at the racetrack, which I took great pride in exercising myself.

I knew of several riding schools in Shanghai, but thought of them strictly as a place for beginners to go to learn to stay on a horse. That one might seriously study equitation or jumping technique, not to mention "dressage," was totally inconceivable to me. Daring and fearlessness seemed all that was necessary to get along in the horse world!

World War II brought a sudden halt to all of my horse activities. My home and horses were confiscated by the Japanese, and I was placed in a concentration camp. One of my favorite Thoroughbreds was shot by the Japanese, and another, a lovely gray mare, was sold. After the war was over, I learned that this mare was still located in a nearby stable. Technically, she should have been returned to me, but formal requests for her return fell on deaf ears.

So one holiday after several champagnes, my husband and I decided to go and see her. An English friend of ours was at the stable, and seeing my sad face as I looked at my mare, she felt very sorry for me. She marched over to us, slapped me on the back so hard that it almost sent me flying and said very firmly, "You just get the halter and take your horse home!" Her encouragement was all we needed, and we did as she suggested. All sorts of fireworks exploded the next day, but fortunately, the official directives were on my side and I was able to settle the matter by a small payment "to save face." At least after the horrors of the war and the concentration camp, I had my dear Blue Star to ride again.

Not too long after this, the economic and political pressures of the world began to change my life again, for it became more and more evident that China was going to go Communist. That is how I happened to become a Californian. The move was a major one for me. It meant again establishing a home, changing cultures, habits and in fact a whole way of life. This took a number of years.

During this period I managed first to find a horse to rent. This was very nice but did not satisfy me, so we purchased two horses. At that time, a horse was simply a horse to me, and I hesitate to tell you what those two looked like, or how they were bred. Let me simply say that I ended up training the one who was a Tennessee Walker (but who had fortunately never learned the Tennessee walk) well enough for my young teen-age daughter to win many jumping and three-day events with him.

By now the showing of hunters appealed to me, so we purchased two conformation hunters and I started working in earnest. Since I now realized that there was much more to riding, I looked for someone to give me lessons. That first instructor came very well recommended, and I was interested in everything he had to say and do. In retrospect, all I remember is that you should *never* touch the sides of the horse with your legs, and must sit with your spine curled under. How far riding in America has come since then!

The showing of hunters was fun, and one could take a great deal of pride in having really good-looking animals. We started going to many shows. However, the jumping was mostly in a ring, and I missed riding cross-country. Then several of our friends suggested that we all band together and start a hunt, and with about five other couples, we founded the Los Altos Hunt (now a full-fledged, recognized hunt). Originally, the field was the staff and the staff was the field, but as the hunt grew, I became an honorary whipper-in, and I loved it. My husband and I both worked very hard for the

Mrs. Franklyn Downton and Kadett, the third successive Pan American Games dressage gold medalists for the United States, at Winnipeg in 1967.

hunt for many years, as did many others, and enjoyed every minute of it. Still, the distances involved in trying to do something like that in California made it very time-consuming.

My showing of hunters continued, but I now sought events at which there were outside courses. One of the first big ones I remember was Pebble Beach, where there was a combination hunter show and three-phase event. A rider could perform a cross-country course in a hunter class and also have it counted in the three-phase. I entered only the hunter classes, and learned, at the end of the show, that I was Reserve Champion. The jumps, the courses, the footing and the people were all so beautiful. Dick Collins, who ran the show, congratulated me and remarked that if I had only entered the dressage class I would have been the winner of the three-phase event as well. *This sparked my first real interest in dressage.*

At first this interest was limited to the rather basic dressage necessary for the three-day events which were just then gaining popularity. I stumbled even on the word "basic," for I suddenly realized that I did not have the "basics" of riding and probably did not know what they really were.

I started reading every book on the training of horses that I could get my hands on. I gradually worked through most of the books and started taking instruction. What a fascinating and challenging field of endeavor dressage proved to be!

It was our intention to take our daughter on a vacation trip to Europe as part of her education, and we decided to attend the 1956 Olympic Equestrian Games in Stockholm. Our trip was marvelous, and we enjoyed the Games along with quite a Californian contingent. The end result of our trip was the purchase of one of the horses that had been on the German three-day team. This wonderful mare had failed to place because of a bad fall near the end of the cross-country course, but she had won the dressage portion of the event. I learned a lot from her, and she produced several fine foals.

Still studying, reading and taking lessons, I was impatient about my progress and the horses I had to work with. However, I knew enough to recognize that dressage was indeed an art form. (I remember a statement in one of the books I read to the effect that dressage was "the ballet of horsemanship.") Dressage was something I decided to pursue diligently, but there was very little activity in this field and so few riders that I did not have much opportunity to observe others working. There was so much I wanted to know and do that I did not feel I was progressing fast enough.

A chance came to purchase a horse in Europe and spend some time there, and I purchased my dear Kadett. Though I thought he was trained to a higher level than he was—the fault of the purchaser and not the seller—I enjoyed my new horse. I loved seeing all the people who were interested in dressage, but still faced many rough questions and problems. How do you teach a horse piaffe, passage, pirouettes at the canter . . . ?

How beautiful the performances I saw in Europe proved to be. Here was a sport in which anyone can participate, at any level, with pride and enjoyment. The enjoyment can be just as gratifying at the low levels as at the higher, for it is the unison and molding together of the efforts of rider and horse that produce the performance. The recognition of this beauty made me work harder and harder. A very strong and fortunate factor in the rapidly increasing interest in dressage is that there are no barriers of sex or age, and riders from all walks of life can compete on an even basis. There are youngsters and grandparents, those who are just struggling along and those who are titled or very wealthy.

The goals that I could see so plainly were a constant driving force. Through many heartbreaks and trials and errors, I finally started making progress. I took instruction from quite a few different people; from some I learned a great deal and from others, not so much. I was always hoping that the total answer would be found around the corner in a single individual, but this, of course, is not and never will be possible. It is the rider himself who must make the progress.

I finally reached the point where I could compete with Kadett at the Grand Prix level of dressage. The Pan American Games in Chicago and the

Kadett and Kyra Downton at the piaffe, at home in California.

Olympics in Tokyo were coming up, and the USET conducted trials for the team. With high hopes, Kadett and I entered and did our best, but it was not good enough and we were not selected. From the heights of aspiration to the depression of rejection can be (and was) a heartbreak! After a while recovery came, as thank God it does, and I returned to hard work again. After training and retraining, I decided to try competing in Europe.

Kadett and I entered many of the large shows in Germany. To see the number of people interested in dressage and to compete with so many riders was highly stimulating. There were many young riders, but there were also many considerably older than I. We did quite well. To take part in the Aachen show, one of the largest horse shows in the world, was especially exciting.

One of the highlights of my trip was tying with the world champion in one of the classes at Cologne. The placings were to be determined by a Kür, in which each rider composes his own test. Unfortunately, the announcement of the conditions was given in German, and I did not completely understand the time allowance. My test went very well, but I unknowingly exited before my allotted time was up, incurring a penalty. I was given seventh place instead of first or second because of this mistake. Again, my initial feelings of elation for tying with the world champion were soon to be followed by depression.

However, when the USET trials for the 1967 Pan American Games at

The "indescribable sensation"—Kyra Downton on the winner's podium at the Winnipeg Pan American Games, listening to her country's anthem as its flag is raised.

Winnipeg were announced, I felt confident in entering Kadett, and this time I was fortunate enough to be selected as a member of the team.

On we went to Winnipeg! I was thrilled to be representing my country, for like the convert in religion, as a naturalized citizen I am in many ways a stronger American than the average.

An aside for those interested in anecdotes: I told one person in California and one in New Jersey that if I made the team, I would win the gold medal. Luckily, my prediction came true in Winnipeg, and I did win the individual gold medal. The sensation of standing on the podium in the stadium and being presented with a medal while your country's national anthem is played and the flag of your country is raised is indescribable!

I returned home full of enthusiasm and fire. Thinking of the possibility of being on the team for the Olympics in Mexico, I felt that I should have some supercharged form of instruction to prepare me for the heightened competition. As several times before, I was looking for the one answer to everything. I know that I erred. I made the team, but my performance in Mexico was a crushing blow; I should and could have done much better. I returned home dejected and crushed, but quickly put myself to work, every minute of the day. Whenever I am unhappy, I work very hard so that I will have no time for self-pity. I started sculpting in wood. In four months I had my first sculptures accepted in a leading gallery in San Francisco. The subject? Horses, of course! My style is a classic contemporary, and I have since sold well and have pieces in a number of galleries around the country. My subjects now vary from horses and other animals to the female form. I find sculpting an artistic challenge similar to dressage, and dressage keeps me fit enough to do the hard work required of a sculptor and play some tennis in addition.

My fervor for dressage continues as strong as ever. I have trained one Thoroughbred to the Grand Prix level and am showing him, and am bringing another Thoroughbred along and hope to have him ready for the Montreal Olympic Trials. (What a quirk of fate that a Russian would buy a horse named Zhivago!) My two granddaughters, Laurie, aged fourteen, and Kyra, aged eleven, both ride, and I hope someday they too may have the opportunity to represent their country.

A Feeling for Dressage

JOHN W. WINNETT JR.

Not many riders have represented their country in both jumping and dressage, but "Jacques" Winnett has done it, and on a championship level at that: as a French resident he rode in the very first world jumping championship at Paris in 1953, some twenty-one years before he captained our dressage team at Copenhagen. Also the captain of our 1972 Olympic dressage squad and the 1975 Pan American gold medalists, Winnett lives in Tuxedo Park, New York, where an excellent cellar attests to his continuing interest in wine.

"WHAT'S DRESSAGE ALL ABOUT?" someone once asked. The best answer was provided by the great French authority, General l'Hotte, many years ago. He said, "To make the horse calm, forward, straight and light." With these words he created a sparkling light which has ever since thrown clarity along the entire road to follow. These words, in essence, gave birth to modern academic equitation, as well as establishing guidelines for competition as we know it in the modern era.

First, a thorough study of the horse's natural abilities had to be undertaken; horsemen had to understand how the horse's muscles and joints coordinated with each other. It was soon found that training was simply a systematic program of gymnastic exercises of the horse's body that led to proper muscular development and the utmost flexibility of the animal's spinal column and joints. The French called this *dressage*.

In order to explain further the meaning of dressage, I would like to take you back a few years. As a young boy, I lived in Paris. My family had little money at the time. It was in 1938, shortly before the beginning of World

230

John Winnett, captain of the gold-medal-winning U.S. team at the 1975 Pan American Games in Mexico, with his Games mount, Leopardi.

War II. My riding was very limited and restricted to pleasure rides on rented stable horses in the Bois de Boulogne.

As I remember, my first break came when I was twelve years old. My uncle arranged a meeting for me with the Duchesse de la Trémouille, a grand old lady who owned the Montevideo *manège* and many top-class jumpers. Madame de la Trémouille, sensing my burning desire to ride, invited me to her stable and turned me over to Vincent Laurent, a Saumur graduate and a formidable teacher/trainer of his time.

I was soon made aware that learning to ride was not always glamorous and fun. In order to earn my lessons, I had to groom, feed and muck out, and was always assigned the worst horses in the stable for my lessons. During these years, M. Laurent seldom allowed me a pair of stirrups, my lessons being restricted to body exercises on horseback.

M. Laurent jumped his horses once a week on the longe line. On these days, he would often order me to jump up on their backs, and without the benefit of a saddle or reins, I would be longed over jumps like a sack of potatoes. It was not uncommon for him to erect verticals of 5′ and in-and-out sets at one stride. Luckily, most of his horses had manes, and I can honestly say that this adornment has since held my deepest gratitude.

Though I looked at M. Laurent as a god, I surely hated his guts. But as I soon learned, that was why he was known to be such a good teacher.

My graduation from the torture of the longe line came unexpectedly one day in the early spring of 1943. There was a horse in the stable whose name I do not recall, but whom I will never forget. He had developed the defense of rearing, and he went at it with such force that he often turned over backward on his owner, causing the poor man great pain and embarrassment.

On this day M. Laurent addressed me by my name, for the first time in three years. Then he ordered me to take this horse out to the Bois de Boulogne and ride him twice around the outer perimeter, adding that I should not return to the stable until this had been done. I can hardly convey my reactions to this command, for they seemed compounded of equal parts of amazement, pride and fear. (Subsequently I was to encounter the same emotion once again, when a flight instructor opened the plane door, hoisted himself out on the end of the runway for a well-deserved rest and muttered the deafening words, "You're on your own.")

Fortunately, during my three years at Montevideo I had made many friends among the grooms, and my camaraderie with old Gaston, the head lad, was to pay off on this day. Gaston told me that my only chance lay in a bottle of red wine. Wine was not a stranger to either of us, and I thought he had something else in mind when we set off for the local drinking spa.

Gaston ordered two brandies and a cheap bottle of red Nicolas. We drank the brandies, and on our way back to the stable, he handed me the bottle of wine and told me, "When he tries to rear, you must hit him between the ears with everything you have."

Armed with thick gloves, a heavy heart and a bottle of cheap wine, I set out with nature's noblest beast at an extended walk for the Porte Dauphine and the entrance of the Bois. For a while, nothing happened, but as we entered the bridle path—very suddenly, he reared.

I was caught off guard and could not immediately react. We continued a few more meters, and then, in a split second, I felt trouble building up again. Before the horse had a chance to rear a second time, I struck a hard

Winnett and his 1972 Olympic mount, Reinald, in the medium trot at Aachen. (Compare this with the extended trot in the preceding picture.)

A deceptively difficult movement: Winnett and Reinald perform the extended walk at Munich in the 1972 Olympic Games.

blow between his ears. The result was equally startling to us both. He fell to his knees as I endeavored to rid myself of what was left of the broken bottle. With red wine dripping everywhere, my mount reluctantly regained his feet and staggered forward. His behavior for the rest of the ride was impeccable, and to the best of my knowledge, he never reared again.

Needless to say, I never revealed either to the owner of the horse or to Vincent Laurent the means of my success, but both gentlemen were ecstatic. The owner had a reformed horse and M. Laurent had a good student. That evening I spent what was left of my allowance on Gaston at the local bistro. It was a good day for everyone.

I relate this incident because it marked one of the most important crossroads in my riding career. From that day on, M. Laurent adopted me as one of his protégés, and began to teach me the basics of low school. This in essence embodies the basic gymnastic development of the horse's body and its longitudinal and lateral flexibility, thus preparing the horse for a career in jumping, eventing or, indeed, high school. The latter embodies the highest degree of suppleness and collection the horse can attain, which is demonstrated through such classical figures as the piaffer, passage, pirouettes and flying changes at every stride.

It was only at this period that I realized what riding was all about. During those three years of basic training, I had somehow developed a strong seat and the ability to coordinate the use of my hands and legs. I had also developed the ability to feel. Without this ability, proper training of a horse would be impossible.

While my lessons became more sophisticated and I was now allowed to ride a few good horses, my tutelage still remained simple. I was not supposed to read books on equestrian theory (although I ventured to read Fillis and Guérinière late at night) which might confuse my progress. I was made to follow M. Laurent's advice, which has since accompanied me

233

through life with its wisdom: "The simplest things are the most difficult. It is through striving for perfection in the elementary movements that the advanced movements become harmonious and easy."

Please forgive me for reminiscing about these personal experiences, but they do underline a few basic laws concerning dressage. Now let me comment on them more directly. First, I must reiterate that the early development of the rider's seat, position and coordination of his hands and legs cannot be overemphasized. No matter how advanced the rider is, he should never stop trying to improve on these fundamentals, for they are his tools.

Next comes "feel," for it has been said that riding is feeling, and surely the rider's feel for the right moment plays a very important part in dressage training. Referring back to the bottle of red wine, what actually happened? We do not have to be concerned whether it was the wine dripping down his face or the hard blow that influenced the horse; what made it work was feel and timing. Because I could feel the defense build and stopped it in a fraction of a second before it exploded, I left an indelible mark on the horse's memory.

In training, we must remember that the psychology of obedience is based on the principle of contiguous association. It works like this: When impressions are produced simultaneously, only one impression needs to register on the horse's memory in order for the other impressions to be communicated immediately to his memory bank. It is then sufficient to follow obedience immediately with a reward and disobedience immediately with a punishment until the horse loses all semblance of resistance. By repetition the conscious associations will transform themselves into unconscious associations, reflexes and absolute obedience.

Earlier I referred to dressage as a systematic program of gymnastic exercises of the horse's body. While this is accurate, it nevertheless is an oversimplification of a great art. There are numerous training methods which, if followed systematically, can produce good results. I have seen riders follow a particular method religiously and attain success. But riders are artists; as prima donnas of their art, they like to think that their chosen method is the only means to an end, and they will argue passionately in its defense. The fact is, they are arguing over different approaches that eventually all lead to the same result.

It is dangerous to be brainwashed by one method, school or, indeed, book. Each horse is different and must be analyzed carefully before his training is undertaken, just as any artist must study his subject. What are the horse's eating habits? Sleeping pattern? Energy? What is his conformation? How are his gaits? Where is his stiffness? The great dressage artist will maintain an open mind and formulate, through study of each horse, a training schedule specially tailored to each subject. He will not train a horse with a book in hand, or always employ the same approach; he will use his experience and intelligence to vary his method to suit the situation.

I spoke of my jumping experience. While many people, especially in our country, do not like to associate jumping with dressage, I would like to express the conviction that jumping and cross-country riding are among the most important phases of training a dressage horse. In fact, I have never seen a good dressage horse who wasn't a good jumper, and vice versa. Jumping is one of the best exercises to obtain longitudinal flexibility, and riding cross-country over varied terrain improves natural impulsion, balance and cadence. Outdoors, the horse is more relaxed and his rider can ride him through the neck at a much earlier stage. Also, when the horse has become sufficiently supple and is ready for high collection, what could be easier than collecting while moving toward the stable on the return home? At this stage a horse will reach his highest degree of animation, and a clever rider can take full advantage of this natural situation to obtain the first steps of piaffer and passage or a few strides of canter on the spot in preparation for pirouettes.

If a horse is to be trained successfully to Grand Prix level, it should, in my opinion, be done in the simplest and most natural way possible. Simplicity and naturalness are the true tests of nobility; so should they be the true tests of beauty in the Grand Prix horse.

If the rider has acquired a good seat and can coordinate the use of his hands and legs, he will be able to feel his way along the long road ahead. While on the road, the rider must always strive to perfect the simple things —"calm, forward, straight and light."

I myself have over the years gained a certain theoretical knowledge by reading articles and books. However, I like to think that the small success I have attained comes not so much from my theoretical knowledge as from the years of practical experience given to me by the many horses I have ridden and loved, and who have given so generously of themselves. Through their generosity and feel they have taught me far more than words ever could.

Winnett and Mario, working at the passage in a practice session at home.

The American
Dressage Outlook

BENGT LJUNGQUIST

A rider since he was ten, Bengt Ljungquist became a career officer in the Swedish cavalry, often competed abroad with its horse-show team and was several times the national dressage champion. Nonetheless, he was a four-time Olympian (and twice a medalist) as a fencer before becoming a dressage Olympian at Tokyo in 1964. After retiring as a colonel, Ljungquist came to the United States in 1970, settling in Potomac, Maryland, where he quickly established himself as an outstanding dressage coach. His first USET assignment was as coach of the 1974 World Championship squad, his second as coach of the gold-medal-winning Pan American Games team the following year.

As is well known, European dressage traditions are much older than those in the United States. Equestrian sports were first included in the Olympic Games in Stockholm in 1912. At that time the military was the backbone of the sport, and all the competitors were officers. The cavalry, the infantry, the artillery and the maintenance and supply units of all armies depended on horses for transportation. Young horses, called remounts, were trained at the regiments by officers, noncommissioned officers and corporals. These men often stayed with the military for many years and acquired considerable skill and experience by virtue of the numbers of horses they trained and the technical help and advice available within their units.

For example, in my regiment in Sweden we had six hundred horses, of whom one hundred were remounts who were trained for two years before being used for duty in the squadrons. Competing with the best of these horses in various equestrian events was considered part of an officer's job. Officers were able to compete regularly, as the entire cost of stabling, transport and grooms was covered. In the 1930s, however, most armies became completely motorized, and the military riders were retrained to handle tanks, armored cars and trucks. This was often the end of their equestrian activity, though some of them did instruct in their free time or after eventual retirement.

After World War II, civilian riders began to dominate the equestrian scene. Of course, as the military riders gradually disappeared, so too did much of their knowledge of basic training, and it became harder and harder to find skilled instruction. Unfortunately, very few of the horsemen trained in the military are still active today, and the problem of finding thoroughly trained instructors has now become acute in all countries interested in equestrian sport.

I believe that finding and using good instructors is essential to the future of the sport. People who are taking up riding for the first time need both help to learn the principles of horsemanship and inspiration to work for excellence. In the last five years the interest in dressage has spread rapidly in the United States; however, the talented people who have been attracted to it must get proper instruction or their interest will drop. If riders and horses don't continue to improve, we will end up with a broad layer of mediocre performers but lack the brilliant riders who serve as an inspiration and challenge to the novice. A sport needs stars to develop.

The United States is not alone in this lack of good instructors, though

Colonel Bengt Ljungquist, shown in uniform as a member of the Swedish Olympic dressage team in 1964. His ride at Tokyo was his fifth Olympic appearance!

it is little comfort that many other countries share the same problem. If we improve the quality of instruction we can rapidly improve the training of our horses. Many Americans now buy dressage horses trained in Europe. Since the really desirable horses are seldom for sale, we often end up with second-rate horses. Hence I believe that our motto should be: American riders on American horses, trained in America.

I'm convinced that this goal is within reach. To attain it, we must spread the knowledge of sound basic schooling throughout the equestrian community. The horses developed by the military riders of old often remained sound and fresh to an advanced age because of the long and careful basic training they received. Too often, nowadays, young horses are asked to accomplish feats for which they are unprepared both physically and psychologically. Thus traumatized, they fail to fully realize their potential. Too many riders are thrilled by the "fancy things," forgetting the basics. It is important to remember that good paces, rhythm, suppleness, contact (when the horse is on the bit), impulsion, straightness and finally collection are the pillars of dressage.

Fortunately, this "fancy things" attitude is gradually changing, and the importance of good basic training is becoming more generally accepted by serious dressage students. It gets increasingly hard to win a ribbon in the lower levels as more and more horses are trained according to correct principles, and that is for the best. It should take a well-schooled horse to win. With correct basics, riders will be able to climb the ladder to the higher international levels.

I cannot emphasize enough the importance of good basic training in those horses destined for international levels. A young rider recently asked me, "Do you think I can perform the collected stuff?" (She meant piaffe, passage, pirouettes and so on.) Of course the skilled rider and the suitable well-trained horse will be able to perform the "collected stuff," but they must have the foundation well laid. So often one sees riders performing the difficult movements without suppleness and ease. Still worse, the paces between these advanced movements are not acceptable, for the horse does not go forward in a relaxed, rhythmical way. A horse does not become a fourth-level horse because he can do a flying change. Advanced schooling takes time, for the horse must develop, muscle up and mature. Only "slow

The 1975 Pan American Games gold-medal-winning team at Mexico (from left) Edith Master, Dorothy Morkis, coach Bengt Ljungquist, John Winnett and Hilda Gurney. Mrs. Morkis and Miss Gurney were the individual bronze and silver medalists, respectively.

The Ljungquist prescription—American riders on American horses, trained in America—as exemplified by Hilda Gurney and the California-bred Keen, individual silver medalists at the 1975 Pan American Games in Mexico.

and steady" will give the right result. Patient daily work pays off in the long run.

The recipe that turns good fundamentals into international-level rides is very simple, but we have not yet developed a sure mechanism for locating the talented riders and horses and bringing them together for training. I believe that ultimately, the dressage community must establish its own permanent training center to bridge the gap between the private individual working alone and the rider who is sufficiently advanced to work with the USET. Prospective horses could be trained both by the experienced members of the team and by prospective members. After all, talented riders who don't have the money to buy a horse or pay for instruction must still be helped or we lose their talent. Such a center could also be open to those instructors who would be influential in raising the dressage standards in their home area, and would be an excellent site for judges' forums.

Our problem is not one of raw material, for in my opinion, there are many talented riders in this country. However, they need instruction as well as a clearer conception of the type of horse necessary for competitive dressage. There are also many suitable dressage horses in this country, but somehow they don't get to the dressage ring. A good horse should make you catch your breath and cause your heart to beat a little faster. Regrettably, I seldom get that feeling when judging the lower levels where the prospective international horses should be; yet I am sure that those special horses exist, undiscovered, in backyards and pastures all around the country.

Nonetheless, the quality of the horses is improving, and it is clear that more and more riders understand what to look for in a prospective dressage horse. I should add that it isn't necessarily the flashy, glamorous horse who has the best potential. There is an Arab saying, "If you look for a horse without faults, you will never have a horse in your barn," and it is true. Indeed, some of the top dressage horses in the world are no beauties, but they move well and straight and are amenable to the training that creates brilliance.

Reschooling spoiled horses from the racetrack or jumping arena is very frustrating. These horses often have temperament problems because their trainers, in trying to produce a quick result, have pushed them too hard. Often their mouths have been ruined and they have no confidence in the rider. It is usually easier to start with a young, relatively untrained horse and give him his thorough basic schooling yourself.

Once we have horses and riders with sound basics reaching the international levels, they must go to Europe for competition, both to gain experience and to become known. It is a fact (though it should not be so) that an unknown rider is usually scored lower than one whose reputation precedes him. Our riders must be able to go proudly—and not entirely at their own expense—to compete with confidence with the European riders. Too often in the past Americans have ridden without the special flair that makes a winner. Our best horses and riders must go with a fighting spirit to meet and beat the Europeans on their home ground. There is no place for excessive humility or an inferiority complex in international competition.

Another part of the recipe is for us to develop a corps of judges who are trained to look for the essential basics in a test, rather than leaning too heavily on technicalities and geometric accuracy. Riders and judges must be in complete agreement regarding performance requirements. This problem is well on its way to being solved, as coordinated judges' forums and

Edith Master (shown here on Sergeant), a member of the 1968 and 1972 Olympic dressage teams, has accomplished most of her training abroad. Ljungquist hopes that such sacrifices will become unnecessary, but acknowledges the need for European competitive experience.

apprentice judge programs gradually increase the number of qualified people. I hope that a "sewing machine" without presence and liveliness will never again be a winner.

I hope, too, that the endless discussions about national dressage styles will be kept in proper perspective. The different styles (German vs. French, for instance) are becoming more or less amalgamated into a single standard defined by the FEI, and the current rulebook is very clear in describing the requirements of the tests. Of course, there will always be small variations of style within the dimensions of the tests, as the individual riders are artists and their performances will not and should not all be cast from the same mold.

On balance, the future for dressage in the United States looks encouraging. From the tremendous interest and devotion that is now evident should come many good riders and horses. The time is ripe for a breakthrough in the international dressage world, for while our interest in dressage is rapidly expanding, most European nations are having increasing difficulties in fielding complete teams. Germany is perhaps the sole exception.

There is a long way to go, to be sure, but with determination, enthusiasm and intelligence, nothing is impossible. It is worth remembering that the Russian dressage team at Helsinki in 1952 made a very poor showing; in 1956 they were much improved, and by 1960 they had a gold-medal winner in Filatov. The U.S. jumping and three-day-event teams have shown that our country's resources in horses and riders, properly developed, are a match for any in the world. Let us do the same in dressage!

Caring for the USET Horses

GEORGE SIMMONS

Born in Massachusetts, George Simmons has spent his whole life "around horses," except for a stint with the U.S. Marines during World War II. A versatile horseman, he held a trainer's license at the New England tracks before joining the USET in 1961. Since then, as USET stable manager, he has been exposed at one time or another to virtually everything that can happen to an international jumper or dressage or three-day-event horse.

BASICALLY, there is nothing very fancy about the way the USET horses are cared for—we simply give them the very best care we know how. We try to deal with most problems by avoiding them, but with the competition horse this is not always possible. Fortunately, when difficult problems arise the team usually has access to the very finest veterinary advice.

Through the years, however, many people have asked me how the USET handles the basic routine of horse care and feeding, and how we customarily deal with the common problems that occur. Perhaps this is a good opportunity to answer these questions.

Ordinarily, the USET horses are fed twice a day. The exact times of feeding vary according to our program. During the winter months when the horses are not showing and are in very light training, our feedings are at 7 A.M. and 4 P.M. In the summer months our normal feeding times are 6 A.M. and 4 P.M. When we're showing in Europe they are fed at 7 A.M. and from 7 to 8:30 P.M., depending on the time we have completed showing.

The particular menu varies, depending upon the individual horse and the type of training the horse is in. We have to control horses' diets because

Among his other duties, a USET stable manager gets a graduate course in building and measuring fences. Here George Simmons (center) confers with Dennis Haley (left) and jumping coach Bert de Nemethy as riders Steinkraus and Kusner await the new combination. The scene is the schooling area at Tokyo in 1964.

some of them retain fat easily; these horses are bedded on wood shavings, while others not prone to weight or to eating their bedding are bedded on straw.

Hay is fed according to the size and the diet of each horse. Some get sixteen pounds per day and then others as much as twenty-four pounds.

We feed steam-rolled oats that are dust-free and toasted steam-rolled barley to horses that get too full of themselves on oats. We also feed a wheat bran and a mixed feed that is very palatable. It is packed in a paper bag, always fresh, easy to eat, quick to digest. It is a molasses blend and light bulky mix that tempts even fussy eaters to dig in and clean up every last bite.

The amount of feed varies according to the horse and his training. In competition and in heavy training the average morning feed is four quarts of oats (or barley) and the evening feed is eight to ten quarts, consisting of four quarts of oats (or barley), three or four quarts of bran and one to two quarts of mixed feed, to which we add carrots and a supplement.

Salt is fed by salt bricks, held by a plastic holder attached to the wall of every stall, and fresh water is in every stall at all times.

When the horses are not in regular training the feed is cut back to two quarts of oats (or barley) in the morning and two quarts of oats (or barley), two quarts of bran and one quart of mixed feed in the evening, plus the carrots and supplement.

After the morning grain the horses are given their hay, and the water buckets are taken out, washed and refilled and returned to the stalls. The stalls are then cleaned out and any additional bedding required is added. Bedding is changed completely every week.

The routine grooming consists of light currycombing and brushing, and

243

picking out the feet. The tail is never brushed, since this excessively thins the hair; instead, we pick the tail out by hand.

For the protection of the front cannon bone, ankle and tendon we use felt galloping boots. For the protection of the horse's quarters (back of the foot above the hoof) we use rubber bell boots. If the horse tends to interfere behind, we use a leather brushing boot. We use the other protective boots more or less routinely.

After every training session, when the horse is returned to the stable the tack is removed and the horse is checked carefully for any possible injuries. In the summer months the horse is generally given a warm-water bath with a dash of astringent bracer. He is then covered with a light cooler and is hand-walked until he is dry, after which he is brushed again and his feet are dressed with a hoof dressing. If the horse has had strenuous work or schooling, his legs are braced with a light liniment or alcohol and then bandaged all around in rest bandages. The reason for the bandaging is to increase circulation, which will help any slight strains or mild bruises. There are times when a horse's hooves will get very dry and hard, so we pack them with hoof packing to keep them moist and flexible. (The horse's foot is like a foundation of any building. Without the proper angle and balancing you can run into difficulties. Therefore, you have to be very careful that the proper shoeing is maintained.)

In colder weather, after the horse has been exercised or schooled he is not given a bath, but the saddle marks are sponged off and the horse is then rubbed dry and groomed again.

When do we braid a horse's mane? Usually when we are competing in a Nations Cup, a Grand Prix or a major jump-off class like the George V Cup, and for all parades. The braids are sewn in with thread to make a neater appearance.

Many people ask how we transport our horses to Europe. We transport them from the stable to the airport by van. There they are unloaded from the van into units of two standing stalls to a pallet (flat metal platform) which is on a conveyor that has rollers. The conveyor is then pulled to the airplane and the pallets are pushed onto a lift which brings them up to the cargo hatch of the plane. The pallets are then pushed from the lift into the plane, whose floor has connecting rollers, and once inside they are pushed back to the tail of the plane and locked in place. The same procedure is followed, two by two, until all the horses are loaded. Hay and water are provided in flight. The airlines provide a leather collar which is placed around the horse's neck and fastened to rings on the stall to keep him from rearing.

On the plane, as a safety precaution, we use head bumpers made of leather and felt to protect the head. We also use a one-half-inch nylon rope made into a war bridle. The ends of the rope are put through rings on the

At right, air transport in the 1950s: Bob Freels leads Reno Kirk down the ramp after the long flight to Hamburg, Germany, in 1956. In those days, stalls were brought into the plane individually and erected one by one. Below, air transport in the 1970s: Big jet aircraft have sharply reduced both flying and loading times. These stalls and their pallet will be rolled onto the scissors elevator being positioned under the cargo hatch; the horses won't leave them until they're on the ground again on the other side of the ocean.

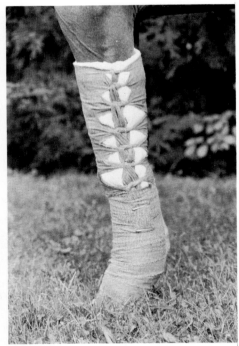

At left, Main Spring models a head bumper and the form of war bridle the USET uses during air shipment. At right, the spider bandage with its supporting short bandage that keeps it from slipping. Note that the knots in the spider are *not* secured, so that they will give a little when the knee is bent.

stall, which gives us much more control of the horse should he become upset.

Are the horses tranquilized before shipping? Certain bad shippers are tranquilized before leaving the stable, and all horses are routinely tranquilized before they are put on the plane and again about one hour before landing.

What are some of the common injuries that occur with a competition horse? One of the more common injuries with jumpers is the big knee. As soon as we see any evidence of this injury, the horse is hosed with cold water for forty-five to sixty minutes, or put in a whirlpool, to reduce the inflammation and to prevent further hemorrhaging. After this a poultice (usually Antiphlogistine) is placed on the horse's knee. The poultice is covered with brown paper before the cotton is applied, and we do the horse up in a spider bandage as well as bandage the leg. We use a spider instead of a regular bandage because it allows the knee more flexibility, and we bandage the leg to keep the spider in place. This treatment may be continued until all the inflammation has disappeared. Then if the knee is still larger than normal we sweat it for several days. As a rule this accomplishes the desired result. If the injury still has not been corrected it may be necessary to apply a blister, but this is not generally resorted to without veterinary advice.

246

The next common problem is the tendon injury. If a horse receives a minor bruise or injury to the tendon while schooling or in competition, we again start treatment with cold water and poulticing. Once the inflammation is out, to tighten the tendon we brace it with a liniment. If the injury is severe and looks like the start of a bowed tendon, we first put the leg in ice for about six hours. Then we poultice it for about eighteen hours, put it back in ice and then back in a poultice, alternating heat and cold until all the inflammation is gone. Afterward we then try to tighten the tendon with a liniment. If this is not satisfactory blistering may be necessary, which means a long recovery period of three or four months.

Obviously, whenever the trauma is severe we consult with our veterinarians, and as stable manager, I also work closely with the team vets in setting up and administering our parasite-control and immunization programs. Further details of team practices in this regard will be found elsewhere in this book.

To conclude, I would like to turn to a few more specialized questions that are often asked:

Do extremes in altitude changes affect horses?
A. A high altitude does affect the horses, and before they can enter competition it takes about a month to get them acclimated.

What do you consider good stabling conditions?
A. It is best for the horses' health to be kept in a stable that has plenty of daylight and fresh air and is kept clean. In summer, the stable should be kept as free of flies and mosquitoes as possible; the stable should be fogged at least once a day, or equipped with metered anti-insect sprays.

Do you believe in paddocking?
A. Yes, I believe that turning a nervous and high-strung horse out in a paddock will do the horse a world of good. Paddocking makes a horse more settled and quiet, and it also improves a good feeling horse. In lieu of paddocking, turns on a mechanical hot-walker can also be beneficial.

How are horses affected by water and feeding in foreign countries?
A. So far in traveling to the various countries we find there is very little effect, but we make a big effort to maintain the quality of feed. At worst, the finicky eaters may back off for a day or two.

Do you allow people to feed your horses sugar, carrots and/or apples?
A. No. We do not like people to feed our horses "goodies" because it contributes to the bad habits of pawing and getting upset. However, we often add carrots directly to the feed.

The Veterinary Aspect

JOSEPH C. O'DEA, D.V.M.

A native of New York State's famous Genessee Valley, Dr. O'Dea first encountered the USET while serving as show veterinarian for the National Horse Show, and shortly thereafter was named the team's official veterinarian for the 1956 Olympic Games. He remained in this post through the 1975 Pan American Games, resigning only in order to serve as the FEI's veterinary technical delegate at the 1976 Olympics. A graduate of Cornell and a past president of the American Association of Equine Practitioners, Dr. O'Dea is himself an active Thoroughbred breeder at his own Roscommon Stud in Geneseo, New York.

Bringing competition horses to peak condition and keeping them there requires considerable veterinary sophistication, and dealing with the kinds of injuries and wear-and-tear that afflict any athlete from time to time is no simpler. Through the years the USET has taken pains to enlist the most highly skilled assistance obtainable, both for horses lent to it and those which it owned outright, and it has been fortunate in having had made available to it the services of some of the most distinguished equine practitioners in the world. Among the many who have given freely of their time and skill it is only fair to acknowledge the special relationships that existed between the USET and a brilliantly innovative orthopedic surgeon, the late Dr. Jacques Jenny. However, mention must also be made of the special contributions of the teaching staffs of the University of Pennsylvania and Cornell University veterinary colleges, and such noted private practitioners

Dr. Joseph O'Dea, at left, with USET President Whitney Stone, seems to be evaluating a dubious soundness case in this picture from the early 1960s. The role of USET veterinarian demands great judgment and wide experience, for much depends on his decision.

as Doctors Lohmeyer, Simenson, Teigland, Wright, Reed, McCashin, Marks, Leslie, and many others who have assisted the team in this country, not to mention the foreign veterinarians who have rendered assistance abroad from time to time.

The first years of the USET's existence were mostly concerned, from the veterinary point of view, with the alleviation of injuries, arthritic degeneration and respiratory problems and the establishment of sound standard procedures for the prevention of disease. In the past quarter-century, advances have been made in all of these areas, and the team has kept abreast with them as well as with the use of some products (such as the tranquilizers and phenylbutazone) that did not exist at all a quarter-century ago.

For the purposes of this article I would like to review the USET's experience and current practices in five separate areas that may prove of current interest and value to other horsemen: (1) immunization procedures and the prevention of infectious disease; (2) parasite control; (3) the use of tranquilizers in shipping; (4) considerations involved in the use of phenylbutazone; and (5) considerations involved in the accommodation of competition horses to high altitudes.

1. IMMUNIZATION PROCEDURES

Probably the area of greatest advance in veterinary medicine in recent years has been in the development and refinement of immunization and testing procedures for various infectious diseases. The following is a summary of the practices the USET has adopted for protection against the more common diseases, and they are the same practices that I would recommend to any horse owner.

249

ESTABLISHING AND MAINTAINING IMMUNITY TO TETANUS ("LOCKJAW")

Tetanus is a wound infection caused by the anaerobic bacterium *Clostridium tetani*. The symptoms are well known and characterized by a high mortality rate once developed, but fortunately they can be easily and efficiently prevented.

All horses should be immunized against tetanus. To effect protection, each horse over three months of age should receive two doses of tetanus toxoid, administered intramuscularly four to eight weeks apart, followed by an annual booster of a single dose of tetanus toxoid.

Though foals from immunized mares should derive substantial protection from the colostrum (first milk) of the dam, the degree of immunity thus obtained is variable. It is suggested that the newborn foal receive 1500 units of tetanus antitoxin subcutaneously to protect against infection via the navel.

Whenever a deeply penetrating puncture, or other wound, is experienced, particularly around the foot, lower leg or face, a tetanus toxoid booster may be administered to horses that have been previously vaccinated with toxoid. If the injured horse has *not* been previously protected with toxoid, it should receive a 1500-unit dose of tetanus antitoxin instead.

Warning: Tetanus antitoxin is made from the blood of hyperimmunized horses. Certain horses may become sensitized to the protein in the antitoxin, and administration of a second dose may result in severe allergic reactions, shock or even death. It is advisable not to administer tetanus antitoxin within six months of a previous administration.

INFLUENZA

Influenza is a generalized disease caused by one or more of the several influenza viruses. It is characterized by a rapid onset, fever, inappetence, sore throat, general muscle soreness, increased respiration rate, cough and sometimes a nasal discharge. The general symptoms usually disappear within a few days, but a cough sometimes lingers. If a horse is put to work before he recovers from the cough, he may develop emphysema (heaves) or unilateral or bilateral laryngeal hemiplegia (roaring), or fall victim to secondary infection, usually in the respiratory tract and associated structures. Some horses become chronic "bleeders."

Horses over three months of age should receive two doses of Flu-Vac intramuscularly four to twelve weeks apart, followed by an annual booster of a single dose. Foals under three months of age usually have good protection from their dam's colostrum, especially if the mare has been injected with Flu-Vac.

Warning: Administration of Flu-Vac to fit horses in advanced training may result in muscle soreness, loss of appetite, fever, general debility and loss of training condition. For this reason, all horses should be vaccinated before they are put into training and receive the boosters between training periods. This warning is most applicable to the racehorse and the event horse. In the event of the untoward reactions described above, Butazolidine or Dexamethasone may be administered. Do *not* administer corticosteroids. Recent studies indicate that a booster should be administered every three to four months if maximum immunity is to be maintained.

RHINOPNEUMONITIS

Rhinopneumonitis is a specific virus disease with symptoms substantially similar to those of influenza. It causes severe respiratory distress, especially in foals and young horses in training, and induces abortion in broodmares if they become infected in the terminal stages of pregnancy (from the beginning of the eighth month through term).

Foals over three months of age and older horses (except pregnant broodmares) should receive two doses of Rhino-Mune, four to eight weeks apart, followed by an annual booster of a single dose.

Pregnant broodmares should receive one dose in the first or second month of pregnancy, followed by a second dose in the fifth to seventh month of pregnancy, followed by an annual booster. It is usually suggested that pregnant mares not be vaccinated after the seventh month of pregnancy, though in the face of an "abortion storm" or severe outbreak, your veterinarian may choose to vaccinate all horses on the farm. Recent reports indicate that the use of vaccine in infected animals seems to have hastened recovery.

Equine influenza and rhinopneumonitis are not infective to humans.

VENEZUELAN EQUINE ENCEPHALITIS (VEE)

Venezuelan equine encephalitis is a virus disease, usually transmitted by the mosquito. It causes an inflammation of the brain and it is characterized by high fever, deranged consciousness, paralysis and prostration; it has a high mortality rate. Vaccination is very effective and stopped the spread of the disease in this country. A single dose of VEE vaccine administered to horses three months of age or older will produce a solid immunity for upwards of three years.

While there have been no known cases of VEE in the United States in over three years, the nature of the disease and existing animal health regulations make it imperative that all horses be vaccinated when this is recommended by state or federal authority.

Warning: If possible, VEE vaccine should be administered during mild weather, and all stress avoided for ten days following administration. In the event of fever or incoordination following vaccination, Butazolidine or Azium may be administered. Do not administer corticosteroids.

251

EASTERN-WESTERN ENCEPHALITIS (EEE-WEE)

This is not a horse disease in the sense that it *cannot* be transmitted from horse to horse, or from horse to human and vice versa. It is a disease of birds and small mammals, which is transmitted by biting insects. Man and horse are terminal victims. It is characterized by fever, inappetence, depression, incoordination, prostration and coma. The mortality rate is high.

Vaccination is elective and is usually recommended only in areas where there is a high pheasant, warbler or small-rodent population and when horses are kept on terrain that is wooded or located close to scrub brush.

If vaccination is elected, it is my opinion that only the intradermal method should be used. This consists of two doses of vaccine administered intradermally ten to fourteen days apart. (A vaccine for intramuscular administration is available but should be avoided, as we have observed lameness, muscle soreness, fever and general debility lasting sometimes up to seven days.)

RABIES

Rabies is seen infrequently in horses. It is a virus disease characterized by pharyngeal and/or facial paralysis, fever, general debility and death; *or* it may take a more violent course characterized by deranged mental state, violence, fear of water and death. Immunization consists of a single dose of vaccine administered intramuscularly. A single booster is administered annually.

Immunization is recommended only when there is a high incidence of rabies in the area in dogs, cats, skunks, etc.

STRANGLES

This is a systemic bacterial infection of horses which is caused by *Streptococcus equi* and is characterized by involvement of the upper respiratory tract, the lungs and any or all of the lymph glands of the body.

Vaccination is recommended in stables where strangles is a recurrent problem, sales stables, and all farms in the face of an outbreak.

For immunization, three 10cc doses of vaccine, administered intramuscularly seven days apart, is recommended. In foals three to six months of age, the dosage may be reduced to 6cc and administered in two sites.

Warning: Do not vaccinate horses that show fever or have had previous symptoms of the disease within one year, or that have been previously vaccinated within one year. Do not continue the vaccination series if the animal shows a hot, painful circumscribed swelling after the first or second dose, as this is indication that active immunity exists. In the event of excessive swelling at the site of injection, Butazolidine or Azium may be administered.

MIXED BACTERIN

Though several mixed bacterins of common bacterial infective agents are presently on the market, these are considered by most practitioners to be of doubtful value and are not recommended.

COGGINS TEST FOR EQUINE INFECTIOUS ANEMIA (EIA)

The Coggins test is not a vaccination but a blood test called the immunodiffusion test to determine if a horse is a carrier of equine infectious anemia, sometimes called "swamp fever."

EIA is a virus disease of horses transmitted from horse to horse by biting insects, injection with an infected needle or other vector. It is characterized in the acute stage by recurrent fever, anemia, severe loss of condition and swelling of the legs, pectoral region and lower areas of the abdomen, including the penile sheath or the mammary gland, as the case may be. In the terminal stages, ulceration of the swollen areas sometimes precedes prostration and death. However, in the chronic carrier state, clinical symptoms may be entirely lacking. At present there is no preventive vaccine, and there is no treatment.

The Coggins test is an official test which is now recognized by the federal governments of the United States and Canada and most states. Each year additional testing requirements will be instituted for shipping and competition, and thus it is essential for all horses now in your stable to be Coggins-tested and all new additions to be tested before being brought onto the premises.

N.B.: If you have not already had all your horses Coggins-tested we would advise you to do so immediately, lest you find yourself denied a shipping certificate or lose a sale or an opportunity to compete because of an unkown silent carrier's being found on your premises.

PIROPLASMOSIS

Piroplasmosis is a protozoan infection in the red blood cells of horses. It is characterized by high fever, anemia and sometimes hemoglobinurea (bloody urine). The transmitting agent is specific: the wood tick known as *Demacentor nitans*. The disease is sometimes mistaken for acute swamp fever (equine infectious anemia) and is somewhat similar, in that the animal may appear to recover and its clinical symptoms may disappear, though the blood of the animal may remain infective for months or even years.

There is no vaccine or preventive agent. Control is through blood testing, to eliminate the "silent" carriers, and through control of the wood ticks. Treatment with arsenicals has been attempted, but it is a very risky process, and results have been variable at best; it is worth trying, however, with valuable animals.

Purchasers of foreign horses, especially those coming from warm climates, should always make the sale contingent upon acceptance of the horse by national and state veterinary authorities in the country to which the horse is imported. If it is feasible, a lot of grief can be avoided if you arrange for a blood sample to be taken before the horse is shipped and submit it to the U.S. Department of Agriculture laboratory at Beltsville, Maryland, for a "courtesy test."

GENERAL CONSIDERATIONS

In general you should talk your vaccination program over with your regular veterinarian, and once it is initiated you should keep detailed records of the products administered, the date of administration and any untoward reactions noted. VEE and Coggins reports should be carefully preserved in case they are required for shipment or sale.

Active immunization procedures are not recommended for foals under three months of age for two reasons: (a) most have a good residual immunity from having received their dam's colostrum; (b) it is very doubtful that a foal under three months of age can generate immunity from the vaccines administered to it. Do not administer corticosteroids to horses that are undergoing immunization procedures, as these will interfere with the development of immunity. In the event of soreness, phenylbutazone (Butazolidine) or dexamethasone (Azium) may be administered without upsetting the immunity.

2. MEDICATION FOR THE ELIMINATION OF INTERNAL PARASITES

The use of Parvex has now been superseded by the availability of Parvex-Plus—the "plus" being the addition of piperazine, thus increasing efficiency for the elimination of ascarids.

Interim worming in the feed is done through the use of Equizole-A or Telmin—both safe, efficient products readily accepted by most horses.

We prefer to avoid all products formulated from organic phosphatase compounds. (Be sure you read the warning on each and every one of the "new products.") Organic phosphatase alters the chemical reactions at nerve endings. If certain products—including anesthetics, certain tranquilizers, etc.—are administered from two weeks before worming to two weeks after worming, untoward and even fatal reactions may occur. Obviously you can never be certain that your horse won't require any of these products in the two weeks following the use of organic-phosphatase worming compounds.

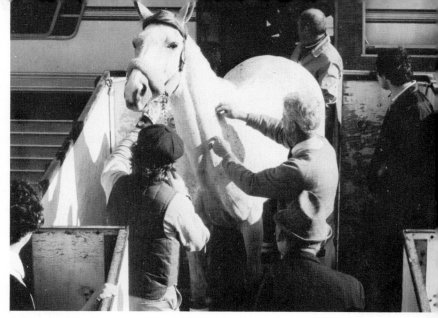

Dr. Joseph O'Dea administering a tranquilizer prior to air shipment. Modern drugs and airport procedures at last have largely eliminated the risk factor in shipping horses by air.

3. THE USE OF TRANQUILIZERS

Before discussing the use of tranquilizers, I would like to emphasize that they all belong to the category of "forbidden substances," as defined by both the AHSA and the FEI, and their presence in the blood and/or urine of any competing horse is strictly prohibited. Since they still have many useful applications for problem shippers, for horses difficult to work around and in the case of standing surgical procedures, it is imperative for all owners, riders, trainers and veterinarians to be thoroughly conversant with the provisions of the AHSA and/or FEI drug rules and testing procedures.

In recent years the tranquilizers used by most equine practitioners have been Acepromazine (azopromazine), Rompun (xylazine) and less frequently, Sparine. Thorazine and *Rauwolfia* have for all practical purposes been abandoned. When the use of a tranquilizer is indicated, the drug of choice is often Rompun.

It is very efficient, has a wide safety margin and can be safely administered per vein, subcutaneously or intramuscularly. Most horses drop their heads and appear to hang in the crossties, but remain quite steady on their feet. For this reason, it is an excellent product for loading horses on a van or airplane, or for shipping, clipping or shoeing a difficult horse.

It is used to facilitate many standing surgical procedures, when accompanied by local anesthetics and/or hypnotics. Remember, however, that horses which are prone to kick with their hind legs will frequently kick just as hard under Rompun, even though they seem deeply tranquilized.

Acepromazine is another very reliable product that can be given per vein, intramuscularly or subcutaneously and produces good, even tranquilization, but is somewhat slower in taking effect than Rompun.

Warning: Some competitors are known to tranquilize with resperine (Serpasil) because of its longer-range effect, and possibly in hopes that its detection will continue to prove more difficult than that of other prohibited substances. Such persons should carefully weigh the advantages sought

255

against the risks involved, for most veterinarians agree that this is an extremely variable and unreliable product in the horse. Its administration has frequently been accompanied by severe gastrointestinal symptoms, violent colic and other unexpected adverse results, and I do not know of any situation in which I could consider it the drug of choice.

4. PHENYLBUTAZONE

Phenylbutazone, usually referred to as Butazolidine, or "bute," is a chemical formulation which has very strong anti-inflammatory and some analgesic (pain-lessening) effects. It may be administered orally or intravenously. It should not be administered intramuscularly or subcutaneously.

Because of the dramatic efficiency of phenylbutazone in the treatment of lameness, its use has been widespread in horses. When administered at prescribed levels it does not have in the horse the untoward and sometimes dangerous effects it has in humans. Though the horse rarely shows any sensitivity to it, excessive overdosage may cause liver insult with severe colic.

It is especially useful in chronic arthritis and bursitis where there is no mechanical damage or mechanical inflammation, and it is frequently used in pedal osteitis, navicular disease, carpitis and similar conditions. Many horses deprived of its use would be cripples. With it they are able to live useful lives, to hunt and to compete.

In racing, the use of phenylbutazone has met with considerable misunderstanding and difference of opinion because of the fear that trainers will run horses "hot and cold," but a system of controlled medication developed in Colorado, Nebraska and California has overcome this objection. Now virtually every state in the Union with the exception of New York (which has lagged behind in establishing a workable medication rule) permits the use of phenylbutazone under controlled conditions. There have also been charges that the use of phenylbutazone will have a deleterious effect on the breeding of horses, but no concrete evidence or even sound theory has been put forward to support the objection.

Even if these objections were valid, they have little bearing on the use of phenylbutazone for showing and eventing. The ethical administration of racing requires (a) protection of the wagering public and (b) protection of the breed and the conduct of events to prove stock for future breeding.

Events conducted under FEI rules, however, are purely a test of the proficiency of horse and rider. There is no standard for soundness, except as related to horse and rider safety, and there is no wagering public. Horses are not being proved for return to the stud. As a practical matter, most are geldings or mares past the usual reproductive age.

Showing under AHSA rules is for the most part comparable, but there are exceptions and I think it is time we reassessed the program.

In my view, in classes wherein intrinsic physical soundness is a specification of the class, phenylbutazone and all comparable medication should be prohibited. This means all in-hand and breeding classes in all breeds and in the conformation-hunter division, especially the green division.

The working-hunter division is different, since only "hunting soundness" is required, and under normal working conditions in the hunting field many steady and capable hunters require normalization with phenylbutazone. The same is true in other working classes, including those for jumpers. In those events performance and score is the standard and intrinsic physical soundness is not judged.

The problem with prohibiting phenylbutazone is that it would probably be replaced with dangerous and deleterious products that are not readily detectable and not easily controlled.

Phenylbutazone when properly used is safe and efficient. If outlawed, it would be replaced with the systematic administration of corticosteroids, which can and do cause the suppression of the adrenal cortex, resulting in fluid and chemical imbalances, etc. Another approach would be repeated intra-articular and/or intrabursal injections, which result in an insidious but permanent damage to the joint or bursa.

Furthermore, if phenylbutazone were outlawed and the newly developed test for exogenous (injected) corticosteroids employed, hundreds of horses, including many that have reached a high level of competency, would be lost to the sport. For example, most horses that reach the Olympic level have a considerable amount of "wear and tear" from years of training and competition. Similarly, many ponies and small horses that have "come down through the family" could not be used without normalization with phenylbutazone. Yet these too are working animals—since only "using" soundness is required, while intrinsic physical soundness is not.

These thoughts on phenylbutazone do not apply to any other product. Each product must be considered individually in the light of its therapeutic properties.

ANABOLIC STEROIDS

Anabolic steroids are natural body products, hormones which help to support the body, effect repair and in part regulate certain physiologic functions.

Excessive amounts can be detected in the body fluids, and promising new tests for the detection of administered steroids are presently under study. However, each time the presence of high levels of anabolic steroids has been the reason for a disqualification, that decision has been upset in civil court.

In the equine, anabolic steroids are used fundamentally as replacement therapy in castrated males and spayed females. Altered animals have lost in part the natural production of anabolic steroids through the removal of either the testicles or the ovaries. Administration of replacement therapy, as the term signifies, lets the horse function at near normal level. Without replacement, many horses suffer muscle weakness, general debility and other undesirable effects of castration and spaying.

5. ACCOMMODATION FOR HIGH ALTITUDE

Although not everyone has occasion to worry about the effects of altitude on equine performance, the USET has had several occasions to explore the matter, and their experience may be of interest to others. On the first occasion, the Pan American Games of 1955 in Mexico City, research was limited to inquiries at the Hipódromo in Mexico City. Trainers there advised of a marked loss of form between the tenth and twenty-first day at high altitude, as compared with performance at lower altitudes. (Mexico City is some 8,000 feet above sea level.) In practice, they advised the team to come late or come early, or to get some altitude training, and the eventual decision was to have the three-day squad train at Colorado Springs, and then ship the whole squad relatively late. This seemed to work out reasonably well, but there was no objective means of evaluation.

The XIX Olympic Games in Mexico City in 1968 caused us to reevaluate this subject and investigate the effects of altitude again. This time we used a much more sophisticated technique, and both the subjective and objective results in the Games appear to justify the measures we took.

In 1968, the Olympic village at Mexico City was opened two weeks early, in order to give all competitors a chance to become acclimated, and our horses were shipped a week before the village opened, and thus about a month before competition, in order to give them ample time to overcome the effects of shipment. While they were still at home in normal training, blood samples were taken to enable us to establish normal values for each individual. Twelve hours after their arrival in Mexico City (or Avandaro, in the case of the three-day squad, at a slightly higher altitude still), samples were taken again, and this was continued every day thereafter. No horse was permitted to resume even light under-saddle work until his packed-cell volume had returned to near-normal level.

The procedure works in this way. As altitude increases, the amount of oxygen in the atmosphere decreases. The lowered oxygen level results in an increase of carbon dioxide in the body. To compensate for the problem, the heart and respiration rates increase, and the increased carbon dioxide in the body produces diuresis, characterized by more frequent urination and the loss of fluid component from the circulating blood. This results in relative increase in the number of red cells per cc of blood. The ability of the blood to transport oxygen in the body and to remove carbon dioxide is directly proportional to total red-cell volume. So by knowing the normal level for each horse, we could graph out his progress in accommodation.

As far as we know, we were the only competing nation that handled the altitude acclimatization by means of a planned medical approach, and we were the only nation that did not suffer one or more untoward effects from altitude anoxia.

Strangely enough, the greatest portion of this change appears to take place in the circulating blood, and few signs of body-tissue dehydration were apparent. Also of interest is that several horses which plateaued-off at a red-cell volume higher than the preestablished norm maintained that higher volume for several weeks when returned to sea level.

An Overseas View
of the USET

DOUGLAS BUNN

A noted juvenile competitor in England before the War, "Duggie" Bunn was riding on the British jumping team when he first came in contact with the USET. Shortly thereafter he established the All England Jumping Course on his own property at Hickstead, Sussex, and rapidly developed it into one of the finest jumping grounds in the world. During the past two decades he has often invited the USET to consider Hickstead its foreign training base, receiving its riders and staff not only like countrymen but, as he says, like family. The USET has had no more generous friend.

As one who first learned to like and admire Americans during World War II, when I was a small boy growing up on the south coast of England, I am probably not completely objective about the American show-jumping team. Be that as it may, one of the great pleasures of my life during the past sixteen years has been to have the USET jumping team frequently staying in my house at Hickstead as guests—no, more as family. I like to think that the opportunities they have had for competition and schooling at Hickstead have contributed to their development and competitive success elsewhere.

Given time to reflect, I could tell a thousand stories about the U.S. show-jumping team. Instead, let me write briefly about the main impressions they made on this side of the Atlantic, and what I consider they have done for the sport.

In my view, the USET contributed a lot of style to the international show-jumping scene in the 1950s, at a time when European riders were

Douglas Bunn's famous All-England Show Jumping Course at Hickstead, with the four finalists for the 1974 World Championship saluting the royal box. (The riders are Frank Chapot; Hartwig Steenken of Germany, the eventual winner; Eddie Macken of Ireland and Hugo Simon of Austria.)

perhaps insecure, a little scruffy and not quite sure whether their sport had much of a future. The Americans showed us that you could still ride like an Englishman (or indeed, like a gentleman) and win big classes. No one else, even the d'Inzeos, made such an impression as Bill Steinkraus.

Moreover, all their horses were immaculately turned out; the tack and equipment was well cleaned and polished; the riders wore well-cut boots and their clothes were invariably spotless. The smartest field in Leicestershire would not have been better turned out. The USET really set a standard for the show jumpers in Europe; they were competitors to look up to, and a marked and general improvement in the sport soon followed.

During this period, the USET's show-jumping activities have been presided over by Bert de Nemethy. Much has been written about Bert, whom I consider to be one of the world's finest "nagsmen." After Bert has ridden a horse for a month or two (and sometimes only a day or two) you may wonder if it is still the same horse. The improvement is sometimes truly startling. More than that, Bert succeeded in establishing and maintaining a splendid standard of team morale and discipline, both in and out of the ring. And in passing, I would like to point out that few people realize how difficult it is to build a team when you are several thousand miles from home for months on end. Developing team unity is never an easy matter, even if you are lucky enough to start with four unattached young men like Steinkraus, Chapot, Wiley and Morris. The task is not unlike the courting of elephants—a great deal of dust gets kicked up, and the result is an unconscionable long time away!

As all the world knows, Bert got his result. And how! Though let me add that in dealing with Bert's era, which roughly coincides with the Hickstead era too, I am dealing with what I remember personally, and do not mean to slight any predecessors.

I could not conclude without recalling a few of the many vignettes of the USET that stick in my memory. First, the young George Morris at Aachen—having shed a little tear on account of Bert's giving him hell over a previous slow round on War Bride, but having made the jump-off—tremulously inquiring, "What shall I do, Bert?"

"Vot you do? I tell you vot: You jump again clean—*but this time you jump f-a-a-s-t!*" (Following orders, George won the class.)

Nor can I forget overhearing team captain Steinkraus, well known for his jawbreaking command of the more obscure half of the English language, being interviewed by a nice, uncomplicated commentator on Irish television at Dublin, and referring to ". . . this amorphous, yet cosmopolitan conglomeration." The poor interviewer's face betrayed his suspicion that he had gotten a member of the Dutch team by mistake. I wonder what they thought in Kerry! Despite his "propensity for linguistic obfuscation," I must say that Bill would give the best horse in the world the best ride in the world. The word "artist" is frequently overworked in sport, but not in his case.

Frank Chapot, who happens to be my eldest son's godfather, is noted for his tenacious competitiveness, and the USET will always be in debt to him for two especially heroic rides—on Trail Guide in the Rome Olympics in 1960, and on White Lightning at Munich in 1972. They call it pulling the fat out of the fire—and Frank is also perhaps not unfamiliar with being in hot water.

The seemingly frail, delicate Kathy Kusner sticks in my mind as having the strongest will of any rider on the team. At one Hickstead meeting at which she swept the board with Untouchable, reporters asked her to comment on her unbelievable speed in a jump-off. "All I do," she replied demurely, "is tell myself that there are no fences between the wings." She meant it—and the fences might *not* have been there, either, for all the trouble they gave her.

I could go on indefinitely, for the USET has brought so many top-class riders to our shores—and so many delightful ones. Long may it prosper. In this tormented world of ours, I find some comfort in the fact that the Stars and Stripes not only remains an important symbol of liberty and enterprise for all freedom-loving people, but represents as well the finest in equestrian sport.

262

APPENDIX

EDITOR'S NOTE

The following appendix, which was compiled by the noted equestrian historian Max E. Ammann on the basis of USET records and his own archives, provides a comprehensive review of the team's major competitive highlights. However, it cannot be considered a complete record of our country's international equestrian participation since 1950, since it omits the results obtained by American riders while studying or living abroad, or while competing as individuals under private sponsorship; unfortunately, these records were not available on a consistent basis. Accordingly, such results have been included only with respect to official FEI championships (in Part II). Elsewhere, the results shown are limited exclusively to those achieved by riders competing as members of official USET teams and only at the more important international shows.

I. OLYMPIC AND PAN AMERICAN GAMES RESULTS

1952 Olympic Games Helsinki, Finland	Jumping:	William Steinkraus/Hollandia	11th
		Arthur McCashin/Miss Budweiser	13th
		John Russell/Democrat	24th
		Team: 3rd place (bronze medal)	
	Dressage:	Robert Borg/Bill Biddle	11th
		Marjorie Haines/Flying Dutchman	17th
		Hartmann Pauly/Reno Overdo	27th
		Team: 6th place	
	3-Day:	Charles Hough/Cassavellanus	9th
		Walter Staley/Craigwood	18th
		John E. B. Wofford/Benny Grimes	31st
		Team: 3rd place (bronze medal)	
1955 Pan American Games Mexico City, Mexico	Jumping:	Charles Dennehy/Pill Box	8th
		Arthur McCashin/Mohawk	9th
		John R. Wheeler/Little Mac	14th
		William Steinkraus/Volco's Duke	15th
		Team: 4th place	
	Dressage:	Robert Borg/Bill Biddle	2nd
		no team	
	3-Day:	Walter Staley/Mud Dauber	1st
		Frank Duffy/Passach	8th
		John E. B. Wofford/Cassavellanus	elim.
		Team: eliminated	
1956 Olympic Games Stockholm, Sweden	Jumping:	Hugh Wiley/Trail Guide	11th
		William Steinkraus/Night Owl	15th
		Frank Chapot/Belair	27th
		Team: 5th place	
	Dressage:	Robert Borg/Bill Biddle	17th
		Elaine Shirley Watt/Connecticut Yankee	30th
		No team	
	3-Day:	Jonathan Burton/Huntingfield	elim.
		Frank Duffy/Drop Dead	elim.
		Walter Staley/Mud Dauber	elim.
		Team: eliminated	

1959 Pan American Games **Chicago, U.S.A.**	Jumping:	Frank Chapot/Diamant Hugh Wiley/Nautical William Steinkraus/Riviera Wonder George Morris/Night Owl No individual competition; team: 1st place (gold medal)	
	Dressage:	Patricia Galvin/Rath Patrick Jessica Newberry/Forstrat Karen McIntosh/Scipio Team: 2nd place (silver medal)	1st 5th 6th
	3-Day:	Michael Page/Grasshopper Michael Plumb/Markham William Haggard/Bold Minstrel Walter Staley/Sebastian Team: 2nd place (silver medal)	1st 2nd 9th elim.
1960 Olympic Games **Rome, Italy**	Jumping:	George Morris/Sinjon Hugh Wiley/Master William William Steinkraus/Riviera Wonder Team: 2nd place (silver medal) (George Morris/Sinjon; Frank Chapot/Trail Guide; W. Steinkraus/Ksar d'Esprit)	4th 7th 15th
	Dressage:	Patricia Galvin/Rath Patrick Jessica Newberry/Forstrat No team competition	6th 12th
	3-Day:	Michael Plumb/Markham Michael Page/Grasshopper David Lurie/Sea Tiger Walter Staley/Fleet Captain Team: eliminated	15th 17th elim. elim.
1963 Pan American Games **São Paulo, Brazil**	Jumping:	Mary Mairs/Tomboy Frank Chapot/San Lucas Kathy Kusner/Unusual William Steinkraus/Sinjon Team: 1st place (gold medal)	1st 4th 15th ret.
	Dressage:	Patricia Galvin/Rath Patrick No team	1st
	3-Day:	Michael Page/Grasshopper Kevin Freeman/Reno Pal William Haggard/Bold Minstrel Michael Plumb/Markham Team: 1st place (gold medal)	1st 2nd 6th elim.
1964 Olympic Games **Tokyo, Japan**	Jumping:	Frank Chapot/San Lucas Kathy Kusner/Untouchable Mary Mairs/Tomboy Team: 6th place	7th 13th 33rd
	Dressage:	Patricia de la Tour/Rath Patrick Jessica Newberry/Forstrat Karen McIntosh/Malteser Team: 4th place	8th 14th 17th

266

	3-Day:	Michael Page/Grasshopper	4th
		Kevin Freeman/Gallopade	12th
		Michael Plumb/Bold Minstrel	15th
		Lana duPont/Mr. Wister	33rd
1967 Pan American Games Winnipeg, Canada	Jumping:	Kathy Kusner/Untouchable	5th
		Mary Chapot/White Lightning	7th
		Frank Chapot/San Lucas	7th
		William Steinkraus/Bold Minstrel	9th
		Team: 2nd place (silver medal)	
	Dressage:	Kyra Downton/Kadett	1st
		Diana Firmin-Didot/Avaune	4th
		Donnan Plumb/Attaché	10th
		Team: 2nd place (silver medal)	
	3-Day:	Michael Plumb/Plain Sailing	1st
		Michael Page/Foster	3rd
		James Wofford/Kilkenny	4th
		Rick Eckhardt/The Stranger	5th
		Team: 1st place (gold medal)	
1968 Olympic Games Mexico City, Mexico	Jumping:	William Steinkraus/Snowbound	1st
		Frank Chapot/San Lucas	4th
		Kathy Kusner/Untouchable	21st
		Team: 4th place	
	Jumping:	(Mary Chapot/White Lightning; Kathy Kusner/ Untouchable; Frank Chapot/San Lucas)	
	Dressage:	Kyra Downton/Kadett	21st
		Edith Master/Helios	23rd
		Donnan Plumb/Attaché	24th
		Team: 8th place	
	3-Day:	Michael Page/Foster	3rd
		James Wofford/Kilkenny	6th
		Michael Plumb/Plain Sailing	14th
		Kevin Freeman/Chalan	elim.
		Team: 2nd place (silver medal)	
1972 Olympic Games Munich, West Germany	Jumping:	Neal Shapiro/Sloopy	3rd
		Kathy Kusner/Fleet Apple	10th
		William Steinkraus/Snowbound	22nd
		Team: 2nd place (silver medal)	
		(Neal Shapiro/Sloopy; Kathy Kusner/Fleet Apple; Frank Chapot/White Lightning; William Steinkraus/Main Spring)	
	Dressage:	Edith Master/Dahlwitz	18th
		John Winnett/Reinald	22nd
		Lois Stephens/Fasching	31st
		Team: 9th place	
	3-Day:	Kevin Freeman/Good Mixture	5th
		Bruce Davidson/Plain Sailing	8th
		Michael Plumb/Free and Easy	20th
		James Wofford/Kilkenny	30th
		Team: 2nd place (silver medal)	

1975 Pan American Games Mexico City, Mexico	Jumping:	Buddy Brown/A Little Bit	2nd
		Michael Matz/Grande	3rd
		Dennis Murphy/Do Right	7th
		Team: 1st place (gold medal)	
		(Michael Matz/Grande; Dennis Murphy/Do Right; Joseph Fargis/Caesar; Buddy Brown/Sandsablaze)	
	Dressage:	Hilda Gurney/Keen	2nd
		Dorothy Morkis/Monaco	3rd
		John Winnett/Leopardi	4th
		Team: 1st place (gold medal)	
	3-Day:	Tad Coffin/Bally Cor	1st
		Bruce Davidson/Golden Griffin	2nd
		Beth Perkins/Furtive	5th
		Mary Anne Tauskey/Marcus Aurelius	7th
		Team: 1st place (gold medal)	

II. WORLD AND EUROPEAN CHAMPIONSHIP RESULTS

JUMPING

1953 Paris World Championships	John Winnett/Sultan and Buffalo	unpl.
1955 Aachen World Championships	John Russell/Bally Bay and Lonie	unpl.
1956 Aachen World Championships	William Steinkraus/First Boy and Night Owl Hugh Wiley/Master William	5th 9th
1958 Aachen European Championships	William Steinkraus/Ksar d'Esprit Hugh Wiley/Nautical	5th 6th
1959 Paris European Championships	William Steinkraus/First Boy and Ksar d'Esprit Hugh Wiley/Nautical and Master William	5th 6th
1960 Venice World Championships	William Steinkraus/Ksar d'Esprit George Morris/Sinjon	4th 10th
1961 Aachen European Championships	Warren Wofford/Hollandia and Huntsman	unpl.
1965 Hickstead Ladies' World Championships	Kathy Kusner/Untouchable and That's Right	2nd
1966 Lucerne European Championships	Frank Chapot/Good Twist and San Lucas William Steinkraus/Snowbound and Sinjon	2nd with- drew
1967 Fontainebleau Ladies' European Championships	Kathy Kusner/Untouchable and Aberali	1st
1970 La Baule World Championships	Frank Chapot/White Lightning William Steinkraus/Bold Minstrel	6th 9th
1974 La Baule Ladies' World Championships	Michele McEvoy/Mr. Muskie and Sundancer	2nd
1974 Hickstead World Championships	Frank Chapot/Main Spring Rodney Jenkins/Idle Dice	3rd 8th

DRESSAGE

1958 Wiesbaden European Championships	Jessica Newberry/Archimedes	11th

1961 Aachen European Championships	Karen McIntosh/Heraldik	19th
1966 Berne World Championships	Diana Firmin-Didot/Avaune	21st
1967 Aachen European Championships	Diana Firmin-Didot/Avaune	17th
	Martha Knocke/Englishman	32nd
	Barbara McGuinness/Four Seasons	34th
1970 Aachen World Championships	Edith Master/Helios	23rd
	Lois Stephens/Fasching	25th
1974 Copenhagen World Championships	Edith Master/Dahlwitz	15th
	Elizabeth Lewis/Ludmilla	15th
	John Winnett/Leopardi	19th
	Sidley Payne/Felix	32nd

THREE-DAY

1959 Harewood European Championships	John E. B. Wofford/Cassavellanus	33rd
1966 Burghley World Championships	Kevin Freeman/M'Lord Conolly	9th
	Rick Eckhardt/Gallopade	elim.
	Kevin Freeman/Royal Imp	elim.
	J. A. B. Smith/Bean Platter	elim.
	J. Michael Plumb/Foster	elim.
	J. Michael Plumb/Chakola	elim.
1967 Punchestown, European Championships	Mason Phelps/Gladstone	15th
1970 Punchestown, World Championships	James Wofford/Kilkenny	3rd
	Mason Phelps/Rowen	elim.
1974 Burghley World Championships	Bruce Davison/Irish Cap	1st
	J. Michael Plumb/Good Mixture	2nd
	Beth Perkins/Furtive	6th
	Edward Emerson/Victor Dakin	14th
	Donald Sachey/Plain Sailing	21st
	Caroline Treviranus/Cajun	ret.
	Team: 1st place (gold medal)	

III. NATIONS CUP RESULTS

1950	Harrisburg	2nd to Mexico
	New York	1st (McCashin/Paleface; Carol Durand/Reno Kirk; Norma Matthews/ Country Boy)
	Toronto	1st (McCashin/Paleface; Carol Durand/Reno Kirk; Norma Matthews/ Country Boy)
1951	Harrisburg	2nd to Canada
	New York	3rd to Mexico and Ireland
	Toronto	2nd to Ireland
	Monterrey	1st (Russell/Swizzlestick; McCashin/Totilla; Steinkraus/Reno Kirk)
1952	London	2nd to Great Britain
	Harrisburg	2nd to Mexico
	New York	2nd to Mexico
	Toronto	3rd to France and Ireland
1953	Harrisburg	1st (McCashin/Rusty; Mutch/Briar Lad; Carol Durand/Reno Kirk)
	New York	4th to Ireland, Great Britain and Canada
	Toronto	2nd to Great Britain
1954	Harrisburg	3rd to Mexico and Spain
	New York	2nd to Mexico
	Toronto	4th to Spain, Mexico and West Germany
1955	London	4th to Italy, Great Britain and Ireland
	Dublin	5th to Italy, Great Britain, Ireland and Sweden
	Le Zoute	4th to France, Great Britain and Belgium
	Harrisburg	4th to Ireland, Mexico and Canada
	New York	3rd to Mexico and Ireland
	Toronto	2nd to Ireland
1956	Stockholm	6th to Great Britain, Italy, Portugal, Spain and West Germany
	Aachen	5th to Brazil, West Germany, Spain and Portugal
	London	5th to Great Britain, Brazil, Turkey and Ireland
	Dublin	4th to Great Britain, Turkey and Ireland
	Harrisburg	2nd to Canada
	New York	4th to Mexico, Ireland and Canada
	Toronto	1st (Chapot/Defense; Wiley/Nautical; Steinkraus/First Boy)
1957	Harrisburg	2nd to Great Britain
	New York	1st (Chapot/Pill Box; Steinkraus/First Boy; Wiley/Nautical)
	Toronto	1st (Dennehy/Pill Box; Steinkraus/Night Owl; Wiley/Nautical)

271

1958	Aachen	2nd to Spain
	London	1st (Morris/Night Owl; Chapot/Diamant; Wiley/Nautical; Steinkraus/Ksar d'Esprit)
	Dublin	2nd to Great Britain
	Ostend	2nd to France
	Rotterdam	4th to France, West Germany and Ireland
	Harrisburg	3rd to West Germany and Canada
	New York	2nd to West Germany
	Toronto	3rd to West Germany and Canada
1959	Rome	1st (Morris/Sinjon; Chapot/Diamant; Steinkraus/Ksar d'Esprit; Wiley/Nautical)
	Paris	3rd to Soviet Union and West Germany
	Aachen	2nd to Italy
	London	1st (Morris/Night Owl; Chapot/Tally Ho; Steinkraus/Riviera Wonder; Wiley/Nautical)
	Harrisburg	1st (Morris/Sinjon; Chapot/Spring Board; Steinkraus/Trail Guide)
	New York	2nd to Canada
	Toronto	1st (Morris/Sinjon; Chapot/Spring Board; Steinkraus/Trail Guide)
1960	Lucerne	1st (Morris/Sinjon; Chapot/Tally Ho; Wiley/Nautical; Steinkraus/Riviera Wonder)
	Aachen	2nd to West Germany
	London	1st (Morris/Sinjon; Chapot/Tally Ho; Wiley/Master William; Steinkraus/Riviera Wonder)
	Ostend	2nd to France
	Harrisburg	2nd to Venezuela
	New York	2nd to Mexico
	Toronto	1st (Morris/Sinjon; Chapot/Ksar d'Esprit; Wiley/Master William)
1961	Harrisburg	1st (Chapot/Night Owl; Kusner/Sinjon; Steinkraus/Ksar d'Esprit)
	New York	elim (winner Argentina)
	Toronto	1st (Chapot/San Lucas; Kusner/Sinjon; Steinkraus/Ksar d'Esprit)
1962	Aachen	1st (Robertson/The Sheriff; Mairs/Tomboy; Chapot/San Lucas; Steinkraus/Sinjon)
	London	2nd to West Germany
	Dublin	2nd to Italy
	Harrisburg	1st (Mairs/Tomboy; Chapot/San Lucas; Steinkraus/Sinjon)
	New York	1st (Mairs/Tomboy; Chapot/San Lucas; Steinkraus/Sinjon)
	Toronto	1st (Mairs/Tomboy; Chapot/San Lucas; Robertson/Master William)
1963	Harrisburg	1st (Mairs/Tomboy; Chapot/Manon; Steinkraus/Fire One)
	New York	1st (Mairs/Tomboy; Chapot/San Lucas; Steinkraus/Sinjon)
	Toronto	1st (Mairs/Tomboy; Chapot/San Lucas; Steinkraus/Unusual)
1964	London	3rd to Great Britain and Italy
	Dublin	1st (Mairs/Tomboy; Kusner/Untouchable; Chapot/Manon; Steinkraus/Sinjon)
	Ostend	1st (Kusner/Untouchable; Hofmann/San Pedro; Chapot/ San Lucas; Steinkraus/Sinjon)
	Rotterdam	2nd to West Germany
	New York	1st (Chapot/Manon; Kusner/Untouchable; Steinkraus/Sinjon; Shapiro/Jacks or Better)
	Toronto	1st (Mairs/Tomboy; Kusner/Untouchable; Steinkraus/Sinjon)
1965	Harrisburg	1st (Mary Chapot/Tomboy; Kusner/Untouchable; Chapot/San Lucas; Steinkraus/Snowbound)

	New York	1st (Mary Chapot/Tomboy; Kusner/Fire One; Chapot/San Lucas; Steinkraus/Sinjon)
	Toronto	1st (Hofmann/San Pedro; Kusner/Unusual; Mary Chapot/Tomboy; Chapot/San Lucas)
1966	Lucerne	1st (Mary Chapot/Tomboy; Kusner/Untouchable; Chapot/San Lucas; Steinkraus/Sinjon)
	Aachen	2nd to Italy
	Harrisburg	1st (Mary Chapot/Tomboy; Jones/Fru; Chapot/San Lucas; Steinkraus/Snowbound)
	New York	1st (Mary Chapot/Tomboy; Steinkraus/Bold Minstrel; Chapot/San Lucas; Kusner/Untouchable)
	Toronto	2nd to Canada
1967	Aachen	3rd to Great Britain and Italy
	New York	1st (Shapiro/Night Spree; Hofmann/Salem; Kusner/Untouchable; Steinkraus/Snowbound)
	Toronto	1st (Jones/Trick Track; Shapiro/Night Spree; Mary Chapot/Anakonda; Kusner/Untouchable)
1968	London	1st (Mary Chapot/White Lightning; Kusner/Untouchable; Chapot/San Lucas; Steinkraus/Snowbound)
	Dublin	1st (Mary Chapot/White Lightning; Kusner/Fru; Chapot/San Lucas; Steinkraus/Snowbound)
	Ostend	1st (Mary Chapot/White Lightning; Kusner/Untouchable; Hofmann/Out Late; Chapot/San Lucas)
	Rotterdam	1st (Mary Chapot/White Lightning; Hofmann/Out Late; Kusner/Untouchable; Chapot/San Lucas)
	New York	1st (Mary Chapot/White Lightning; Hofmann/Salem; Chapot/San Lucas; Steinkraus/Bold Minstrel)
	Toronto	1st (Shapiro/Trick Track; Mary Chapot/White Lightning; Chapot/San Lucas; Hofmann/Salem)
1969	Harrisburg	1st (Shapiro/Trick Track; Brinsmade/Triple Crown; Chapot/San Lucas; Steinkraus/Bold Minstrel)
	New York	1st (Brinsmade/Triple Crown; Kusner/Wicked City; Chapot/San Lucas; Steinkraus/Bold Minstrel)
	Toronto	2nd to Canada
1970	Lucerne	1st (Shapiro/San Lucas; Fargis/Bonte II; Kusner/Silver Scot; Steinkraus/Snowbound)
	Aachen	3rd to West Germany and Great Britain
	La Baule	3rd to Canada and France
	Harrisburg	2nd to West Germany
	New York	2nd to West Germany
	Toronto	2nd to West Germany
1971	Fontainebleau	4th to West Germany, Italy and Great Britain
	Aachen	1st (Fargis/Bonte II; Homfeld/Triple Crown; Shapiro/Sloopy; Steinkraus/Fleet Apple)
	Dublin	4th to West Germany, Great Britain and Italy
	Harrisburg	1st (Fargis/Bonte II; Shapiro/Sloopy; Chapot/San Lucas; Steinkraus/Fleet Apple)
	New York	2nd to Canada
	Toronto	2nd to Canada
1972	Lucerne	3rd to West Germany and Switzerland
	Aachen	3rd to West Germany and Argentina

	Harrisburg	1st (Shapiro/Duke's Honor; Kusner/Triple Crown; Chapot/Good Twist; Steinkraus/Main Spring)
	New York	1st (Shapiro/Duke's Honor; Kusner/Triple Crown; Chapot/Good Twist; Steinkraus/Main Spring)
	Toronto	1st (Shapiro/Trick Track; Kusner/Triple Crown; Steinkraus/Main Spring; Chapot/Good Twist)
1973	Washington	1st (Jenkins/Idle Dice; Chapot/Main Spring; Matz/Snow Flurry; Cone/Triple Crown)
	New York	2nd to Great Britain
	London	1st (Cone/Triple Crown; Matz/Mighty Ruler; Jenkins/Idle Dice; Chapot/Main Spring)
1974	Lucerne	4th to Great Britain, West Germany and Switzerland
	La Baule	2nd to West Germany
	London	2nd to Great Britain
	Dublin	3rd to Great Britain and West Germany
	Washington	1st (Brown/Sandsablaze; Hardy/Comming Attraction; Murphy/Do Right; Jenkins/Number One Spy)
	New York	1st (Brown/Sandsablaze; Hardy/Coming Attraction; Murphy/Do Right; Chapot/Main Spring)
	Toronto	4th to France, Canada and Great Britain
1975	Washington	1st (Shapiro/Jury Duster; Smith/Radnor II; Homfeld/Old English; Jenkins/Idle Dice)
	New York	1st (Brown/Sandsablaze; Matz/Grande; Murphy/Do Right; Jenkins/Idle Dice)
	Toronto	1st (Brown/Sandsablaze; Murphy/Do Right; Ridland/Southside; Jenkins/Idle Dice)

IV. MAJOR EUROPEAN VICTORIES
(For Nations Cups, see Part III.)

1952	Düsseldorf	Team class	McCashin/Totilla; Russell/Rascal; Steinkraus/Hollandia
		Preis St. Georg	Arthur McCashin/Miss Budweiser
	Hamburg	Derby	John Russell/Rattler
	Dublin	Class No. 4	William Steinkraus/Baldoyle
1955	Le Zoute	Prix Savoy Hotel	William Steinkraus/Night Owl
1956	London	King George V Gold Cup	William Steinkraus/First Boy
		Country Life Cup	Frank Chapot/Matador
	Dublin	Class No. 3	Frank Chapot/Matador
		Class No. 5	Frank Chapot/Defense
1958	Aachen	Preis Philips	William Steinkraus/First Boy
		Preis Glas Industrie	George Morris/War Bride
		German Federation Trophy	William Steinkraus/First Boy
	London	Manifesto Stake	William Steinkraus/Ksar d'Esprit
		Foxhunter Stakes	Hugh Wiley/Nautical
		King George V Gold Cup	Hugh Wiley/Master William
	Dublin	Puissance	Hugh Wiley/Nautical
		Américaine	George Morris/War Bride
		Ball's Bridge Stake	George Morris/Sinjon
		Irish Trophy	George Morris/Night Owl
		High Jump	Hugh Wiley/Nautical
	Ostend	Prix Pesage	George Morris/Sinjon
		Prix Kursaal	William Steinkraus/Ksar d'Esprit
		Grand Prix	William Steinkraus/Ksar d'Esprit
		Prix Vainqueurs	Hugh Wiley/Master William
	Rotterdam	Puissance	William Steinkraus/Ksar d'Esprit
		Grand Prix	William Steinkraus/Ksar d'Esprit
1959	Wiesbaden	Puissance	William Steinkraus/Ksar d'Esprit
	Paris	Prix Tuileries	Hugh Wiley/Master William
	Aachen	German Championship	William Steinkraus/Riviera Wonder
	London	Manifesto Stake	Hugh Wiley/Nautical
		Horse and Hound Cup	Hugh Wiley/Nautical
		Nizefela Stake	William Steinkraus/First Boy
		King George V Gold Cup	Hugh Wiley/Nautical
		Daily Mail Cup	Hugh Wiley/Nautical
1960	Wiesbaden	Grand Prix	William Steinkraus/Riviera Wonder

	Lucerne	Preis Bürgenstock	George Morris/Sinjon
		Preis Pilatus	George Morris/Sinjon
		Preis Ermitage	William Steinkraus/Riviera Wonder
		Preis Gütsch	George Morris/High Noon
	Aachen	German Federation Trophy	George Morris/High Noon
		Puissance	William Steinkraus/Ksar d'Esprit
		Grand Prix	George Morris/Night Owl
		3rd Qualification	William Steinkraus/Riviera Wonder
	London	Horse and Hound Cup	George Morris/Sinjon
		Tankard Stake	William Steinkraus/Riviera Wonder
		Lonsdale Puissance	William Steinkraus/Ksar d'Esprit
	Ostend	Prix Janssens	George Morris/Sinjon
		Prix Kursaal	Hugh Wiley/Master William
		Grand Prix	William Steinkraus/Ksar d'Esprit
	Venice	Puissance	William Steinkraus/Ksar d'Esprit
1962	Aachen	Puissance	William Steinkraus/Ksar d'Esprit
		Preis Philips	Frank Chapot/Night Owl
		1st Qualification	William Steinkraus/Sinjon
		2nd Qualification	William Steinkraus/Sinjon
	London	Country Life Cup	William Steinkraus/Sinjon
	Dublin	Pembroke Stake	William Steinkraus/Sinjon
		Puissance	Frank Chapot/San Lucas
1964	Hickstead	Emerald Stake	Kathy Kusner/Untouchable
	London	Imperial Cup	Mairy Mairs/Anakonda
		George V Gold Cup	William Steinkraus/Sinjon
		John Player Trophy	Mary Mairs/Tomboy
	Dublin	Pembroke Stake I	Frank Chapot/Manon
		Pembroke Stake II	Kathy Kusner/Untouchable
		Irish Trophy	Kathy Kusner/Untouchable
	Ostend	Prix Royal Palace	Kathy Kusner/Untouchable
		Prix Wellington	Carol Hofmann/Can't Tell
	Rotterdam	Pre-Olympic	Kathy Kusner/Untouchable
1966	Wiesbaden	Grand Prix	Frank Chapot/San Lucas
	Cologne	Grand Prix	Crystine Jones/Fru
	Lucerne	Preis Neu-Habsburg	Mary Chapot/White Lightning
		Preis Seeburg	Kathy Kusner/Untouchable
		Grand Prix	Kathy Kusner/Untouchable
	Aachen	Preis Feuerversicherung	Frank Chapot/Good Twist
		Preis Landschaftsverband	Frank Chapot/Good Twist
		Puissance	Kathy Kusner/Untouchable
		Américaine	Crystine Jones/Fru
		Röchling Preis	Frank Chapot/Good Twist and San Lucas
		Grand Prix	Neal Shapiro/Jacks or Better
	Essen	Grand Prix	Mary Chapot/Tomboy
1967	Cologne	Grand Prix	William Steinkraus/Bold Minstrel
	Aachen	Preis Olympische Gesellschaft	Frank Chapot/Good Twist
		Puissance	Kathy Kusner/Aberali
	Hickstead	Class 34	Frank Chapot/Good Twist
		Class 41	Frank Chapot/Good Twist
1968	Hickstead	Ireland Stake	Kathy Kusner/Untouchable
		Parcours de Chasse	Carol Hofmann/Out Late
	London	Nizefela Stakes	Kathy Kusner/Fru

	Queen Elizabeth Cup	Mary Chapot/White Lightning
	Daily Mail Cup	William Steinkraus/Snowbound
	Last Chance	Neal Shapiro/Night Spree
Dublin	Shellstar Stake	Carol Hofmann/Out Late
	BP Chase	Carol Hofmann/Out Late
Hickstead	Wills Stake	Kathy Kusner/Fru
Ostend	Prix Henri Serruys	Carol Hofmann/Out Late
	Prix Wellington	Mary Chapot/White Lightning
	Prix du Champion	Frank Chapot/Good Twist
	Grand Prix	William Steinkraus/Blue Plum
	Puissance	William Steinkraus/Blue Plum
Rotterdam	Jockey Club	Carol Hofmann/Out Late
	Américaine	Kathy Kusner/Fru
	Grand Prix	Carol Hofmann/Out Late
1970 Lucerne	Preis Bürgenstock	William Steinkraus/Snowbound
	Preis Seeburg	William Steinkraus/Bold Minstrel
	Preis Kanton Luzern	William Steinkraus/Snowbound
	Preis St. Georg	William Steinkraus/Bold Minstrel
	Preis St. Gotthard	Robert Ridland/Blue Plum; Kathy Kusner/Night Hawk
	Preis Gütsch	William Steinkraus/Bold Minstrel
Wülfrath	Grand Prix	Kathy Kusner/Silver Scot
Aachen	Hilko Preis	William Steinkraus/Snowbound
	Américaine	Kathy Kusner/Fru
	Preis Actienbrauerei	William Steinkraus/Snowbound
	Orlik Preis	Frank Chapot/White Lightning
La Baule	Class No. 3	Frank Chapot/San Lucas
	Class No. 6	Frank Chapot/San Lucas
	Relay	Robert Ridland/Blue Plum; Kathy Kusner/Fru
1971 Aachen	Preis Kreissparkasse	Robert Ridland/Charles Stewart
	Hilko Preis	William Steinkraus/Fleet Apple
	Röchling Preis	William Steinkraus/Snowbound and Fleet Apple
	Grand Prix	Neal Shapiro/Sloopy
Hickstead	Three Castle Stakes	William Steinkraus/Fleet Apple
London	Horse and Hound Cup	Neal Shapiro/Sloopy
	John Player Trophy	William Steinkraus/Fleet Apple
1972 Wiesbaden	Grand Prix	Kathy Kusner/Triple Crown
Lucerne	Gübelin Preis	William Steinkraus/Main Spring
	Heliomalt Preis	Kathy Kusner/Nirvana
Aachen	Münchner Versicherung	William Steinkraus/Main Spring
	Rheinland Preis	Robert Ridland/Almost Persuaded
	Juvena Preis	Frank Chapot/White Lightning
	Zentis Preis	Kathy Kusner/Nirvana
La Baule	Criterium Champions	Kathy Kusner/Triple Crown
	Class No. 3	Neal Shapiro/Duke's Honor
1974 Lucerne	Relay	Buddy Brown/A Little Bit; Robert Ridland/Flying John
	Grand Prix	Robert Ridland/Almost Persuaded
La Baule	2nd Qualification	Michele McEvoy/Mr. Muskie
Hickstead	Chasse	Dennis Murphy/Do Right
	Speed Stake	Dennis Murphy/Tuscaloosa
London	King George V Gold Cup	Frank Chapot/Main Spring

	John Player Trophy	Rodney Jenkins/Number One Spy
	Calor Glass	Buddy Brown/A Little Bit
	Puissance	Robert Ridland/Almost Persuaded
Cardiff	1st Leg Championship	Rodney Jenkins/Number One Spy
	Match Play	Rodney Jenkins/Idle Dice
Dublin	BP Chase	Buddy Brown/Sandsablaze
	Top Score	Dennis Murphy/Tuscaloosa
	Six Bars	Rodney Jenkins/Idle Dice
	Irish Trophy	Buddy Brown/Sandsablaze

V. NORTH AMERICAN FALL CIRCUIT VICTORIES
(For Nations Cups, see Part III.)

1950	Harrisburg	Low Score 2	McCashin, Durand
	New York	Low Score 1, 2	McCashin, Durand, Matthews
1951	Harrisburg	Fault and Out	Arthur McCashin/Paleface
		Championship	Arthur McCashin/Totilla
		Low Score 2, 3	McCashin, Durand, Russell
	New York	Drake Memorial	John Russell/Blue Devil
	Toronto	Fault and Out	Arthur McCashin/Totilla
		Relay	McCashin, Russell, Steinkraus
1952	Harrisburg	Henry Trophy	William Steinkraus/Democrat
		Low Score 2, 3	Steinkraus, McCashin, Durand
	New York	Royal Winter Air Trophy	William Steinkraus/Democrat
		Good Will Trophy	William Steinkraus/Democrat
		President of Mexico Trophy	William Steinkraus/Democrat and Hollandia
		Low Score 1, 2	Steinkraus, McCashin, Russell
		Stake	William Steinkraus/Democrat
	Toronto	Stake	William Steinkraus/Democrat
		Championship	William Steinkraus/Democrat
		Fault and Out	William Steinkraus/Democrat
1953	Harrisburg	Low Score 3	Durand, McCashin, Mutch
	New York	Stake	Carol Durand/Reno Kirk
		Championship	Carol Durand/Reno Kirk
		Low Score 1, 2	Durand, McCashin, Mutch
1953	Toronto	Low Score 1	Durand, McCashin, Mutch
		Puissance	Carol Durand/Reno Kirk
		Low Score 3	Durand, McCashin, Mutch
		Fault and Out	Mutch/Matador
1954	New York	West Point Trophy	Arthur McCashin/Paleface
	Toronto	Puissance	Charles Dennehy/Black Watch
1955	Harrisburg	Penn State Police	Charles Dennehy/Altmeister
		Low Score 2, 3	Dennehy, Wiley, Steinkraus
	New York	President of Mexico Trophy	William Steinkraus/Saxon Wood and Can Can
		West Point Trophy	William Steinkraus/Saxon Wood
		Stake	William Steinkraus/Saxon Wood
		Winter Fair Trophy	Charles Dennehy/Altmeister

	Toronto	Low Score 2, 3	Dennehy, Wiley, Steinkraus
		Fault and Out	Charles Dennehy/Pill Box
1956	Harrisburg	Henry Trophy	Frank Chapot/Matador
		Low Score 2, 3	Chapot, Steinkraus, Wiley
	New York	Drake Memorial	Hugh Wiley/Nautical
		Stone Trophy	Frank Chapot/Defense
	Toronto	Class A	William Steinkraus/First Boy
1956	Toronto	Puissance	Hugh Wiley/Nautical
		Team Class A	Chapot, Steinkraus, Wiley
		Two and Two	Chapot, Steinkraus, Wiley
1957	Harrisburg	Henry Trophy	Frank Chapot/Moonflight
		Low Score 3	Wiley, Steinkraus, Chapot
	New York	West Point Trophy	Hugh Wiley/Nautical
		Stone Trophy	Hugh Wiley/Nautical
		Stake	Hugh Wiley/Nautical
		Low Score 2, 3	Wiley, Steinkraus, Chapot
	Toronto	Individual	Frank Chapot/Pill Box
		Fault and Out	Hugh Wiley/Nautical
		Puissance	Hugh Wiley/Nautical
1958	Washington	Stake	Frank Chapot/Trail Guide
1958	Harrisburg	Penn Stake Police	Hugh Wiley/Nautical
		Stake	William Steinkraus/Ksar d'Esprit
		Low Score 2	Chapot, Steinkraus, Wiley
	New York	West Point Trophy	Hugh Wiley/Nautical
		President of Mexico Trophy	William Steinkraus/Diamant and Ksar d'Esprit
		Low Score 1	Chapot, Steinkraus, Wiley
		Good Will Trophy	William Steinkraus/Ksar d'Esprit
		Stone Trophy	Hugh Wiley/Nautical
	Toronto	Fault and Out	Frank Chapot/Trail Guide
		Jumping Table C	Hugh Wiley/Nautical
		Championship	William Steinkraus/Ksar d'Esprit
1959	Harrisburg	Championship	William Steinkraus/Trail Guide
		Stake	Frank Chapot/Springboard
		International Team	Chapot, Steinkraus, Wiley
1959	Washington	Two Horse	William Steinkraus/Ksar d'Esprit and Trail Guide
		Preliminary	Frank Chapot/Tally Ho
		Speed	Hugh Wiley/Nautical
		Table A	Hugh Wiley/Nautical
		Speed	Hugh Wiley/Nautical
		Table A	Hugh Wiley/Master William
	New York	Democrat Trophy	William Steinkraus/Trail Guide
		Drake Memorial	William Steinkraus/Riviera Wonder
		Puissance	William Steinkraus/Ksar d'Esprit
		Stake	Hugh Wiley/Nautical
		Low Score 2	Steinkraus, Wiley, Chapot
		Championship	William Steinkraus/Riviera Wonder
		Two and Two	Chapot, Steinkraus, Morris
	Toronto	Fault and Out	George Morris/Sinjon
		Championship	William Steinkraus/Trail Guide
		Stake	William Steinkraus/Trail Guide
1960	Harrisburg	Penn Lodge Trophy	Frank Chapot/Tally Ho
		Low Score 1, 2, 3	Chapot, Wiley, Morris

	Championship	Frank Chapot/Tally Ho
	Stake	Frank Chapot/Trail Guide
Washington	Abendroth Trophy	Frank Chapot/Diamant
	Humphrey Trophy	George Morris/Sinjon
	Martin Trophy	George Morris/High Noon
	Puissance	Hugh Wiley/Ksar d'Esprit
New York	West Point Trophy	Frank Chapot/Trail Guide
	Good Will Trophy	George Morris/High Noon
	Stake	Hugh Wiley/Nautical
	Low Score 1, 2, 3	Chapot, Morris, Wiley
Toronto	Puissance	Hugh Wiley/Ksar d'Esprit
	Jumping Table C	George Morris/Sinjon
	Team Class A	Chapot, Morris, Wiley
	Two and Two	Chapot, Morris, Wiley

1961 Harrisburg	28th Infantry Trophy	William Steinkraus/Ksar d'Esprit
	Fault and Out	Frank Chapot/Diamant
	Puissance	William Steinkraus/Ksar d'Esprit
	Penn Lodge Trophy	William Steinkraus/Lilly Buck
	Stake	Frank Chapot/Night Owl
	Gamblers Choice	William Steinkraus/Ksar d'Esprit
	Championship	William Steinkraus/Ksar d'Esprit
Washington	President's Cup Qualification	Frank Chapot/San Lucas
New York	Fault and Out	Kathy Kusner/High Noon
	Championship	Frank Chapot/San Lucas
Toronto	Puissance	William Steinkraus/Ksar d'Esprit
	McKee Stake	Frank Chapot/San Lucas
	Team Class A	Chapot, Steinkraus, Kusner

1962 Harrisburg	28th Infantry Trophy	William Steinkraus/Sinjon
	Fault and Out	Frank Chapot/Shady Lady
	Puissance	William Steinkraus/Fire One
	Scurry	Frank Chapot/Shady Lady
	Gamblers Choice	Frank Chapot/San Lucas
	Stake	William Steinkraus/Fire One
Washington	Chechi Trophy	Mary Mairs/Tomboy
	Martins Trophy	Carol Hofmann/Le Bon Chat
	President's Cup	Kathy Kusner/Unusual
New York	McKay Trophy	Frank Chapot/San Lucas
	Democrat Trophy	William Steinkraus/Sinjon
	Murray Memorial	Steinkraus, Mairs, Chapot
	Good Will Trophy	William Steinkraus/Fire One
Toronto	Welcome Stake	Frank Chapot/San Lucas
	Puissance	Frank Chapot/San Lucas

1963 Harrisburg	Preliminary	Frank Chapot/Shady Lady
	Fault and Out	William Steinkraus/Sinjon
	Puissance	Frank Chapot/Manon
	Championship	Frank Chapot/Manon
	White Trophy	Frank Chapot/Shady Lady
	Stake	William Steinkraus/Sinjon
	Qualifying	tied { William Steinkraus/Fire One / Kathy Kusner/Untouchable
Washington	Ecuador Trophy	Frank Chapot/Manon
	Puissance	Frank Chapot/San Lucas

281

		Martins Trophy	Frank Chapot/Shady Lady
		Washington Stake	Mary Mairs/Tomboy
	New York	Good Will Trophy	Frank Chapot/Manon
		Stake	William Steinkraus/Sinjon
	Toronto	Team Class A	Chapot, Mairs, Kusner
		Welcome Stake	William Steinkraus/Sinjon
		Puissance	Frank Chapot/San Lucas

1964	Harrisburg	Puissance	Neal Shapiro/Jacks or Better
		Fault and Out	Neal Shapiro/Jacks or Better
		Preliminary	James Saurino/Blenheim's Buck
		Speed Class	Carol Hofmann/Can't Tell
		Gamblers Choice	Neal Shapiro/Jacks or Better
		Two Horse Class	Bill Robertson/Norwich and The Sheriff
	New York	Democrat Trophy	Kathy Kusner/Untouchable
		Mackay Trophy	Kathy Kusner/Untouchable
		Pennsylvania Trophy	Frank Chapot/Shady Lady
		Puissance	William Steinkraus/San Lucas
		Good Will Trophy	Frank Chapot/Manon
		Grand Prix of North America	Kathy Kusner/Untouchable
		Murray Trophy	Chapot, Kusner, Shapiro
	Toronto	Welcome Stake	Kathy Kusner/Untouchable
		Puissance	tied { Kathy Kusner/Untouchable / Frank Chapot/Manon
		Maple Leaf	William Steinkraus/Sinjon
		Rothman Stake	William Steinkraus/Sinjon
		McKee Stake	Kathy Kusner/Untouchable
		Team Class A	Chapot, Kusner, Steinkraus

1965	Harrisburg	Preliminary	Kathy Kusner/Untouchable
		Table A	Frank Chapot/Anakonda
		Fault and Out	Kathy Kusner/That's Right
		Jump-Off	Mary Chapot/Tomboy
		Take Own Line	William Steinkraus/Snowbound
		Table A	Mary Chapot/Manon
	New York	Team Speed	Chapot, Kusner, Steinkraus
		West Point Trophy	Frank Chapot/Manon
		Americana Trophy	William Steinkraus/Sinjon
		MacKay Trophy	Kathy Kusner/Unusual
		Puissance	Frank Chapot/San Lucas
		Good Will Trophy	Mary Chapot/Anakonda
		Stake	Mary Chapot/Tomboy
		Black and White Trophy	Kathy Kusner/Unusual
		Grand Prix	William Steinkraus/Snowbound
	Washington	Ringmaster Trophy	Kathy Kusner/Fire One
		Martins Trophy	Mary Chapot/White Lightning
		Ecuador Trophy	Kathy Kusner/Unusual
		Puissance	Frank Chapot/San Lucas
		President's Cup Preliminary	Kathy Kusner/Unusual
		President's Cup	Frank Chapot/San Lucas
		Stake	Frank Chapot/San Lucas
	Toronto	Team Class A	Chapot, Chapot, Kusner
		Gamblers Stake	Mary Chapot/Tomboy
		Doubles and Trebles	Frank Chapot/Good Twist
		Welcome Stakes	Mary Chapot/Tomboy
		One Chance	Carol Hofmann/Can't Tell

		Puissance	Frank Chapot/San Lucas
		North American Championship	Frank Chapot/San Lucas
1966	Harrisburg	Time Class	Mary Chapot/Anakonda
		Puissance	Frank Chapot/San Lucas
		Stake	Mary Chapot/Tomboy
		International Individual	William Steinkraus/Snowbound
	New York	West Point Trophy	Kathy Kusner/Aberali
		Democrat Trophy	William Steinkraus/Snowbound
		Good Will Trophy	Kathy Kusner/Untouchable
		Black and White Trophy	Kathy Kusner/Untouchable
		Pennsylvania Trophy	Mary Chapot/White Lightning
		Royal Winter Fair	Frank Chapot/Good Twist
		Grand Prix	Mary Chapot/Tomboy
	Washington	Martins Trophy	Carol Hofmann/Salem
		Puissance	Kathy Kusner/Untouchable
		President's Cup Preliminary	Frank Chapot/Good Twist
		President's Cup	Crystine Jones/Trick Track
		Stake	Kathy Kusner/Untouchable
	Toronto	One Chance	Frank Chapot/Good Twist
		Puissance	Frank Chapot/San Lucas
		Doubles and Trebles	Frank Chapot/Good Twist
1967	Harrisburg	28th Infantry Trophy	William Steinkraus/Bold Minstrel
		Puissance	William Steinkraus/Bold Minstrel
		Doubles and Trebles	Crystine Jones/Ksarina
		Tandems	William Steinkraus/Bold Minstrel and Snowbound
		Grand Prix	Mary Chapot/Anakonda
	Washington	President's Cup	Neal Shapiro/Night Spree
	New York	West Point Trophy	Mary Chapot/Manon
		Democrat Trophy	Neal Shapiro/Night Spree
		Puissance	William Steinkraus/Bold Minstrel
		Good Will Trophy	Carol Hofmann/Salem
		Black and White	Mary Chapot/Anakonda
		Pennsylvania Trophy	Kathy Kusner/Aberali
		Royal Winter Fair	Carol Hofmann/Salem
	Toronto	Welcome Stake	Kathy Kusner/Aberali
		International Stake	Mary Chapot/Anakonda
		Scurry Stake	Mary Chapot/Manon
		Gamblers Stake	Neal Shapiro/Night Spree
		Doubles and Trebles	Kathy Kusner/Untouchable
		Championship	Kathy Kusner/Untouchable
1968	Harrisburg	28th Infantry Trophy	Jared Brinsmade/Triple Crown
		Puissance	Joan Boyce/In My Cup
		Doubles and Trebles	Gay Wiles/Manon
		Stake	Jared Brinsmade/Triple Crown
	Washington	President's Cup	Jared Brinsmade/Triple Crown
		Ringmaster Trophy	Gay Wiles/The Senator
		Puissance	Neal Shapiro/Trick Track
		Table A	Neal Shapiro/Trick Track
		Jump-Off	Jared Brinsmade/Triple Crown
	New York	MacKay Trophy	Kathy Kusner/Fru
		Stake	Carol Hofmann/Salem
		Grand Prix	Mary Chapot/White Lightning
	Toronto	Bate Trophy	Carol Hofmann/Out Late

		Puissance	Frank Chapot/San Lucas
		Doubles and Trebles	Mary Chapot/White Lightning
		Speed Stake	Carol Hofmann/Out Late
		McKee Stake	Frank Chapot/San Lucas
1969	Harrisburg	National Horse Show Trophy	William Steinkraus/Bold Minstrel
		28th Infantry Trophy	Neal Shapiro/Manon
		Fault and Out	Frank Chapot/White Lightning
		Grand Prix	Jared Brinsmade/Triple Crown
	Washington	Eisenhower Trophy	Jared Brinsmade/Golden Gavel
		Ringmaster Trophy	Jared Brinsmade/Golden Gavel
		President's Cup Preliminary	Frank Chapot/White Lightning
	New York	West Point Trophy	Frank Chapot/White Lightning
		Democrat Trophy	William Steinkraus/Bold Minstrel
		MacKay Trophy	Frank Chapot/White Lightning
		National Horse Show Cup	Kathy Kusner/That's Right
		Stake	William Steinkraus/Bold Minstrel
		Royal Winter Fair	William Steinkraus/Bold Minstrel
	Toronto	International Stake	Frank Chapot/San Lucas
		Scurry	Frank Chapot/White Lightning
		Doubles and Trebles	Kathy Kusner/That's Right
		Speed Stake	Jared Brinsmade/Rome Dome
1970	Washington	Opening Class	Conrad Homfeld/Bonte II
		Eisenhower Trophy	Carol Hofmann/Salem
	New York	Democrat Trophy	William Steinkraus/Bold Minstrel
		Puissance	Frank Chapot/San Lucas
		Good Will Trophy	Frank Chapot/White Lightning
1971	Harrisburg	Opening Class	Joe Fargis/Bonte II
		Puissance	Frank Chapot/San Lucas
		Police Trophy	Joe Fargis/Bonte II
		Grand Prix	Neal Shapiro/Sloopy
	Washington	President's Cup Preliminary	Joe Fargis/Bonte II
	New York	Democrat Trophy	William Steinkraus/Fleet Apple
		MacKay Trophy	Carol Hofmann/Salem
		Volco Trophy	Frank Chapot/White Lightning
		Good Will Trophy	Neal Shapiro/Nirvana
		Stake	Joe Fargis/Bonte II
		Grand Prix	Robert Ridland/Almost Persuaded
	Toronto	Rothman Stake	Carol Hofmann/Salem
		Relay	Frank Chapot, Carol Hofmann
		Américaine	Joe Fargis/San Lucas
		Championship	Joe Fargis/San Lucas
		McKee Stake	Frank Chapot/Good Twist
		Fault and Out	Frank Chapot/Good Twist
1972	Harrisburg	Preliminary	Frank Chapot/Good Twist
		International Individual	William Steinkraus/Main Spring
		Puissance	Kathy Kusner/Nirvana
		International Individual	Kathy Kusner/Nirvana
		International Individual	William Steinkraus/Main Spring
		International Individual	William Steinkraus/Main Spring
		Grand Prix	Frank Chapot/Good Twist
	Washington	Fault and Out	Kathy Kusner/Nirvana
	New York	Cavcote Trophy	Kathy Kusner/Nirvana
		Democrat Trophy	Frank Chapot/Good Twist

	MacKay Trophy	Frank Chapot/Good Twist
	Puissance	Neal Shapiro/Trick Track
	Volco Trophy	William Steinkraus/Main Spring
	Table A	Kathy Kusner/Nirvana
	Stake	William Steinkraus/Main Spring
	Fault and Out	Frank Chapot/White Lightning
	Table A	Frank Chapot/Good Twist
	Grand Prix	Frank Chapot/Good Twist
Toronto	Class	Neal Shapiro/Trick Track
	Fault and Out	Mac Cone/Bomber
	Championship	William Steinkraus/Main Spring
1973 Washington	Welcome Stake	Rodney Jenkins/Balbuco
	Bonus Class	Frank Chapot/Main Spring
	Puissance	Rodney Jenkins/Idle Dice
New York	MacKay Trophy	Frank Chapot/Good Twist
	Volco Trophy	Frank Chapot/Main Spring
	National Horse Show Cup	Rodney Jenkins/Idle Dice
	Grand Prix	Rodney Jenkins/Idle Dice
Toronto	Rothman Stake	Frank Chapot/Good Twist
	Scurry	Rodney Jenkins/Idle Dice
	Fault and Out	Rodney Jenkins/Idle Dice
	Puissance	Rodney Jenkins/Idle Dice
	Championship	Frank Chapot/Main Spring
1974 Washington	Inverness Trophy	Rodney Jenkins/Number One Spy
	Accumulator	Dennis Murphy/Tuscaloosa
	Speed Class	Rodney Jenkins/Idle Dice
	Martin Trophy	Rodney Jenkins/Idle Dice
New York	Democrat Trophy	Buddy Brown/Sandsablaze
	Puissance	Dennis Murphy/Do Right
Toronto	Doubles and Trebles	Rodney Jenkins/Number One Spy
	Hit and Hurry	Rodney Jenkins/Idle Dice
	Fault and Out	Dennis Murphy/Tuscaloosa
	Puissance	Dennis Murphy/Do Right
	Championship	Frank Chapot/Main Spring
	Fuller Speed	Dennis Murphy/Tuscaloosa
1975 Washington	Speed Class	Rodney Jenkins/Idle Dice
	Accumulator	Rodney Jenkins/Idle Dice
	President's Cup Preliminary	Rodney Jenkins/Number One Spy
	Speed Class	Rodney Jenkins/Idle Dice
New York	Democrat Trophy	Dennis Murphy/Do Right
	MacKay Trophy	Rodney Jenkins/Idle Dice
	Volco Trophy	Rodney Jenkins/Number One Spy
	Classic Magazine	Rodney Jenkins/Idle Dice
	Stake	Rodney Jenkins/Number One Spy
	Grand Prix	Rodney Jenkins/Number One Spy
Toronto	Welcome Stake	Rodney Jenkins/Number One Spy
	Rothman Stake	Rodney Jenkins/Idle Dice
	Open Stake	Dennis Murphy/Do Right
	Fault and Out	Rodney Jenkins/Idle Dice
	Puissance	Robert Ridland/Almost Persuaded
		Buddy Brown/Sandsablaze
	Jigsaw	Robert Ridland, Buddy Brown
	Championship	Robert Ridland/South Side

PICTURE CREDITS

The editor gratefully wishes to acknowledge the generous cooperation of the photographers listed below, whose work appears on the pages indicated. The hardy souls who specialize in photographing equestrian sport have much in common with the competitors they depict, for both share a passion for horses and must endure the same environment. Often the only things either can show for his efforts are the same—a tired body, a pile of wet and dirty clothing, and a few pictures. But what memories some of these photos conjure up, even decades later!

Allen Photos, 159; Jean Bridel, 31, 39, 44, 69, 167; Budd Studios, 12, 24, 41, 67, 90, 98, 103, 107, 249; Oscar Cornaz, 66, 192, 194; José Castro, 185, 197, 231, 239; Milan Czerny, 175; Finlay Davidson, 163; Werner Ernst, 89, 147, 151, 178, 187; Dublin Evening Argus, 115; June Rice Fallaw, 139, 141; Kevin Ferry, 2; Mark Fiennes, 167; Freudy Photos, 161; Greyhound Racing Association, London, 33; Clive Hiles, 71, 77, 96, 111; Stacy Holmes, 173; Dublin Independent Newspapers, 37; Ray Jones, 118; Victor Lafrenz, 14; L. G. Lane, 57, 261; Patrick Lynch, 81; Margulies Photodienst, 28; Foto Mitschke, 61, 210, 233; Monty, 86; Udo Schmidt/Theodor Janssen, 64, 76, 117, 232; Larry Stevens, 87; H. Sting, 215; Foto Tiedemann, 29, 43, 55, 88, 143, 155, 156, 211, 214, 243; U.S. Army, 122, 124, 127, 128, 203–205; U.S. Olympic Committee, 157; Greg Van Zandt, 235; Th. Volmer, 51; Warner Studio, 255; Guido Wedding, 75. Pictures not otherwise identified are from the USET files.